For Kathryn Turner
— sublime artist —
with appreciation
January 2020

A Trail of Light

The Very Full Life of Dr. Anita Figueredo

Sarita Eastman

A Trail of Light
The Very Full Life of Dr. Anita Figueredo

iUniverse books may be ordered through booksellers or by contacting:

iUniverse
1663 Liberty Drive
Bloomington, IN 47403
www.iuniverse.com
1-800-Authors (1-800-288-4677)

ISBN: 978-1-4759-9307-3 (sc)
ISBN: 978-1-4759-9308-0 (ebk)

Printed in the United States of America

iUniverse rev. date: 05/23/2013

For my mother and her mother,

and for Brent

Now and then you must have seen a shooting star leave a radiant wake in its course through the sky. You may also have seen the plodding tracks of turtles in the sand. We human beings are like that. There are those who live, creating a trail of light as they pass, and there are those who leave a track of tears.

You, my beautiful and good Anita, have lived radiantly, shedding light wherever you pass, fulfilling your mother's great dreams, making sweet the twenty-four hours of every day…

And you, Sarita, look back on the luminous trail you have left in your passage through life. Contemplate the splendid fruit of your labor. All Costa Rica has watched your struggle, and your example is a beacon lighting the path for your countrywomen.

-Ignacio Cornejo

from a letter to Sarita Villegas on the occasion of the wedding of her daughter Anita Figueredo, August 1942

Contents

Author's Note and Acknowledgements

The original edition of this book left Anita Figueredo in her 70s, still practicing medicine and engaged in most of the things that had ever engaged her. By the time of the first release of *A Trail of Light* (2009), Anita had lost two of the major figures in her life and in this book, her husband Bill Doyle at 85, and her friend Mother Teresa of Calcutta.

Anita herself went on waking every morning in her bedroom by the sea, sharing the big house with son Charlie, daughter-in-law Dian, and daughter Anita Maria, who moved back home from Montana to join the siblings providing care. Around the time Anita turned 90, Charlie and Dian were away a single night and Anita Maria not yet come, so I had a chance to observe my mother dawn to dusk in our old home, and the flood of memories engendered a poem I will let stand as a final portrait, just before the epilogue.

The publication this year of *A Trail of Light* in Spanish (*Una estela luminosa*), in turn prompted this English revision. The prospect of the Spanish translation of her biography was very joyful for Anita. She was delighted by our developing friendship with Costa Rican historian Jorge Saenz Carbonell, whose painstaking work became so much more than a simple translation. Over the course of six months, Jorge

Saenz and I forged a true historical collaboration, during which he uncovered hundreds of pages of primary source materials and little-known memoirs, and transmitted them to me for my review and for the amplification and correction of the smallest details in the book. Every Friday morning I would take to Anita the new treasures Jorge had sent that week, and we would read them together, to her great, great pleasure.

The first edition of *A Trail of Light* would never have seen the light of day without my sister Anita Doyle who decided that fifteen years in manuscript was long enough. Her affectionate shepherding and sense of design are pervasive in the project. Our brother Charles Doyle is the wizard who produced the photographs over countless hours.

I am very grateful to my original editor and dear friend, Sandra Lambert, who read the earliest drafts of the book and pronounced them worthwhile; and to Lila Byock, who made the last edits and final blessing.

PROLOGUE

I had a remarkable mother and so did she.

Anita Figueredo and Sarita Villegas were strong women, steady and relentless and probably fearless. They were striking models for a young girl growing up in the North American 1950s.

My mother Anita's beautiful face and the ever-growing list of her achievements were recorded by the press from the time she was a girl; and several nights a year throughout my own childhood I was a guest at formal events where praise was heaped upon her. Seated at those round tables in my party dresses, looking up at her on the dais, I was first aware that other people found her extraordinary. For one thing, they seemed impressed by the contrast between Anita Figueredo's small size and large works.

In her doll-like shoes (actually factory samples, size 4B) she stood just about five feet tall, and when she was not pregnant she had a trim little figure unbolstered by any of the confining underpinnings of the day. Her long dark hair, prematurely streaked with gray, was pulled back from her high forehead into a simple bun at the nape of her neck, and drops of gold and pearls dangled from her small pierced ears. She had a lovely fair complexion, brown eyes lit with intelligence and good will, and a luminous smile. She seemed

1

magnetically attractive to both women and men, and I gathered that this was the secret of her effortless leadership.

But as time passed and I began to understand the limits of most people's energy, including my own, I saw that she could do magic with an ordinary day, that the hours were enchanted for her, and never slipped away half-used but were crammed to the very brim with all her works and prayers. She was like a star burning steadily with limitless fuel at its core, radiating light and warmth in all directions.

Anita Figueredo is a surgeon, one of the first two women in the world trained in the surgery of cancer, and the first to perform any kind of major surgery in the county where she lives. She is also a humanitarian, a friend of the poor in general, and specifically a friend of Mother Teresa of Calcutta. She has been married more than half a century and still delights her husband. She had many children, ultimately nine, whom she cheerfully admits were more the result of religious acquiescence than any particular bent toward motherhood. Yet the great joy of her life was this enormous family gathered around her, not so much the infants, who were more nuzzled and nurtured by my father, but the children who could speak, who had ideas and dreams. She herself was bursting with ideas and dreams, fed by an intense spirituality, the conviction that all her days were filled with the rhythm of the work of God. This conveyed upon her a quite perfect freedom, an immunity to the conventions of her sex and time. She did what she wished to do -- or perhaps she wished to do what she saw needed to be done -- and the works of her acute mind and generous heart were to be seen everywhere around, rippling out in waves from home to office and hospital, school, church and town, and eventually across international borders to the regions of desperation.

Her command post, at least for the last thirty years, has been the sunroom of a Spanish colonial house overlooking the Pacific Ocean in La Jolla, California. Here we each have had our own territory. Mine, when I was growing up, was the upstairs northwest corner, a cool, white-walled bedroom with its small private bath in sea-green tiles and its pillared balcony under the deep overhang of red roof. I dressed and studied and slept with the smell and the comforting roar of the sea. My father's haven is still his living room library with its sungold walls and Persian rugs, and the wonderful colors of paintings, sculptures, objets d'art, books in fine bindings and the seductive brown leather chair for losing oneself in the classical and romantic composers.

My mother's place, by contrast, is the realm of action in the sunny back half of the ground floor, and her medical office converted from the two-bedroom guest-house. The sunroom faces directly south into a walled garden with an enormous Torrey pine, its big old limbs braced and stretched over lily ponds and a long low pool banked with masses of birds-of-paradise. A profusion of flowers blooms nearly year-round, the most dazzling of which are the roses, red, pink, white, yellow and velvet peach, which spill into the house in spring, into the crystal vases in the living room and the carved brass pot on the dining room table. The table is a Costa Rican masterwork, a ten-foot polished mahogany slab on pedestals thick with scrolls and acanthus leaves, and girded by twelve chairs dense with clustered grapes and birds. In the dining room, too, are the potted bulbs, prodigious blue iris and red amaryllis allowed inside for their moments of yearly perfection. They form a still-life at the sunlit window with the tropical green of the patio, great fans of palm and fern, and the dripping brilliance of fuchsia and scarlet Christmas cactus.

My mother's desk overlooks all this glory. The legs of this desk are cut down to her diminutive size, and its soft green leather surface is piled high at all times with the papers of her projects, lists, letters, checks, bills, medical journals and invitations to speak. From this station through the years she could keep an eye on almost everything in her charge, simultaneously typing, telephoning, acknowledging the signals of her office nurse, and assessing the halting progress of my grandmother down her patio stairs.

3

Of course Anita did not stay long in any one place. Her routine evolved over the years, according to the numbers in the household. At one time in the 1960s there were fifteen regular mouths to feed at home, never mind the hungry elsewhere. Her medical practice was huge. Patients from all over San Diego and from adjacent counties and states came for examinations and minor surgery to her cottage across the patio; and for major operations, it was only a few steps from her office, across the street and up the hill, to the beautiful old village hospital. There she stood on stools, one or several according to the height of the assisting surgeon, and did the elegant, precise oncological surgery she learned from the titans at Memorial Hospital for Cancer and Allied Diseases in New York. Early in the morning and late at night and at lunch time she did community service, and she had an expansive notion of community.

It was not really all this activity, however, which impressed me, as an affectionate observer. What I found marvelous was how energized my mother was by action -- it was inactivity, when she occasionally tried it, which tired her out -- and how serene and good-natured she was. It was practically impossible to anger her. She saved her moral outrage for such things as world hunger and poverty. She lived in the present, accepting life as it unfolded to a degree that the rest of us could scarcely comprehend. She was misunderstood sometimes, especially when she failed to collapse under the weight of the family tragedies which hammered at her over the years, but her way was to bend misery into the shape of something good, or at least tolerable. Most remarkable of all, I think, she was a woman of extremely high personal standards who was immensely tolerant of everyone else.

Growing up, I shared the general view that my mother was extraordinary, and from an early age I wanted to record her life, and also to understand how she was made. The journalists who wrote about her and the masters of ceremonies who spoke at all those banquets repeated her own explanation. "Tonight's honored guest [distinguished physician, Woman of the Year, Mother of the Year, Humanitarian of the Year, receiving her papal medal, civic plaque, silver tray, honorary doctorate] attributes her success to the strength of character and single-minded devotion of her own mother." The outline of this story was that my grandmother, then a young woman of twenty-five in the obscure Central American nation of Costa Rica, had listened to her little girl's wish to become a doctor, and had left husband and family and comfortable home for the privations of a seamstress in New York, so that her child could accomplish her goal. An admirable story, surely, but with hints of disappointed love, feminist salvos, and general unorthodox carrying-on.

What I wanted to know was, what element of this history was the key? Was it Costa Rican birth? Fatherlessness? Deprivation in New York? Only childness and the undivided attention of her mother? (In which case her own nine, well-fed, well-fathered, American-born children were forever barred from greatness?) Or was there something in the genes that might be passed along?

Not curious herself about the past, my mother was patient with my questions, but she had very little information. I determined to ask her mother, Sarita Villegas; this was a reasonable idea. I wanted to ask her father; but Roberto Figueredo was a ghost who had vanished from his daughter's life.

Anita Figueredo had been that rarest of fatherless girls who simply accepted her mother's poor opinion of him. It was only when I began to practice pediatrics myself and to listen to the wistful talk of the children of divorce that I realized how unusual this was. I cannot remember many of these children, especially adolescent girls, who did not dream about their absent fathers and re-make them in their fantasies. But Anita Figueredo was not a dreamy child. She was practical and focused, and understood that her life's connection was to her mother. In a stream of touching letters from a succession of boarding-school bedrooms she acknowledged over and over her debt to her mother and her adoration of her. By the time I asked about her father forty years later, it was the habit of her lifetime to disregard him, although Roberto Figueredo had been famous in his

5

time and place, and strangers now and again recognized the name and something of the face and small strong body in his daughter.

I began with my grandmother.

Her name was Sarita but we called her Lita, from the affectionate Spanish *abuelita* meaning "little grandmother." Lita moved to La Jolla from New York in 1953, after her seventh grandchild was born. She was fifty-six years old, a young fifty-six, healthy, good-looking and energetic, and I think it cost her a good deal to leave New York.

She had visited us many times, occasionally taking full charge while our parents took a brief holiday. But it was a huge step to close the door on thirty years of independent life in what she thought was the most wonderful city in the world, where she had close friends, a trade she enjoyed, and both privacy and late-night poker. I suppose she dragged her feet. But finally there were all these little grandchildren three thousand miles away from her, and she opted for us. The first three years, before we moved into the big house by the ocean, she lived down the street from us at the home of a widow named Mrs. Miller. Lita slept at Mrs. Miller's and breakfasted there, then spent the day at our house, supervising the housekeeper, grocery-shopping and chauffeuring all us children around from school to Brownies or Little League or whatever; then we'd have a family dinner at six o'clock, and she'd go home to Mrs. Miller's. That first year she came to stay, the oldest child Billy was eight, and that made the rest of us seven, five, four, three and one, plus the baby. (The other two came later.)

The new house we moved into in 1956 had, among its other charms, a separate apartment for Lita. Our home had been built by an artist and this was his studio, a suite of spacious rooms with a fine north light above the several garages. There was a sign, "*La Casa de Lita*", in hand-painted tiles at the crest of her stairwell, which she loosely translated as "no trespassing" for any unaccompanied child.

Lita practiced a Latin style of child-rearing, a lot of smoky kisses and Spanish imprecations, and we almost never showed her sufficient respect or obedience. I believe she felt that the ideal number of children is one, and I know that while she was still in New York my mother waited longer and longer in each pregnancy to tell her a new baby was on the way. But, having cast her lot with us, she plunged into the running of the household much like the old shop steward she was.

I do think Lita was generally happy during those years. She was a handsome, intelligent woman of medium height, which meant that she was a head taller than her only child. She had soft waves of white hair brushed back from her face, a good figure and good taste in clothes, something she'd acquired in her days working in the New York garment district. She spoke English quite well but with an accent like Ricky Ricardo's on the "I Love Lucy Show," and she liked saying "What the hell" for dramatic effect. More than anything she loved to have fun, to smoke and drink one or two awful rum cocktails and play cards and horses. She found San Diego sadly tame after New York, but she discovered Las Vegas and slot machines, and she made good friends. Still I noticed that as gay and lighthearted as she was with outsiders, she had a darker side at home, and the dark side intensified over the years.

I left for college when Lita was sixty-five, and I was gone for over a decade before returning with my husband to live again in La Jolla. It was then that I began studying my grandmother, circling around her, looking her over and trying to figure her out.

By this time Lita was flinty. She was hard to live with, and I realized that she had not lived with anybody she loved for very long until she was past the usual age of accommodation. Now in her late seventies, she had lost much of the language of affection and preferred to talk about old disappointments. She was not senile; her brain was too alive with angry sparks to let senility get a toehold. Time had not worn down her edges. It had cut across her like a river through granite, sharpening the facets of her Latin soul.

Ancient codes of honor and fierceness percolated through her, now and then erupting into the most astonishing breaks with old friends. Her daughter and grandchildren were the only persons known to have survived her wrath and be returned to reasonable good grace. In the case of her daughter, her only child, the love was no longer expressed, only implicit in the concern and pride she voiced in public. In their private or familial encounters, my grandmother's conduct toward my mother was outrageously bad. "Daughter," she would call to her. "*Mánde*," my mother would reply -- "Order me" -- and Lita would: bring me milk, coffee, crackers; fix the cushion on my chair, the slippers on my feet. She never spoke a "please" or "thank you," and there was nothing in her face to suggest any civility was intended.

I had long ago decided that the grandchildren stood in the most favorable place, enough a part of her to be loved with some tolerance, yet not so precious as to require the exclusive love that my mother had once pledged, but had long since shared with my father, and with us and, for that matter, with all the world. Lita fascinated me, and for years I paid her a ritualistic call on Thursday mornings, before her television programs began for the day. She took the soap operas as a kind of tonic, knocking them back two at a time with TV sets operating simultaneously in different rooms, on different channels. If I arrived at the wrong time I had to sit on the sofa and talk at Lita as she paraded back and forth between the sets, dropping inch-long cigarette ash on the carpet as she went.

By this time the grandchildren had all grown up. Her driver's license had not been renewed, and she could no longer lurch along the freeways to her bingo halls and poker games. A standing motorcycle had pinned her to the ground and broken her hip when she wrestled with it for being improperly parked. No matter that the grandchildren came to visit, that six hundred dollars' worth of driving lessons bought back the license for a while, that the hip was pinned, and re-pinned. She began spending the day in her robe, a disreputable, unquilting, ash-burned pink one, limping about with one leg slightly askew to feed her plants. She did not feed herself much, and she became thin and fibrous.

I was very conscious then of racing time. It seemed all-important to reach the "real" Lita, the woman who had made the most remarkable decisions, who had borne and borne away my mother. Mostly I wanted to get past the failing old lady to the girl and young bride and disappointed wife, and to the brave immigrant, self-sacrificing mother, worker and midnight gambler -- all the women she'd been by the time she was my age. It seemed to me then that my knowing her as a whole person would resurrect her from the half-life, or half-death, into which she had slipped. She was tired of living by this time, and was bitter about things both spoken and unspoken. But I noticed that outrage sapped her strength, and that the tirades were, in fact, tiring. If I listened respectfully and waited, Lita would shift the emotional key to something pleasantly nostalgic, and now and then cheerfully scandalous. Our ordinary language of conversation was Spanish, which she exacted as a sort of tribute when receiving court in her own apartment.

She had no notion of time, and if I pressed her for dates she would make them up. But she did remember relationships, and most faces in photographs, and she had a fat old album with crumbling vellum clinging to its black silk cord and photos and news clippings stuck in at all angles; and a box of letters, all the loving, brave ones from her darling girl away at school, and some others from Costa Rica that were sixty years old. She did tell me much of her story before she died; and by the time my mother took her mother's ashes "home" to her beloved Costa Rica to be buried with her sisters and brothers, her parents and grandparents, I had begun to understand.

The stories that follow, about Costa Rica and also about the early years in New York, are based on the treasures I dug up in Lita's house, though these were passionate fragments, and the trick was to know what was true and what was fanciful. With time, I learned the tools of the historian, and eventually had drawers and binders crammed with letters from the living and the dead, vital records,

9

histories and gazetteers a hundred years old, and chronologies based on volumes of transcribed oral recollections.

When there were still gaps and inconsistencies, I returned to Costa Rica with my mother (and my own little daughter) in January 1988. During the day, I navigated about the central city of San José on foot, against a strong breeze bending the palm fronds and even some off-season raindrops, uncovering the wealth of the Civil Registry and the National Library, the National Archives and Institute of Genealogy, and the Metropolitan Curia which holds the ancient ecclesiastical records of the Catholic Church. And at night I sat with Anita at the emotional and geographical center of the Costa Rican family, in the kitchen of her cousin Gladys Fischel, and heard how it really was.

In the tales of the Rich Coast, I have invented some conversations in an attempt to bring the characters to life. Otherwise, all details are as true as documents and living memory.

When the story becomes Anita's own, in the mid-nineteen twenties, it is based on a cache of written material brought to light from the backs of closets and the depths of cardboard boxes, and on hundreds of hours of interviews. The Thursday mornings with Lita gave place, after her death, to Friday mornings with Anita, many months of precious half-days on which we hid away at my house from patients and children and Anita's tyrannical phone, and together reconstructed a life.

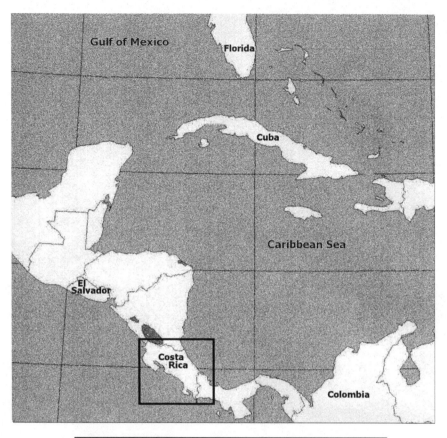

PART ONE

The Rich Coast
Costa Rica, 1855-1921

"I am not overenthusiastic nor disposed to exaggerate,
I believe, when I assert, that if one-fiftieth part of
the inhabitants of the North had the faintest approach
to a true idea of the Republic of Costa Rica,
its superb mountains,
its inexpressible loveliness of valleys,
its atmosphere of eternal May,
its remarkable advancement in ways of civilization,
its cultured, courteous, hospitable people,
not all the hotels in San José could begin to
accommodate the eager crowds that would pour down by
every steamer."

- from the Editor's Introduction to
Joaquin Calvo's
Republic of Costa Rica
1889[1]

THE FAMILY CAST OF CHARACTERS

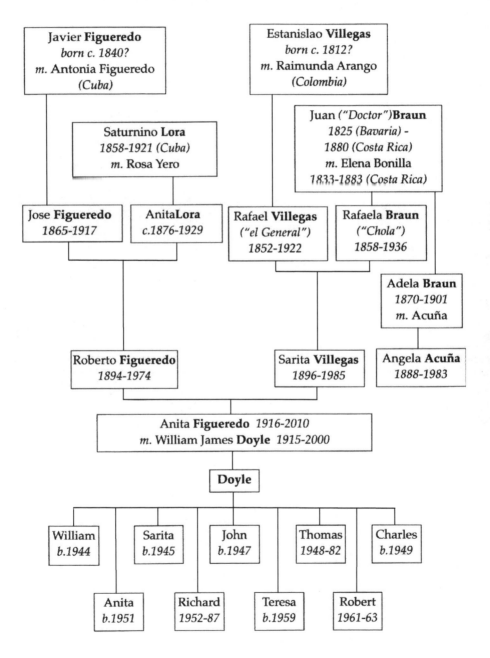

Javier **Figueredo**
born c. 1840?
m. Antonia Figueredo
(Cuba)

Estanislao **Villegas**
born c. 1812?
m. Raimunda Arango
(Colombia)

Saturnino **Lora**
1858-1921 (Cuba)
m. Rosa Yero

Juan *("Doctor")***Braun**
1825 (Bavaria) -
1880 (Costa Rica)
m. Elena Bonilla
1833-1883 (Costa Rica)

Jose **Figueredo**
1865-1917

Anita**Lora**
c.1876-1929

Rafael **Villegas**
("el General")
1852-1922

Rafaela **Braun**
("Chola")
1858-1936

Adela **Braun**
1870-1901
m. Acuña

Roberto **Figueredo**
1894-1974

Sarita **Villegas**
1896-1985

Angela **Acuña**
1888-1983

Anita **Figueredo** *1916-2010*
m. William James **Doyle** *1915-2000*

Doyle

William
b.1944

Sarita
b.1945

John
b.1947

Thomas
1948-82

Charles
b.1949

Anita
b.1951

Richard
1952-87

Teresa
b.1959

Robert
1961-63

14

CHAPTER I

The Rich Coast

Anita Figueredo was born in 1916 in a sleepy province of Costa Rica but was spirited away at the age of five by her formidable young mother, to be raised in the dazzle and stir that was New York City in the 1920s. Sarita Villegas, the mother, turned her back on a particular set of thorny circumstances, but not on the little country she loved and always expected to reclaim. She raised her daughter as a Costa Rican, on an extended work-study program abroad, as it were, and the two of them were heroines back home.

The entire population of Costa Rica in 1916 was less than half a million people who could have crowded themselves into one large neighborhood on Manhattan Island.[2] Costa Ricans were not bumpkins. In fact, by world standards they were highly literate. But they had no medical school[3] and no woman doctor; and, of course, the idea of a woman doctor was still a novelty everywhere in the western hemisphere, not excluding the United States. So the story of young Anita Figueredo deciding to be a doctor, and of Sarita Villegas taking this seriously, was a captivating one. Bulletins on their progress appeared in the Costa Rican papers for at least twenty years, mostly in wildly florid prose and occasionally even in verse.

As it happened, the self-imposed exile of Sarita Villegas ended only when the ashes of her very old bones were returned to San José. But it was not supposed to be that way, and it is not possible to understand the trajectory of Anita Figueredo's life without considering Costa Rica.

When Anita Figueredo was growing up in New York, she was obliged to explain now and again that Costa Rica was not a familiar island in the West Indies, that is to say, not Puerto Rico, but a small temperate Central American nation just north of the Panama Canal. If people were vague about geography, they had at least heard of the great canal which had recently shrunk the world.

Anita Figueredo's birthplace, Alajuela, is clustered with all the other major towns four thousand feet above the sea on the high *meseta central,* in a climate often described as eternal spring. [4]

Despite the name, which means "Rich Coast" and derives from the wishful thinking of Christopher Columbus, neither the Admiral's heirs nor waves of Spanish adventurers drawn there afterwards could ever find much wealth. Moreover, there was no centralized Indian empire to be conquered, as in Mexico and Peru, but only small, ferocious bands whose members were rarely made into slaves or wives; they simply died under Spanish "protection" or vanished into the jungles. There was little gold to plunder, few natives to convert or to be harnessed to vast plantations. This and a terrain of high mountains and valleys produced an isolated, self-sufficient colony of European farmers working family plots of land. [5]

Costa Rica's population remained very small until well into the nineteenth century, by which time there were a few small cities. A national census of 1824 lists 57,000 souls. [6] Since there was little real wealth to defend and no indigenous people to oppress, there was thus no military tradition. What did develop were notions of democracy and universal education.

In 1821, Costa Rica declared herself independent of Spain (which scarcely protested) and briefly joined a Central American Federation, but withdrew again from her fractious neighbors in 1838. In a century-and-a-half of self-government, Costa Rica has had a relatively orderly succession of presidents, with only briefly successful "strongmen" and few coups d'etat. A short civil war in 1948 set up what has been called the "fairest and free-est electoral machinery in the world"[7] and also abolished the army, thus sparing Costa Rica the rain of blood and bullets that falls on the rest of the isthmus.

In Anita Figueredo's family tree the men are soldiers and writers, often both, with a recurring penchant for medicine. The women are "domestic officers" (in the quaint phrasing of old vital records); they are also strong-minded and not above leaving a husband who does not suit. Anita's ancestors include one thoroughly Costa Rican great-grandmother descended from a Spanish *conquistador*[8]. Otherwise, her Costa Rican roots, though spiritually deep, are genetically tenuous. Her father, Roberto Figueredo, was Cuban, as were all his forbears for many generations. Her mother, Sarita Villegas, was born by chance in El Salvador to a German-Costa Rican mother whose Colombian husband was chasing outlaws after the latest Salvadoran revolution.

CHAPTER 2

Betrothal

From a distance of nearly a century, it is easy to look back and see that the marriage of Anita's young parents, Sarita Villegas and Roberto Figueredo, could have been a success, at least by standards of the time and place. Certainly, when their betrothal was announced toward the end of 1915, the match was considered brilliant by the press of San José, Costa Rica, which reported:

> News of the engagement of young don Roberto Figueredo to the lovely señorita Sarita Villegas has been received with great pleasure in all the social circles of this capitol, as well as in the province of Alajuela.
>
> Roberto Figueredo is one of those young men who has distinguished himself among his fellows as much in intellectual endeavors as in athletics where he has won the most impressive trophies.

> Sarita Villegas is a delicate flower of our San José garden whose natural charms combine physical beauty and a high-minded, noble spirit.[9]

Not surprisingly, some of this was true and some off the mark. Roberto Figueredo was, at twenty-one, a celebrated athlete, a star *futbolista*, or soccer player, in a part of the world where soccer was the great game. He had a box of gold medals on multicolored ribbons. Most were for soccer, others for pole vault and long jump.[10]

Intellectually, Roberto Figueredo was distinguished more by promise than achievement. At the time of his betrothal he was *pasante de abogado* or bachelor of law, which meant that he had finished a law school course but not yet taken the bar. He was romantic and wrote poems, some of which were published.[11] He was not self-supporting.

The bride herself was perhaps never a "delicate flower" but, at nineteen, did possess both beauty and spirit. She was as tall as her fiancé, about five feet five, with the womanly figure still admired before the 1920s, and with wavy brown hair marcelled to cascade over one hazel eye. She was also restless, chafing at routine and the burdens of her mother's house.

Sarita's father, Rafael Villegas Arango, was a decorated Costa Rican soldier[12], though not a native. He was born in Colombia,[13] a tenth child in a stupendously fertile and hardy ancestral line; his father was the oldest of twelve, and his grandfather one of eighteen, mostly males and all of them somehow enduring the 18th and early 19th century long enough to reproduce.[14] Rafael Villegas was the first of his clan to leave Colombia, and was now a General[15] in the army of a nation which was mostly at peace. He was also a writer, and roamed around Central and South America wielding both sword and pen. General Rafael Villegas was what is called *un hombre andero*, a romantic, passionate, elusive man who was rarely at home; his marriage had not survived. Sarita Villegas adored her father and now was determined to marry a man much like him.

CHAPTER 3

The General and Chola Braun

In 1885, Anita Figueredo's grandfather, General Rafael Villegas, traveled as a visiting dignitary to the western province of Costa Rica called Puntarenas. He was to be entertained by the governor, one Recaredo Bonilla, whose other guest was his niece, Rafaela Braun.[16] (As the protagonists of this story share the same odd Christian name - and as the woman hates it, in any case - we will call her Chola, as her family does.)

All the good families of that isolated place must have leaped at the diversion of a ball in the General's honor. They would have come on foot or by carriage, ignoring the heat in their formal clothes, and pushing through the doors of the tropical house which served as the governor's mansion. Governor Bonilla stood to receive them, flanked by his houseguests: on his left, the distinguished soldier, resplendent in his long grey tunic with its double row of gilded buttons, gold starred epaulets and oak leaves[17]; and on his right, a slim young woman whom the villagers knew to be the governor's orphaned niece. Rafael Villegas was thirty-three when they met, celebrated, tall and thin, gravely courteous and never-married. And

Chola Braun was a serious woman past her prime, whose life had fallen apart.

When Rafael Villegas first saw her, she was heartsick, and too distracted even to notice his first attentions. At twenty-seven, Chola Braun was a spinster and fledgling schoolteacher, who had just found herself head of a family of seven orphaned and unattached females, including a six-year-old child.[18] She was in mourning. Later on, it would sometimes amuse her to think that Rafael pursued her because she was so obviously indifferent.

Here she was in her five-year-old black dress (donned, first of all for her father, the German physician, and then for her mother, and now for her only brother.)[19] She was surrounded by younger girls with hopeful mothers clustered discreetly where they could view the young General's progress. And yet after a decent interval of polite dancing and small talk he came to sit by Chola's side.

Rafael Villegas was a thoughtful man, voraciously well-read, and given to pondering the mysteries of human behavior. He wrote essays on Spanish chivalry and more than once had been described in print as "Quixote-esque."[20] Rescuing a lady in distress was his style, and may have been the basis of his pursuit of Chola Braun. As he watched her sitting there quietly, talking and nodding with a sober expression, Rafael may have supposed her profound; but the truth is that she was naturally reserved and careworn.

The only surviving pictures of Chola Braun date from the end of her life when she was remarkably wrinkled. But Rafael Villegas had an eye for beauty which he often expressed in sensuous prose, and Chola would eventually produce several handsome children. She had also grown up in a household cascading with books, under the eye of a Teutonic classical scholar. Very likely she was better taught than most women of her generation in Costa Rica, as Rafael Villegas would have known, and prized. But Rafael perhaps forgot that he would also need a wife who could be lighthearted and adventurous. It was the chief misunderstanding of their courtship.

Rafael was so certain they should marry. He wrote long, persuasive, funny letters, brushing away Chola's misgivings. At first, she refused him. She would not let him visit her at home in San José, and rarely went out except to school, to church and to classes in dressmaking. The General went to sewing class and waited at the door. He proposed again; she demurred. Her family pressed forward. They thought it scarcely credible that a girl in such straits could refuse any real suitor, let alone General Villegas. And finally they were married, in the simple church of El Carmen in San José on July 19, 1886 after the blood lineage and dogmatic purity of bride and groom were established by witnesses. [21] Chola Braun had agreed to exchange one set of hardships for another.

Within days of their wedding, Chola found herself installed in a cabin among the banana trees near Carrillo, the last stop on the unfinished Atlantic railway, and an all-day ride on a good horse from San José. In her luggage jolting behind were the household goods Rafael had requested in his last premarital letter:

> 1 dozen soup bowls, plates, cups and saucers
> 1 dozen teaspoons, knives, forks and soupspoons
> 1/2 dozen glasses
> 2 large serving spoons
> 1 soup tureen
> 1 dozen sheets and pillowcases
> blankets and towels
> "Menier" chocolate
> a barrel of our favorite cookies
> 100 dozen fans to keep you cool

He had added:

> Don't forget to look for a good woman for the house, and another to serve you. As a precaution, see that the women are ugly because, if not, they will turn the house into a carnival. You do not yet know the extraordinary value of an ugly woman.

> Take good care of yourself, and take heart, as I know
> you are not above bolting at the church door, though
> the priest has hold of your arm.[22]

And she had been on the verge of bolting, but Rafael had promised to care for all her sisters.

Chola Braun was a woman gently reared, a child of the city. And yet the first decade of her married life played out in a series of camps, mining and military camps, in the hot lowlands of Costa Rica and in similar backwaters of El Salvador and Guatemala.[23]

In the early days Chola kept faith with the notion of normal family life. She had servants to help her, but housekeeping in the outback required as many hands as one could find. The native washerwomen had to be persuaded to use the boards and tubs she had hauled from San José, or else they whipped the clothes on large river stones, wearing them to rags.[24] Mornings, rising from her bed, Chola trod on carpets of crawling things, and looked about warily for scorpions and snakes.

Sometimes, oppressed by heat and dirt, and perhaps by Rafael's preoccupations, Chola fled back to San José. Her husband's affectionate fretting pursued her through the mails:

> What I mostly request is that you take good care of
> yourself, and don't lock yourself up in the house, but go
> out as much as you can. For the body to be healthy, the
> spirit must be gay. Don't worry about me...The port is
> very healthful now, without a single case of fever. [25]

Possibly Chola's early visits home stretched into semi-permanent removals, as nearly four years passed before she gave birth in San José to her first child, Elena.[26]   But if the new mother hoped this event would issue in a more regular domestic life, she was soon disappointed. A month after the baby's birth, General Rafael Villegas got word of a military coup in Salvador which killed his friend, President Menendez; at this, Chola Braun's fiery husband went underground plotting counter-revolution. Rafael persuaded his reluctant wife to join him in one remote village after another where a burst of fertility produced a boy and another girl in quick succession, before Anita Figueredo's mother was born in 1896.

CHAPTER 4

The Birth of Sarita Villegas

On the 30th of September 1896, the wife of General Rafael Villegas was in labor for the fourth time. She lay in a rented bed in Santa Tecla, El Salvador[27], and was angry about it.

Chola Braun, when she stood upright and was not damp and blotched with pain, was still a handsome woman. Her bearing was good, her features regular and even attractive when she smiled. But she rarely smiled; her face was creased with anxious lines, and her natural reserve had hardened with time and disappointment. Not yet forty, she was slowly stiffening into what her granddaughter would call *una mujer seca*, an arid woman.

Now, between pains, Chola wondered again why she was here. At thirty-eight, she had been married ten years to Rafael Villegas and had never had a proper home. At present, her husband was governor and commanding general of the three western and central provinces of Salvador - Sonsonate, La Libertad and Cuscatlán - an area of approximately two thousand square miles which he roamed by train where he could and by mule and horseback otherwise. Chola was desperate to return to the sanity of Costa Rica, where a woman and her children could ride out in a carriage without fear for their lives. El Salvador was a God-forsaken asylum with her husband as chief warden.[28]

September is the most unpleasant month in Salvador.[29] Monotonous rain beat against the house and set it adrift in a sea of foul-smelling mud. The three older children quarreled, penned up inside. Chola could hear their shrill voices coming near; she hoped a maid would corral them before they burst through her door and onto her hot and disheveled body.

The midwife moved around the airless room arranging things: a crucifix, and a small shrine to the Virgin Mary, as well as water and towels, a clean knife, cord. "Señora, drink," she said, and pressed a thick cup to Chola's lips. The laboring woman sipped a pungent tea which was an improvement over the Indian concoction, a magical brew of her own braided hair, which she was persuaded to swallow during her last confinement in Guatemala.[30]

Childbirth no longer frightened Chola very much, but she longed to be among the women of her family, the aunts and cousins and six younger sisters who filled the house at the time of her first confinement. The isolation from her sisters was unnatural and hard. The mails were scarce at best, three times a month from San José.[31] But at this time of year the lumpy sacks of mail heaved onto the wharf at La Libertad sat there until the weather broke, and then were pulled and shoved into oxcarts under the fitful sun. After that, the twenty miles to the high valley of Santa Tecla might as well be a hundred, as axles broke and carts slid into mud holes.

Chola tried to believe it was love that made her husband drag her around after him through the mountains and swamps of the isthmus, from one wretched hamlet to the next. Wherever he went, he wrote, begging her to follow:

> Dearest Cholita, You know I had to leave there because I was wasting away for lack of exercise and stimulation... now I am fit again and the only thing I miss is my

pretty wife. The weather has improved, the nights are
magnificent and even the scorpions have left the house.
I would be the happiest man in the world if you were
here with me.[32]

Chola kept the letters in a box under the bed, and when she let her
arm fall against the side of the lumpy mattress, she could almost touch
them.

Well, where was Rafael now? And why even expect him here? For that
matter, why torment herself with wondering?

Rafael Villegas was, as nearly always, on the road, although the road,
in September, was more a remembered concept than a specific place
on which to plant a mule. When dry, the trails linking the towns of
his jurisdiction were simple cuts in the hillside wide enough for two
carts to pass; when wet, they were shifting ditches sometimes "fixed' by
the authorities with bundles of twigs and loose earth, and sometimes
not.[33]

This day, General Villegas was riding slowly along at the head of a
small military party. He was forty-four years old, tall and very lean
with a long romantic face, full moustaches and a graying, trim goatee.
His bearing and his grave, chivalrous manner were striking in the rude
environs. He was chasing bandits. The route to his current position in
El Salvador had been circuitous. Basically, he was a celebrated Costa
Rican soldier and when his own country was at peace, which was most
of the time, he was sometimes drafted into other people's wars. The
job he had now arose in the bloody wake of a counter-revolution in
Salvador, staged by the General and his friends two years before. They
were victorious, but at a price.

The last desperate act of the losing government, before it fell, was to
open the jails and arm the common thugs and thieves, who - when they
perceived the fight was lost - vanished with their government rifles into
the hills. Within a very short time travelers and outlying villagers were
terrorized by roving bands of assassins; and it fell to Rafael Villegas to
clean them out.

Not a day passed without the General having word of an assault on the farms or on the roads. A messenger arrived at headquarters choking on a story: that a troupe of "acrobats" had appeared in the village of San Pedro, mesmerized the townsfolk at a stage on the edge of town, and then robbed the houses and treasury, knifing the ill and elderly left behind, and slitting the collective throats of the village council.

Or a telegram called the General to a farmhouse with the heads of a man and woman nailed to the door. Inside on the floor he found the naked torsos joined obscenely, out on the patio a machete-hacked child sprawled in the sun, and in a ditch nearby the surviving girl, filthy and wild with terror.

Saddlebags spilled jewels over dead horses and riders. Business notes and invoices, in ledgers covered with fine inlaid silver, found their way as gifts from teenaged assassins to prospective mothers-in-law. A lead-eyed man needing target practice splattered his neighbor's brains on the wall behind his chair.

Now and again General Villegas scaled the hill to a hideout and flushed a bandit over a cliff. More often he sat under a spreading *ceiba* tree in the plaza of a violated town, and mused on man's inhumanity to man as he carried out his heavy duties of investigating officer, chief of police, coroner, judge and jury, and director of executions combined.[34] Meanwhile, Chola Braun and her children waited, in a cheerless house in the rain.

With one last push, the newest baby slid out into the strong hands of the midwife, and from there into the folds of a soft quilt. The house had been very quiet for an hour or so, after a whispered consultation at the bedroom door. Chola had vaguely supposed that the children must all be asleep. But then the baby's cries brought a thunderous answering noise, including the unmistakable sound of a man's boots and spurs on the tiles, and the figure of Rafael Villegas, entwined with small clinging bodies, filled the room.

"Rafael," Chola said slowly. "We have another girl. Are you sorry?"

He did not answer the question she asked, but the one he heard, which was, Are you willing to raise our daughters in a place like this?

Chola knew that as soon as she could leave this bed she would take her children home, take this newest daughter, Sarita Villegas, with her clenched eyes and fists and downy hair, home with her brother and sisters to San José. The lonely day, flung upon a stored weight of disappointments, broke through Chola's heart like lead through a splintering floor. She would remember her anger, guard it against the melting force of Rafael's soft speech and the joy in his children's eyes. They would go home, and Chola and her children would never leave again, though Rafael Villegas might travel to the corners of the earth, and his beautiful letters break their boxes and ribbons and spill from all the windows and doors.

CHAPTER 5

A Household of Women

Chola Braun returned to Costa Rica, resuming her place among the capital-dwellers, the thirty thousand or so *Josefinos*[35] (natives of San José) to whom she belonged by reason of birth and her mother's ancestral line. In the first years of the 20th century, the capital of Costa Rica was a pleasing mixture: a few European-style buildings with stone facades and marble balustrades, alongside simple one-story adobes with roofs of corrugated tin rippling the tropical light.[36] Chola Braun's house was one of these. Her family, which ultimately included her five children, her last unmarried sisters and an orphaned niece, bulged in half a dozen rooms around a working patio where laundry was pummeled under a spreading guava tree; an open corridor led from the main house to quarters in the back for the servant girls and their children.

Her husband came and went. The General's fervid letters were more often addressed to his children; at the tender age of eight, his oldest daughter was hammered by his demanding affection:

> You must not fail to write to me by every post. Your letters are like cool refreshment for me in this feverish

> life, and without them I have nothing with which to calm my fierce and tormented spirit.

> ...It is now necessary for you to think more about educating than amusing yourself. There will be time enough for the latter, but always too little for the first. Much attention and constant industry will save you years of fatigue, because I do not intend to let you rest until you have learned everything I wish you to know.[37]

During the long intervals between wars, General Villegas turned his attention elsewhere. He made arduous trips as a military adviser to such places as Quito, Ecuador, riding mules over mountains so high that "the cold slices the skin, and the rarified air causes the travelers' blood to flow from their noses and ears;" where he saw magnificent funeral coaches of crystal, ebony and bronze pulled by matched black horses with gilded hooves, and chapels filled with such gold and light that the altars seemed on fire.[38] Gradually Rafael Villegas became less a soldier and more a writer. He fleshed out his military pension[39] by free-lance work for journals and reviews of various kinds, and contributed regularly to the local papers.[40] By 1907 he was described in the travel book *Excursion through America* as the "eminent" Costa Rican writer holding court in a little salon in San José and reciting word for word the most celebrated essays and poems of the Spanish language.[41][42]

About this time, when Sarita Villegas was just adolescent and prey to her own moods and storms, the rather unlikely marriage of Rafael Villegas and Chola Braun gave way for good. Together little enough, they nevertheless quarreled fiercely. Chola Braun one day told her husband to leave and he did, vowing that nothing, not even death, would bring him home again.[43] But he did come home once: on the Sunday morning in 1916 when his youngest daughter Sarita was married to Roberto Figueredo.

When Sarita Villegas first met Roberto Figueredo, she was still in school at *El Colegio de Señoritas*, the Academy for Young Ladies, still tucked into the demure uniform of striped blouse with leg-of-mutton sleeves, long suspendered skirt and floppy bow tie. Secondary school for girls was fairly new in San José, but the five-year educational plan was reasonably ambitious. By 1909, when Sarita Villegas attended, the course list included:

> mathematics, geography, physics, chemistry, natural sciences, history, Spanish, English and French, home economics, singing, drawing, manual training, calisthenics, morals and religion, pedagogical psychology, and the practice of teaching.[44]

For all the girls of Sarita Villegas' generation, with one exception, this good finishing school curriculum was the highest education available. The exception was Sarita's orphaned and precocious cousin Angela Acuña. Angela's intellectual gifts were so commanding that, after graduation from *El Colegio de Señoritas* at the head of her class, she was provided a government grant to study in Europe and spent the next four and a half years attending school in France and Belgium and in England, where she saw the militant suffragette Emmeline Pankhurst chained to the railing of Buckingham Palace. Although she was also living a "gay social life" in the Belgian castle of the Marquis de Peralta, Costa Rican envoy to several European governments, attending balls and parties and becoming an accomplished horsewoman, the escalating struggle for women's rights was not lost on Angela, and she was not shocked by the occasional violence. She said later:

> I realized that the position of women in England was different from ours. British women were struggling for a chance to earn their living, while in Costa Rica and throughout Latin America women led a secluded life in the home, provided for by their husbands. In those days very few women, except schoolteachers and domestic servants, worked for a living.[45]

35

The teenage Angela learned what she could about the feminist movements in Europe, especially in Scandinavia, where women had already won the vote, and she was gradually transformed into the first great feminist and suffragette in Costa Rica. Ultimately it would be she who prodded Sarita Villegas to educate her gifted daughter in the United States.

From the age of twelve when she was orphaned (in 1901), Angela had lived with her Aunt Chola and Uncle Rafael Villegas, and she often spoke of Rafael Villegas as "a great scholar, whose youthful mind and spirit were always an inspiration." On her return from Europe to Chola's house in 1910, Angela resumed her close friendship with Sarita Villegas, who was more like a younger sister than a cousin; the Spanish phrase *primas hermanas* (cousin sisters) expresses their relationship exactly. Sarita paid attention as Angela considered the state of higher education in Costa Rica. The University of Santo Tomás, where their German grandfather Dr. Juan Braun had been professor, and which had faculties of law and medicine as early as 1843, no longer existed; it closed in 1888, the ironic casualty of reform aimed at providing free and compulsory education to everyone, as the government decided that "university education was a luxury the country could not afford and that resources would be better spent at the secondary level."[46] The only educational institution in the country now resembling a college was the Liceo de Costa Rica, or Lyceum for Boys, on the outskirts of San José. In 1908, the student body at the Lyceum consisted of 241 boys;[47] soon after, at the insistence of Rafael Villegas, amongst all those boys was one girl, Angela Acuña. She received her Bachelor of Humanities in 1912[48] just as her cousin Sarita, down the street at El Colegio de Señoritas, was graduating into the status of marriageable young woman and caught the eye of Roberto Figueredo.

CHAPTER 6

The Cuban Connection

By all accounts, Roberto Figueredo was a charming young man. Long after his young wife left him, he was a great favorite of Sarita Villegas' family in San José. He always had the time to speak when they chanced to meet in the street, knew them all by name, and asked with real interest about the undulating rivers of their lives. Husbands and wives alike thought Roberto *inteligente, cariñoso, agradable, encantador* (intelligent, affectionate, gracious, charming.) "In fact," a niece would say, "Sarita Villegas is the only person we ever knew who didn't like Roberto Figueredo." But Sarita had liked Roberto once.

Roberto Figueredo was Cuban by birth, the younger son of José Figueredo and his wife Anita Lora. The Figueredo family in Cuba was a sizable clan at the eastern end of that long and sinuous island.[49] Theirs was the "dream city" of Santiago, the beautiful old colonial capital with its rainbow houses, sea-green and mauve, royal purple and indigo, climbing up the hill above the sea.[50] José Figueredo, like Rafael Villegas, was a soldier before he went to school.[51]

The Spanish Empire in the New World was in its death throes, but still Spain could not be persuaded to withdraw on good terms from Cuba, her lovely "pearl of the Antilles." Costa Rica, poor jungle backwater that it was, had disengaged itself from Spain without firing a shot forty years before. But Cuba was the rich and beautiful gateway to the Americas, and much prized by her keepers.[52] After a dozen or more generations, the Cuban-born descendants of the conquerors were still the social and political inferiors of any peninsular Spaniard, however recently come to the island; and the Spanish governors of the nineteenth century were hard and small-minded men. As a consequence, there was nearly continuous insurrection on the island for thirty years, beginning with the Ten Years' War in 1868 and ending in the conflagration of the so-called "Spanish-American War" in 1898. All these insurrections began in the eastern province where the Figueredos lived, as far away as possible from the Spanish capital of Havana on the northwest coast. The boys and men who fought these wars were José Figueredo's peers, and it was only during the brief and unsettled peace between failed campaigns that he could educate himself or even work enough to help his family. War was the real profession of his whole generation of Cubans who only farmed, or hammered iron, or baked bread to keep busy between campaigns.[53,54,55]

When José Figueredo was about twenty-six, he married Anita Lora, the teenage daughter of a rebel leader, Saturnino Lora, who lived in the village of Baire. The year was 1891,[56] and Cuban patriots were agitating for the final expulsion of Spain from the Western Hemisphere.

During the next three years, as ferment brewed, Anita Lora and her mother Rosa both had babies[57]; Anita's first son Viriato was born in 1893[58] and, barely nine months later, his brother Roberto Figueredo on September 13, 1894.[59] Within three months of Roberto's birth the women and all their children were sent away to Costa Rica, because Saturnino Lora saw that the ultimate war with Spain would soon be upon them.[60]

Saturnino Lora was thirty-six years old and had been preparing for this all his life. Now he methodically sold his property, concluded his business affairs, and sent his family into exile. His married daughter Anita, the wife of José Figueredo, at first refused to be separated from her husband. Eighteen years old and with her second son Roberto at her breast, Anita begged to remain behind. In the end, José convinced her that she would be endangering them all if she stayed; and so she sailed away from Santiago harbor, clutching her two babies, nine hundred miles southwest around Jamaica to exile in Costa Rica.

The household the women established in Costa Rica was supposed to be sustained by monies given them by Saturnino Lora when they sailed. Within a few months, though, these funds were exhausted, and Rosa and her second daughter Isabel went to work as pastry-cooks and seamstresses while Anita Lora cared for the children.

Meanwhile, drama was playing out in Cuba. The long-awaited command for revolt was received in Santiago in the early weeks of 1895, and the precious paper hand-carried by José Figueredo to Saturnino Lora at Baire. José galloped, Paul Revere-style, the forty miles to the Lora farm to hand his father-in-law the order of insurrection.

Over the next few days, Saturnino Lora gathered his personnel, infantry and cavalry with whatever arms they could muster, mostly the machetes they used in the cane fields; and then on the 24th of February, he led a column of more than four hundred men into the plaza at Baire. There he stood up in his stirrups and ignited the Spanish American War with his *Grito de Baire* (Shout at Baire): "The moment has come," he cried, "to break the chains which yoke us to the iron cart of tyranny!" With that, he drew his pistol and fired six shots into the air, while the passionate throng shouted "Vivas" for a free Cuba and for the strength and courage of the patriots.[61]

It was three and a half years before the blood stopped spilling into Cuban soil and when independence came, with a push from the United States, Saturnino Lora had fought nearly seventy battles. An authentic hero, he retired to his farm with the highest rank of General of Division.[62] At the end of 1898, his wife and younger children returned from Costa Rica, and resumed the country life they left in Cuba.[63]

His oldest daughter, Anita Lora, however, bid farewell to her mother and brothers and sisters and stayed behind. The war had been shorter for her husband, Lt. Col José Figueredo, whose seditious activities so angered the Spanish authorities that a warrant was issued for his arrest and execution, an order which he barely eluded by escaping into exile himself.[64]

But it appears that José Figueredo left one sort of battle for another when he first came to Alajuela expecting domestic peace. Anita Lora, who had prospered on her own, was teaching high school by then with no intention of giving up her work and staying home. José demanded, tempers flared, bitter words flew; Anita abandoned the house not once but twice, and José even sued for divorce (in 1896!) – but gave it up when the judge told the pair to go home and try again.[65] So there they were in 1898: José Figueredo, of the Cuban Revolutionary Army, retired, and his wife Anita Lora, on their own in Alajuela, Costa Rica with their two young sons. José had no particular profession, but he turned his hand to commerce and before long was an importer of general merchandise, and a representative of important foreign and national commercial firms.[66] The store prospered and after a time the family bought the large home next door, overlooking the central park.

The boys, Viriato and Roberto, went to local schools and then to the Boys' Lyceum in San José where they encountered the extraordinary Angela Acuña, cousin of Sarita Villegas. Both Figueredo boys did well in school, though Roberto spent more time in the ample gymnasium, distinguishing himself as an athlete. Small and quick, he excelled most dramatically at soccer, the national pastime and passion, and was a star at a young age.

There arose in the Figueredo household in the first decade of the new century a debate about what should become of the boys when they leave the Lyceum. Then, as now, a successful merchant sought to establish his sons in professions, primarily medicine and law. The university in San José had been closed for twenty years. But, oddly enough, one university department survived and that was the Faculty of Law steadily producing, some said, a nation of lawyers.[67] It was not possible, though, to study medicine at home. A talented boy had to go abroad, usually to Europe, and for several years.

It is a persistent family story that Viriato Figueredo wished to study law and Roberto medicine, but that their father insisted on the opposite. The reason given was that Viriato was sober and studious and could be relied upon to resist distraction even several thousand miles away; and that the attractive and expansive Roberto had to be kept on a shorter leash closer to home. What is certainly true is that Viriato Figueredo was sent to study medicine at the University of Lyons, France; that he finished the course but had his fledgling practice interrupted by World War I, and was sent to safe haven in Rome as Costa Rican consul; that he returned to Costa Rica briefly in 1920 and set up medical practice in his father's old office in Alajuela[68] only to leave again for Europe for reasons unknown; and that he remained with the diplomatic mission in Geneva[69] until he died in 1940 on a trip to The Hague, just as Europe was collapsing in war again.[70, 71, 72]

Roberto meanwhile went to law school in San José. He lodged with an elderly widow named Magdalena Fernandez and her orphaned granddaughter. Doña Magdalena and the girl, Claudia Mora Fernandez, were completely charmed by Roberto, as were most of the people who ever knew him. He was memorably handsome. There is a wonderful composite photograph of the Figueredo family which appeared in The Blue Book of Costa Rica, 1916 (a look at the land and the people, intended to attract tourists and investors.) There are separate formal portraits of José Figueredo and Anita Lora and each of their sons: the father has rounded, prosperous-looking features and bristling moustaches; the mother's face is slender and fine with wary eyes, and Viriato looks exactly like her, intelligent and over-sensitive. Roberto's face has the father's strength and the mother's gentility, and his gaze is direct and confident.

Roberto did not take to the law, but was intrigued by medicine; his attentions to his friends often included herbal potions which he carried in flasks in his pocket. He did actually finish his legal studies and, though he never practiced law except in matters concerning his own family, he came to know everyone of substance in the social and political circles of the capital.

And Roberto lived for games of all kinds. In Alajuela he worked tirelessly to interest young men in *futbol* (soccer) – recently transported from England and catching on rapidly in Costa Rica – and to teach the fundamentals to all comers. In 1919, Roberto founded the *Liga Deportiva Alajuelense (Alajuelan Soccer League)*, which is still the most respected in the province, and was elected its first captain.[73] His countrymen saw him as the "life, heart and soul of athletic prowess" and sporting events of all kinds. Many years after Roberto Figueredo's days of glory, an Alajuelan historian wrote,

> "he was a champion at every game he played and became
> the absolute idol of our youth. His name should be

sculpted in marble or bronze as the most celebrated athlete of his time."[74]

By the year of her formal courtship, 1915, Sarita Villegas was eighteen years old; in snapshots from ancient cameras her hair flies loose around her shoulders, and she looks as though she relishes her freedom from school. She went with her set to the *Club Unión* and had her picture taken at the New Year's Ball: slender, in a complicated tunic and long straight skirt, full breasts cupped above a high, enormous bow - an effect of innocence undermined by a glittering snake-bracelet winding around her upper arm into her sleeve. She was headstrong and daring, and not above hiding away from the eyes and ears of a chaperone.

Costa Rican society in 1915 was primitive technologically, but highly structured socially and typically Latin. Generally, the young men studied and worked, as the society had no true leisure class. The young women, once they left school, studied mostly the rhythms of their households, working with their mothers when needed, and gathering at one another's houses for tea and cards in the wet afternoons. At night they promenaded arm in arm around the park, nodding and smiling at the men they favored, who strolled nonchalantly in the opposite direction. Or they danced with languid grace at the Union Club in the company of their watchful mothers and aunts. The young people of every several-year age span knew one another and followed intricate rules advancing toward respectable alliances.[75]

Sarita greatly admired independence and self-sufficiency and an active, worldly life. Consequently she idolized her father (the English word she would always use for the General was "lovely"), and had only a thoughtless kind of affection for her mother, whose strength was of a type she did not yet appreciate. Chola was so strict, after all, and Sarita believed that she must have a husband in order to win even the smallest freedom of movement. And Roberto Figueredo was apparently hard to resist.

Roberto may have surprised himself by proposing marriage. He was very young and indulged, and his star was still rising. He might have made an excellent match a decade later, living unconstrained in the interim. But he wanted Sarita Villegas and was unused to self-denial.

CHAPTER 7

Fire and Ice

There could be no church ceremony as Roberto was a freethinker both by birth and inclination. Roberto Figueredo Lora and Sarita Villegas Braun were married in the home of the bride's mother on the Sunday morning of January 30, 1916, in the presence of the governor of the province, after "the contracting party Villegas Braun, being underage, obtained from her father the necessary permission to execute her marriage."[76]

That afternoon their grave, handsome faces appeared in both city papers and the clippings somehow survived the later storm.[77]

They spent their honeymoon on the edge of a volcano.

In 1916, a hotel and park transformed the ancient Poás Volcano into a splendid new attraction. Before the construction of the Hotel Poás and the rough path leading to it, the approach to the volcano had been wilderness; and though the hotel was really just a simple wayside inn, one long story with its sloping corrugated roof, it had become a romantic destination for travelers from San José.[78] Roberto and Sarita, on honeymoon the first year it opened, made their trip in several stages, first by train from their wedding in San José to Alajuela. The approach to Alajuela by rail was over the crest of a rise with the town laid out below against the mountains in an unobstructed view, like a village in a child's picture book. The red dome of the cathedral gleamed in the afternoon sun. As she alighted from the train, Sarita could look along winding narrow streets to houses which were generally simple painted cement, most old and casually-kept. But still the town had a particular charm which seemed related to its undulating hills and great old trees. José Figueredo's home, which would soon be hers as well, stood on the south side of the square facing the park and the church and all that was most vital in the town.

By horse drawn coach the newlyweds proceeded to the hillside village of San Pedro Poás, and then in the morning by horseback, out in the lush green among trees embellished everywhere with orchids, to the crest of the volcano and the inn. The crater was reached by footpath to the rim. There was swirling fog, but when it briefly cleared the lovers could see the great pit and its white-hot lake, and perhaps consider the cauldron of their own emotions.

They returned from their honeymoon to the home of Roberto's parents, and it was apparent soon enough that Sarita Villegas was pregnant. This seemed to make her in-laws very happy. José Figueredo and Anita Lora, called don Pepe and doña Anita, were kind to her, warm and accommodating, and anxious to make her comfortable. The newlyweds were installed in a large room with a beautiful four-poster bed. Seated at the writing table in her bedroom, Sarita could look inward to the morning sun in the garden or out to the cool street and the park. There were servants, and she was not required to do housework except as she wished. Moving about her new home and on the streets of Alajuela, she wore clothes of fine fabrics, imported by don Pepe for his store.

Provincial capital though it was, Alajuela had only six thousand people in 1916[79] and, except for the limitations of ankle-length skirts, one could walk the town end to end in a leisurely stroll. In any case, it was not long before Sarita's condition prevented her from going out in public, and it mattered little that she was away from the relatively bright lights of San José. She sat at home with doña Anita, who had time to talk with her in a way that her mother could not, and the two women became deeply attached. Sarita thought her mother-in-law both beautiful and loving. Doña Anita, for her part, had no female relatives in Costa Rica and no daughters. The coming of this pensive, affectionate girl filled a great void in her life.

Roberto Figueredo, however, was restless. He had not lived at home for several years and, not having taken the bar, could only work as a law clerk in San José until his examinations. He still played soccer in La Sabana stadium on Sundays, and shot billiards with finesse, but there was no money to be made in these pursuits. He installed his wife at home with his parents primarily because it was the custom of the times; he had no income with which to maintain her elsewhere, in any case.

Sarita perceived that the coming of the baby both pleased and vexed him. He enjoyed the idea of a son, but admired beautiful and lively women and did not seem to find the physical changes in his bride particularly attractive. Beyond that, she could not accompany him anywhere very much, and after a time he left her to his mother and rode back and forth to the capital alone.

Except for the inattention of Roberto, Sarita's pregnancy was easy, and the birth of her daughter in the big bed at dusk on a rainy day was equally uncomplicated. She was attended by an old doctor, by her mother Chola Braun, and by doña Anita.

The entry in the registry of births in the Province of Alajuela reads:

ANITA GUARINA FIGUEREDO VILLEGAS

born at 6 o'clock in the evening, on 24 August 1916, legitimate daughter of Roberto Figueredo Lora, Cuban, bachelor of law, and Sarita Villegas Braun, housewife.[80]

The morning papers were more lyrical:

FIGUEREDO IS NOW A FATHER

> Our friend, the charming don Roberto Figueredo, has become a father. Heaven has sent our friend Figueredo and his esteemed wife Sarita Villegas the blessing of a beautiful heiress born in great happiness.

> May the Good Fairy adorn with roses the path of the tiny beauty who has made Roberto so proud.[81]

But, as Sarita saw, the father of the tiny beauty was really rather disappointed, and except for agreeing that she should be named for his mother, showed only perfunctory interest and stayed at home no more than before.

What Sarita would complain of most bitterly about Roberto is that he did not pay attention, neither to her nor to their baby daughter. He was not dramatically unkind. On the contrary, he was courteous, but absent. During the week now, he stopped even the appearance of returning home on the afternoon train, and rejoined the household of doña Magdalena Fernandez, renting the old room which he'd had in law school. The other great affront was that he gave his wife no money of her own. She was humiliated by the need to ask don Pepe for a coin to buy stamps, or for the 75 centavos for the train fare to visit her mother.

Several times a month after the baby was born Sarita took the train to San José and played the role of married daughter in such an ordinary way that no one suspected her growing frustration and anger. She was so proud that she hardly confronted her own disillusion, much less spoke of it aloud. But mortification was eating at her, slowly transforming her natural reserve into something colder, more rigid and unapproachable. Still, her frequent letters to her family were like her visits, superficially gay and sentimental, solicitous, with no mention of any trouble of her own, until she wrote her cousin in May of 1917.

The letter that forever changed Sarita Villegas' life was not really meant for her father's eyes. She wrote in a wild sort of unhappiness to Adelita Acuña, Angela's sister, and told her what others had written to her: that Roberto Figueredo had taken up with Claudia, the teenage granddaughter who lived in the house of Magdalena Fernandez, and had been seen with her in public in the capital.

In the house in Alajuela, Sarita said nothing. Her husband's parents were entranced with the baby, who was now nine months old with a cap of light hair and dark eyes, and who was crawling happily over their rugs and tiles. If doña Anita understood Sarita's state of mind, she did not say so, perhaps hoping that what was unmentioned would cease to be; and really, when the three of them were alone together, grandmother, mother and baby, Sarita could sometimes put down her bitterness and just bask in doña Anita's affection. It pleased her that at least her mother-in-law was deeply happy with her company and with her baby.

Meanwhile in San José, Adelita Acuña presented herself at the house of General Rafael Villegas and showed him Sarita's letter. The general was outraged, both by the public humiliation of his youngest daughter and by her private misery, and he rode to her rescue on the next train to Alajuela.

A loud knocking interrupted the play of grandmother and granddaughter, and doña Anita was astonished to see the gaunt, black-suited form of General Villegas in her doorway. She greeted him courteously; he made a grave bow, and then looked beyond her to his daughter, who was standing pale and unsmiling, gazing at the partly crumpled letter he held in his hand. "Sarita," he said, "you have a father. You do not need to stay with this husband. Get your things, and I will take you home."

So she went to her lovely room and packed a bag, and then took her baby from doña Anita's trembling arms, kissed her, and left her marriage.[82] She was twenty years old.

CHAPTER 8

Interlude

When General Rafael Villegas, silhouetted in the doorway at Alajuela, told his daughter Sarita he was taking her home with him, he was speaking poetically. Where Sarita and little Anita went when they left the Figueredos was back to her mother Chola, her maiden aunts, her sister Tita and little brother Rafael and a boarder or two who helped keep the simple roof over all their heads. Chola Braun might be strict and straight-laced, but she understood about errant husbands and welcomed her youngest daughter and grandchild without much fuss. She was not demonstrative, but she did not pry.

Sarita Villegas had come home to social limbo. In that era a separated wife was "dead" socially - *matada*. If she stayed at home she was *loca*; if she ventured out, she was "looking for men." It was still unusual for women to work outside their homes, although a few in the family were trying it. Her sister Tita Villegas was already one of the country's first graduate nurses, and was set on her life's course of developing the profession of midwifery for "genteel" women.[83] Angela Acuña was pressing to become the first woman admitted to the Costa Rican School of Law.[84]

But Tita and Angela were single. It was quite another thing for the mother of a small child to take a job when her own father could support her, and in any case there were no particular female positions. Clerks and secretaries, bank tellers and so on, were male, and a factory job was beneath consideration. Divorce and remarriage were not then legal options although the irony is that Sarita Villegas could have done both, since her marriage had taken place outside the Catholic Church. But she never wanted to marry again. She would say later that it had never entered her imagination.

Within a few weeks of leaving Roberto Figueredo, she wrote her cousin Francisco Herrera in Dallas, Texas where he was in school. Francisco was a very dear friend. He answered the letter on July 22, 1917:

> My dearest Sarita:
>
> I am very grateful to you for the picture you sent me of your precious little girl, and I congratulate you on her being quite as beautiful as her mother. The picture occupies a special place in my room...
>
> Your separation from Roberto has disturbed me greatly, but I know you are aware of the sincere affection which I have always felt for you, and I have thought a great deal about you and your little one.
>
> The only advice I can give you now is to dedicate yourself completely to your enchanting little daughter; educate her well, teach her to love and respect you, and show Roberto what kind of wife he has lost.

When Sarita Villegas boarded a boat for the United States at the end of 1921, she carried this letter with her; and she would keep it through a dozen moves within New York, and then through the final translocation to California in 1953. Decades later still it would be found among her effects, by then a sixty-six-year-old tattered rectangle with a five-cent intercontinental stamp.

During the four years Sarita Villegas stayed on in Costa Rica after leaving her husband's house, she remained devoted to his mother, doña Anita. One brilliant day, about two months after mother and child abruptly departed for the capital, the young parents came together again in Alajuela for the baby's baptism,[85] and Anita Lora dared to hope for signs of reconciliation; but there was no approach on either side, and they soon went away as before.

Then three months later, on October 14, 1917, Roberto's father, José Figueredo, was shot to death a few feet from his own doorstep at the edge of the great park.

CHAPTER 9

The Death of José Figueredo[86]

On the last day before her husband died, Anita Lora was almost happy. Although she was worried by the Cortés affair, her son was in her house because of it, and her pleasure in Roberto rose like heat in her mind, lifting out the concern.

She served her men at table for the joy of it, dismissing her servants to the back of the house in order to savor the privacy and the compliments. She served *arroz con pollo* colored gold with *achiote* and fat brown plantains, she served crusty hot bread and coffee with steaming milk, and mangos and papayas, she served cakes and tea in the wet afternoon, and listened to her dear husband and her dear son talking and planning. Sometimes one or the other reached for her hand and held it as he talked.

"Papa," Roberto was saying, "don't you think the whole town of Alajuela knows the injustice of this? Whom do they respect in this place, if not you?"

"Well," José Figueredo said, "for one, they revere Dr. Roberto Cortés. He delivers their babies; he was a hero in the last epidemic. Perhaps they don't know or care how bad his politics are. Colombians like Cortés think like thugs when it comes to government."

Roberto said, "Pretend I'm an impartial judge. I have before me on one side Hernán Cortés, a hotheaded nobody, always in the shadow of his dignified father. He accuses José Figueredo of "immoral acts" with a beggar girl – actually files a complaint with the police, who stand watch at don José's office door and recognize a disgusting scheme by a family behind in their rent, who use their child as a pawn. The police dismiss the charges out of hand: Hernán Cortés has slandered an innocent man[87].

"Now I look down from my bench, and I see on the other side the accused don José Figueredo, strong hands resting on his famous cane, and who is he? The town's most prosperous merchant, yes, but besides that what? Its mayor, its National Congressman, the chairman of its Hospital Board, School Board, Orphan Asylum, and every other charitable and civic Board and Trust in the Department of Alajuela, Costa Rica.

"The case is over before it begins."

The back parlor was quiet and comforting despite the buzz of gossip in the great park opposite the house. Across their table fell sunlight stained scarlet by the *poro* tree in their garden. All the rooms looked back into this garden, and waking, walking, bathing one saw sapphire birds, ruby orchids. Next door the same brilliant colors filled the family store which offered merchandise imported from around the Caribbean and the world. The whole establishment taken together, house and supporting store, stood square and solid facing the talkers in the park - the men of all ages who had gathered as long as anyone could remember under the heroic old mango trees, men who talked politics and news, both now centered in the persons of *los señores Cortés y Figueredo*, fathers and sons.

Sitting in the parlor, head back and eyes closed because she slept poorly, Anita Lora allowed herself to be soothed by Roberto's words. Perhaps it would be that simple. It had been one week since Hernán Cortés presented himself to the Chief of Police and had José Figueredo summoned from his office - like a criminal! - to answer the charge of immoral acts with a child. When her husband returned home he was white-faced and trembling with rage. To have to answer to Hernán Cortés! That gangsterish clown who thought politics was a matter of guns and whiskey! How did his father allow it?

The merchant and the doctor had been political opponents for twenty years - not even precisely that, since they were members of the same political party, but contenders for the same party posts. They had their differences, they spoke of them, but they were gentlemen. To be interrogated by the Chief of Police he had hired himself! It was insupportable!

Since the turbulent early years of their marriage, when José Figueredo and Anita Lora had finally vowed to live together in peace, his wife had never again seen him lose control of his emotions. He had been a revolutionary soldier, tender bridegroom, delighted father and a grandfather who had recently sorrowed to see his only grandchild swept away from his house; he had been everything else that Roberto has just been enumerating, but however keenly he felt, he was always in control. That day a week ago, Anita Lora had watched her husband pace, and drag his fingers through his hair, and gesticulate wildly with his cane, and she felt alarm like a thief was ransacking her dwindling stores of pleasure and peace.

These five months without Sarita Villegas and the baby and, of course, without Roberto, had been bleaker even than she had expected. There was not enough to do to fill her heart. The chance of a dutiful letter from her older son Viriato had begun to seem like a reason to go out, but the war in Europe had reduced even these to a rare surprise. While Viriato had been able to stay on in France, the letters had arrived in sporadic little batches whenever a boat could get through; but they became shorter and more curious as the war dragged on, tight scrawls on the backs and sides of paper scraps and sometimes scissor holes in the middle of a page. Anita Lora wondered whether the French censors read Spanish or whether they cut things up just in case.

Viriato's going left such an empty space. He was supposed to come home after medical school. But then the war exploded and they were all frozen in place, until just the past month when Viriato escaped from Lyons to Rome on a diplomatic passport. His father's friends arranged to make him Costa Rican consul in Rome and thought they were making him safer. But all this week the news from the Italian front had been disastrous. Anita Lora considered wiring Viriato about the Cortés affair, but gave it up as impossible and probably pointless.

But thank God that Roberto's friends had told him about it. As enraged as José Figueredo had been, he wouldn't hear of her calling Roberto for help. She supposed he wished to see if their son would turn up on his own, and when he did, she noticed that her husband was as glad as she.

It was not Roberto's style to confront unpleasantness directly. He was so used to being loved. Anita Lora never really thought of that before as a disability. But she had studied her son a little more critically since the defection of his wife, and she perceived that Roberto could not believe that Sarita Villegas had stopped loving him, or indeed that she could really live without him. No pleas from the heartsick grandmother had any more effect than lectures about responsibility from the exasperated grandfather. Roberto smiled at them both fondly and assured them that all would eventually be as it was, but took no steps that they could see in the direction of Sarita Villegas and her baby daughter.

Well, but now he was here, speaking thoughtfully and sensibly about this outrageous business. He had been home six days, a long time for Roberto to be out in "the provinces," and he was gracious enough to hide his restlessness. During the long night before his train arrived from the capital, Anita Lora had considered the problem from every angle and hit upon a plan. What was really intolerable to José Figueredo was that his accuser was that idiot boy; he felt debased even to defend himself. Thus Roberto Figueredo had no sooner washed the dust from his face and hands and seated himself in a chair, than his mother told him he must go and speak to Hernán Cortés.

"Mother," he had said calmly, "we must wait a bit. You see the state Father is in, and you know the Cortés family must all be the same or worse. They will have heard that I am home, and will likely ask to see me in a day or so."

Anita Lora had looked down and folded her hands to steady herself, then answered, "Roberto, there are times when one must wait, and times when one must act. Hernán Cortés hates your father now, and no doubt hates you as well, but you are his counterpart in this affair, and can spare your father the disgrace of dealing with him at all. Go to his house now and insist that he speak to you. We don't even know what the doctor thinks about this; perhaps you can arrange a meeting with him and your father." She could see that Roberto was impressed by the tone and the logic of this small speech, and was perhaps even considering doing what she asked, when he was saved by his father. José Figueredo was sitting down, but still agitated in that frightening way.

"Anita, what are you saying? I will not allow it! They have offended me. Would you now give them the satisfaction of the sight of my son on their doorstep, hat in hand, begging an interview? The shame of it!"

"But, my love..."

"No!" Her husband's fingers were digging into the fat arms of his chair, and Anita Lora stopped in mid-sentence. Another sad novelty of this affair, to be silenced by José. But she understood that it was unbearable for him; that he could not hear of Roberto Figueredo, his gifted son, approaching such a one as Hernán Cortés, a mediocrity, a non-entity.

The rest of that day was quite odd for the three of them. José Figueredo went out to his office as usual, but his manager's face scarcely looked familiar; the young man's mouth was moving, yet don José could not seem to make out the words. The effort to control his rage cost him his hearing and much of his vision, causing him to walk by customers and friends without the courtesy of a nod. He was only conscious of wanting to appear serene and unaffected, that they not have the gratification of distressing him.

His wife moved aimlessly about the house, trying to think what should happen next. She wanted desperately for Roberto to take charge of the situation, now that he was here; and Roberto, for his part, seemed willing, except what was it exactly he should do?   Anita Lora was aware that much of her son's extraordinary personal success (really it was no exaggeration to say that at twenty-three years of age his name was better-known than most in the country) was based on natural charisma. She supposed that was one secret of his charm, that it was effortless.   Roberto smiled on people, and they turned to him like plants toward the sun. Of course he was talented; but there were other young men with talent who were not universally admired. Roberto had no enemies, in a romantic culture where having at least a few enemies of the right sort was almost a badge of honor. (Anita Lora hoped that Sarita Villegas was not an enemy, although she realized that lovely complex girl was a deepening mystery to her, and probably to Roberto.)

Had no enemies, she had been thinking. But now there was Hernán Cortés, who might spit on any of them in the street. And here was Roberto with no experience of being disliked, expected to do something about it. His relief at being forbidden to approach the adversary was obvious. Yet Roberto had come home, with considerable dramatic flourish, accompanied by a crowd of sympathetically indignant friends to the train station, in order to help his father, who had never needed his help before. For all our sakes, Anita Lora thought, we must find a way to let him do it.

While his mother was looking out her window thinking these things, Roberto Figueredo sat in his father's study fingering the grape leaves and odd little birds on the elaborately carved mahogany desk, and considered his options. Piled neatly in front of him were nearly three hundred pages of manuscript in José Figueredo's elegant hand; this was a history of his beloved Cuba, a project begun when his sons left home, and attacked with a vengeance when baby Anita Figueredo Villegas no longer occupied his early mornings and late afternoons. Roberto idly read the last page, and was impressed to find it finished.[88] He had assumed that these memoirs were the sort of thing that went on forever. But, no, that was not his father's way. José Figueredo was a man of action who abhorred unfinished business - which brought Roberto around to the business at hand.   He thought that he needed, first of all, to inform himself better about the case and then to engage the best attorney. To that end, he posted notes to several friends, inviting them to meet him for lunch at their accustomed place; and after a time he went out.

When the family gathered later for supper, Roberto was expansively reassuring. "I have talked to everyone," he said, "Juan Dávila, Tomás Fernandez Barth, Ricardo Acosta, people who have known us and the Cortés family all their lives, and they tell me they can't believe what Hernán has done. They think he's a fool; they're laughing at him. But people don't think we should let him stew too long in this craziness. He has filed a formal complaint, we must answer it, and we need an attorney who can dispose of the thing quickly. I have wired San José for the best man available, and we should have his reply in the morning."

Well, Roberto had come on Monday morning, the attorney on Tuesday night, and now three more days had passed and everything was quiet. The three men, José and Roberto Figueredo and their counsel, had talked the matter through for hours on end. Anita Lora sat quietly by, sewing and listening for comfort. There was much said that should have been reassuring. The attorney was as optimistic as his training allowed, and their friends and neighbors brought word that the whole town was incensed on their behalf. But José Figueredo's indignation did not subside; indeed, it was a growing thing, which he covered with outward serenity like a blanket over a hawk, but the thing was in there, struggling.

Anita Lora pleaded that the younger men settle the quarrel. But the only contact between the two sides that week occurred when don José and Roberto Figueredo entered a public building together in town and encountered the obviously nervous Hernán Cortés, whom they passed with a dismissive smile. Later witnesses would testify that Hernán was obsessed with the humiliating certainty that the great Roberto Figueredo would easily beat him in a fight and, for that reason, was carrying a gun.

The next day, which was Sunday, Roberto would be leaving for a few hours. There was to be a soccer match at La Sabana stadium in San José with teams made up of the outstanding players in the country, and

Roberto had long since agreed to play. "But," he told his mother, when he saw her anxious face, "I'll come back to Alajuela on the afternoon train." So that was alright.

Early Sunday morning Roberto Figueredo left home without disturbing his mother. It is not recorded if he spoke to his father, but José Figueredo was an early riser, and the two men may have had some conversation before Roberto walked the pleasant distance to the early train. What passed between husband and wife is also not known; ordinarily they would have taken breakfast together in the dining room and talked of familiar things.

Then, a few minutes before eleven, José Figueredo took up his cane, which was made of a silvery steel lined with wood, and left his house for the post office to pick up the day's correspondence. He did not vary his customary walks in the face of the current tension, and he did not think to arm himself, although he owned a gun, for the simple reason that he considered himself the injured party. His was the next move, he thought, and he believed it was **his** right to decide how to defend his honor on a personal level, after his complete exoneration in a court of law. His revolver lay in the safe in his office.

He walked along the sidewalk at the edge of the park, passing in front of the home of the Cortés family (who were near neighbors), turned at the northeast corner of the park, crossed the street and entered a shop. A few moments later he came out again and walked along the same sidewalk going west. It was his misfortune that at that very moment, Hernán Cortés was closing his law clerk's office for the mid-day meal, and his office stood on the same side of the street along which José Figueredo was proceeding. Cortés shut the door, turned east toward his home and found himself face to face with his father's enemy.

There were "strong words" and an immediate physical struggle. José Figueredo struck out with his cane, and Hernán with his fists. Soon after the violence began, Cortés was hit hard on the hand, and this seemed to enrage him. He suddenly stepped back a few paces, leapt sideways into the street, drew a gun from inside his coat and fired. The bullet entered José Figueredo's chest near the fifth rib, and witnesses said that he lifted his hand to his chest and felt the blood, but continued walking forward.

At that exact moment, Dr. Roberto Cortés, Hernán's father, arrived on the scene. He shouted some words, possibly meant for both men, urging them to halt, or possibly directed only at the wounded man. And on hearing this, José Figueredo turned with his hand still over his heart toward Dr. Cortés, said something to him in a furious voice, and brought his cane down upon the doctor, bruising the man's right hand. On seeing this, young Cortés shot again. One bullet passed through an arm, and as soon as the third shot was heard, José Figueredo fell headlong in the street and died.

Within a few minutes hundreds of people gathered, and four men lifted the body and carried it home to where Anita Lora stood white and trembling in the doorway. She kissed her husband's hands and forehead before sinking into the arms of people standing by. Hernán Cortés was taken into custody without protest and handed over his revolver with the three empty chambers. His father retired to his own house where he, too, was arrested soon afterwards, and a colleague was called to examine the wound on his hand. José Figueredo's cane, its steel and wood bent by the powerful blows, was delivered to the Criminal Judge. Dr. Joaquin Berrocal, officer of public health, performed the autopsy, which determined that the fatal wound was the first; that the bullet which killed José Figueredo passed through his heart and lungs before lodging near his liver, that the arm wound was insignificant, and that the third bullet missed altogether.

While his father was dying, Roberto Figueredo was playing soccer in San José with his usual skill and enthusiasm, to the acclamation of the large stadium crowd. When the game was over he proceeded downtown with some teammates and other companions to the Cafe La Geisha for a drink. It was there that other friends who had heard the news from Alajuela found Roberto. In the consternation, Roberto on his feet with his blood pounding, his comrades in a shouting crowd around him, a message arrived offering Roberto the use of the automobile belonging to the director of the Pacific Railway; and at this he stormed out on foot with his friends to the station and the waiting car. A few of the crowd flung themselves into the vehicle with him, and they drove wildly off to Alajuela where they were met by a waiting throng of hundreds, all of whom accompanied Roberto home.

That night the body of José Figueredo lay in a dark green casket in the house he had loved for twenty years, where his only grandchild was born and lived for the few months he knew her. A sort of candle-lit chapel was made in the parlor and all of Alajuelan society and much of San José streamed through to pay their respects. Through the whole long night, there were never fewer than two hundred persons in the house; and with daybreak, some two thousand mourners formed a funeral cortege. At ten o'clock on a clear October morning José Figueredo was laid to rest under a mountain of flowers sent by ordinary people, by three Presidents of the Republic, and by his estranged daughter-in-law, Sarita Villegas.

CHAPTER 10

A Digression on Family Medicine

The death of don Pepe, whom Sarita loved, left his wife doña Anita completely alone. Like the acts of a tragic play, the great joys of one year became the desolation of the next. Sarita Villegas and her little daughter traveled often to Alajuela on the train, in reverse of the journeys they had once taken toward San José, and it gave both unhappy women much pleasure to sit together in the quiet house and watch their precious child.

Little Anita had the look of a Figueredo. She had her father's face, and grace, and her mother saw to it that she was *bien educada*, which does not mean well-educated (though she will become that also) but well-bred. Sarita Villegas was loving but very strict. Her daughter was becoming her life's work, and she took her task seriously, requiring courtesy and quick obedience of a child who seemed happily compliant. It was becoming apparent that Anita had the sort of intelligence that merits thoughtful planning; and it seems to be actually true that the little girl began talking about becoming a doctor from the age of three or four.

Medicine first emerged, in Anita Figueredo's family, from the dusty saddlebags of her maternal great-grandfather. Dr. Johann Braun, of St. Alban, Bavaria[89], rode into the center of San José in 1855 and soon volunteered as Costa Rican Army physician in the so-called War of the Filibusters (against the odd and maniacal William Walker of Tennessee, who briefly installed himself president of Nicaragua[90].) Although Dr. Braun rarely practiced medicine after the war - holding forth instead as professor of classical languages, geography and history at the fledgling University of Santo Tomás - he was better educated than most physicians in the world and particularly those of the western hemisphere.[91]

The records of the University of Munich show that Johann Baptist Braun was a student there from 1843-46, reading philosophy for two years and medicine for one.[92] In Bavaria at that time, "philosophy" meant general education and included mathematics and the natural sciences of zoology, botany, mineralogy, chemistry and physics, as well as history, and ancient and modern languages. (Before embarking on this strenuous preparatory course, the student had already spent nine years at a secondary school called *Gymnasium* where he "learned to learn" and where emphasis was laid upon the mastery of Latin and Greek; during the first half of the nineteenth century Latin was still the language of medical faculties in the German states.) After two years in "philosophy" at the University of Munich, the prospective physician sat for his admission examination to the school of medicine,[93],[94]and then his professional studies consumed another year before he abruptly left the country after 1846.

War in Europe drove Johann Braun to Chicago, Illinois where he encountered a much more primitive state of affairs. It was the era of Andrew Jackson's "common man," when pluck and grit were valued above the niceties of a formal education. The American system of medical training was then a combination of apprenticeship and public lectures, and there was almost no regulation of faculties or requirements for the "degree." Proprietary schools were the rule, with self-appointed professors who set their own standards, and the pressure of unregulated competition forced standards to a low ebb.[95]

The family account states that Johann Braun took a specialty course in Botany at the "University of Chicago". However, the earliest form of that institution (which failed) was not established until the 1860s,[96] and it is likely that the young man studied medicinal plants in a storefront school or possibly in the parlor of an immigrant German professor.

From Chicago, Johann Braun moved on to San Francisco just ahead of the Gold Rush, and there encounterd the Hanoverian consul to Costa Rica,[97] who persuaded his young countryman to join him on the rough trek down to San José. Dr. Braun was captivated by Costa Rica and soon by a young lady named Elena Bonilla Carrillo. (As an interesting aside, Elena's grandmother and great-aunt, doña Catarina Nava de Bonilla and doña Manuela Nava de Escalante, were revered herbal healers – the first in San José and the second in Cartago.[98]) The date of the marriage of "Juan Braun" and Elena, March 23, 1856, suggests urgency, because in that same month the first Costa Rican troops marched north to war and Dr. Braun rode off to serve his adopted country through a long year of enforced marches and occasional battles, in which cholera was as deadly as bullets.[99] Effective medicine of the time was mostly surgery, of a quick and brutal kind. For suturing wounds and for amputations, Dr. Braun may have had the use of ether anesthesia, which was first used publicly in Boston ten years before[100] or, at least, chloroform which was then being used for extractions of Costa Rican teeth.[101] But he was nearly helpless in the face of cholera, which kills by rapid dehydration. Nostrums were plentiful but useful drugs few, mostly aspirin, quinine, digitalis and laudanum[102]; and none of this pitifully small pharmacopoeia was of any use against the morbid flux of cholera.

But in May of 1857 the war ended. The ravaged troops straggled home, Dr. Juan Braun reclaimed his wife, and their daughter, Chola Braun, arrived within the year.[103]

A half century later, when the Figueredo brothers were interested in medicine in 1910, there was still no medical school in Costa Rica, as we have seen. There actually were schools of medicine elsewhere on the isthmus[104] but, as they were considered inferior and the roads leading to them even worse, Anita's uncle Viriato was sent to France.

By 1919, when Sarita Villegas began contemplating emigration, Europe had been shattered by a terrible war, and the United States of America had emerged as the richest and most powerful nation in the world. Cousin Angela Acuña wanted to travel to the United States; she had a brother in New York, and was convinced that the U.S. was the most enlightened of countries in regard to women. Female suffrage was actually about to be guaranteed by constitutional amendment. (Angela had decided that in order to accomplish a feminist agenda in her own country, she would have to go to law school, despite the fact that the charter of the Costa Rican School of Law specifically excluded females. Undaunted, she persuaded her family's friends to pass a special act of Congress overriding the charter. She entered the School of Law in 1919, and would graduate in 1925 as the first woman attorney in all of Central America.[105]) Meanwhile, she was taking a thoughtful look at her little cousin, Anita Figueredo, and advised Sarita that she had better raise the child in the United States.

In March of that same year 1919, no doubt due to his friendship with President Federico Tinoco and his brother José Joaquín, as well as to his own popularity as an athlete, Roberto Figueredo was elected Deputy from Alajuela to the national Congress in San José. However, the government was by then notoriously unpopular, virtually a dictatorship with jails full of political prisoners. In August of 1919, after the assassination of his brother, President Tinoco fled the country and shortly afterward Congress was dissolved, putting an end to the brief political career of Roberto Figueredo.[106]

But before the fall of the regime, Roberto had the opportunity to display great chivalry in regard to an old friend of his murdered father - don Tranquilino Chacón Chaverri who was writing a secret account of the abuses of the Tinoco government. As related by an Alajuelan journalist,

> ...don Roberto Figueredo arrived at his home and told him: "Don Tranquilino, in this labor of history, you are running a grave risk of being denounced and almost certainly imprisoned. Here are the keys to the office in my own house. I beg you to take them and continue writing your history, out of danger." Don Tranquilino extended his hand and answered: "You do not discredit your noble lineage. I accept with thanks.

In spite of his friendship with the Tinocos, Roberto was himself taking a great risk. Had he been found out, he would doubtless have been arrested and probably tortured, as had happened to many other adversaries of *tinoquismo* – at times for much less serious offenses than harboring under one's roof a writer of a secret chronicle condemning the regime.[107]

Sarita Villegas, for her part, displayed no interest in the politics of her estranged husband and was fixed on a plan of emigration with Anita.

However, the war also reawakened in Americans an old paranoia about foreigners and produced The Immigration Act of 1917 which severely hampered immigration. Following the law's enactment, there was a take-over of Ellis Island by the U.S. military as a way station for returning sick and wounded servicemen; and then news flashed around the world of thousands of American citizens dying in the plague-like horror of influenza.[108] All this, together with the dismay of her family and the absolute opposition of Roberto Figueredo, kept Sarita and her daughter at home, biding their time.

CHAPTER 11

Taking Leave

At Christmas of 1919, there was a wistful letter from doña Anita:

> Dearest Sarita:
>
> The little bonnets are so darling...if you only knew how unhappy it makes me to have to fold each one into a box for mailing, because they can't get to you any other way...Do you think you'll come the 25th? You forgot the toy; it's here on the armoire. The pictures of me are gone but I saved one for you.
>
> I have heard nothing from Viriato.
>
> Ana[109]

Sarita did regret the thought of leaving doña Anita and even more of her beloved father, General Villegas. At the end of 1920, the frail old man was actually called back into military service to help lead a brief campaign against Panama; the newspapers describe his gallant figure, tall and bone-thin, passing along the sunlit beach in the midst of a company of young soldiers, inspiring them to bravery and sacrifice. The whole country watches him depart, burdened with his nearly seventy years, his shoulders hunched, his hands tremulous, but his gaze fierce and his spirit whole...[110]

Finally in the United States, immigration restrictions eased again and the influenza burned itself out. New York had become the most exciting city in the world, where women cut off their hair and wore short skirts and smoked and did what they pleased.[111] [112] Sarita's family gradually ceased listing all the reasons not to go, perhaps silenced by the old General.

But it was strictly illegal for a mother to leave Costa Rica with a child without the father's permission, and Sarita interviewed many lawyers who explained that their hands were tied. At last she found her man, one Señor Zelaya who was "hungry and *sin verguenza*" (shameless), and who told her, "I'll fix it for you. Wait until Roberto leaves the country, or he'll take the child away."

While she waited, Sarita had their passport picture taken, one of those astonishingly clear, enduring portraits of a dark-haired mother in black and a fair little girl in white; the mother with the diamond of her broken marriage reset in an ornamental pin; and both of them, mother and daughter, touchingly serious and beautiful.

Sometime in 1921, Roberto Figueredo left Costa Rica for Guatemala where he enrolled (surprisingly) in the school of Agriculture; and while there he led Costa Rican athletes to the Central American Olympic Games in honor of Guatemala's Centennial of Independence. As the local press was rapturously describing Roberto's medals in 400 meter relay, discus, high jump, pole vault and soccer[113], Sarita Villegas and Angela Acuña seized their opportunity. Together they booked passage on the "Great White Fleet" of the United Fruit Company, which had half a dozen new steamships carrying the produce and peoples of the tropics to New York, and which advertised luxurious appointments including large and airy staterooms, open to a view of sea and sky.[114]

And at last, on November 5, 1921, a small party of women and one young girl set out for the east coast of Costa Rica by train. At the pier in Port Limón sat the white bulk of the *S.S. Ulua,* largest of the line and pungent with bananas. Holding the hands of her mother and *Tia* Angela, five-year-old Anita Figueredo walked sturdily up the gangplank. The ship pulled back from the pier and churned into the open ocean, as a wave of white handkerchiefs vanished in the mist.

Sarita Villegas and her parents. Rafael Villegas, writer and army general, emigrated from Colombia to Costa Rica where he married Chola Braun in 1886. Their fourth child, Sarita, was born in El Salvador where *El General* was restoring order after a coup; soon after her birth, the family returned to Costa Rica. Sarita Villegas is twelve in this picture and already looks determined.

Roberto Figueredo and his parents. Jose Figueredo and Anita Lora were Cubans who fled to Costa Rica during the Spanish American War, shortly after the birth of their second son, Roberto, in 1896. Jose Figueredo became a prosperous merchant in Alajuela, Costa Rica; he was shot by a political opponent in 1917. Roberto Figueredo wears medals for athletics, principally *futbol* (soccer.)

Anita Figueredo and her parents. Sarita Villegas and Roberto Figueredo had a brief, fiery courtship and marriage. They separated a few months after the birth of their only child on 24 August 1916, in Alajuela, Costa Rica.

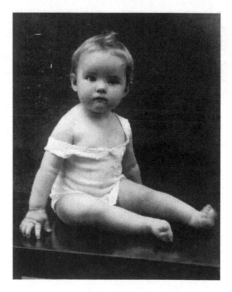

Anita Figueredo, age 4 months, with her Villegas cousins,
L to R, Elena "Neno" Mora, Gladys "Glitos" Mora, baby Anita,
Maria Cecilia "Chila" Mora and Carmen Villegas.

Taking leave. Angela Acuňa, brilliant cousin and suffragette, escorts Sarita Villegas (25) and Anita Figueredo (5) aboard the *S.S. Ulua* bound for New York City, November 1921.

PART TWO

This Side of Paradise
New York, 1921-1947

It is only by risking our persons from one hour to another that we live at all. And often enough our faith beforehand in an uncertified result is the only thing that makes the result come true.

- William James, 1897

CHAPTER 12

Risking the Person

Eight days out of Port Limón, on the morning of the 13th of November 1921, the *S.S. Ulua* slipped through The Narrows at the entrance to New York harbor.[115] Word flowed below decks, and the passengers, United States citizens and aliens alike, dropped their breakfast napkins on their heavy plates and crowded up from the dining room to the portside rail for a glimpse of the Statue of Liberty. The sea air was cold. Sarita Villegas and Angela Acuña huddled against the wind in their thin coats with Anita's little body wedged between them and strained their eyes in the mist, past gulls and jaegers screeching at the bow.

Gradually the great city rose to starboard, and then, west toward the opposite shore on her own small island, *Liberty Enlightening the World*. The stupendous green goddess was still young in 1921, only a few years older, in fact, than the Costa Rican cousins whose eyes unexpectedly filled with tears at the sight of her. The colossal figure seemed to stride forward in a gesture of welcome, and then to stand erect and saluting as they passed.[116]

The clamor of the harbor, bells and horns and engines, called to greet them. They watched as a tug like a sheepdog nudged the *Ulua* into line among the ships of all nations seeking berths along the Hudson River, and ultimately into the waiting arms of Pier 9.

Stewards distributed landing cards. The cousins gathered up cases and hats, and joined a line weaving through the lounge toward United States customs. As these were all first and second-class passengers, an immigration officer had boarded ship. Things were different off Battery Park where the occupants of steerage class stumbled gratefully onshore, only to be herded onto ferries for transfer to Ellis Island. But visitors who could pay their way were presumed not to need social services, and there on the *Ulua* no one expected to go to Ellis Island.

Sarita filled in the blanks on her card. She wrote "yes" to the critical question, "Do you have $50?" She did not fool the inspector who waited impassively while she rummaged about in her empty purse, then stamped "no" across her card and told her to step out of line and let the others pass. By noon the *Ulua* had disgorged all her travelers, including Angela Acuña, into the noise and late-autumn cold of New York City - all except one young woman with slightly shaken bravado and a little fair-haired girl.

Sarita Villegas and Anita Figueredo were detained on board when they could not produce the money they claimed they had. At home in Costa Rica Sarita struggled for the minimum funds; she did competent needlework but still had to borrow from her family and sell her sewing machine to make passage. The pittance left over was mostly used up on the voyage.

So Sarita Villegas and her daughter were left behind with the crew. They rattled about in the empty ship, sitting propped together among the piled-up deck chairs on the promenade and alone in the dining saloon like a pair of impoverished royals, until at last they were officially declared "L.P.C." ("Likely Public Charge") and delivered by the captain to Ellis Island.

There they spent another day and night in the private bedrooms provided for higher-class passengers, eating free and nourishing meals ("2 breakfasts, 4 dinners, 2 suppers") in the huge cafeteria while the judges studied their semi-fraudulent documents. That year on Ellis

Island the staff were processing one immigrant per minute of every twenty-four-hour day,[117] and while Sarita waited her turn in the Great Hall she encountered people who stayed in her memory after much else had fled. An over-friendly agent, who made the wrong assumption about a single woman traveling with a child, draped an arm around Sarita's waist and was banged with her guitar. (The guitar was a casualty, cracked the length of the box, but the story of the instrument protecting her honor gave Sarita as much pleasure as playing it ever did.) A Puerto Rican prostitute made the same wrong assumption and sat companionably by Sarita in the hall, filling her genteel ears with cheerfully vulgar advice.

The Costa Rican consul arrived, fortyish, with a pompadour of thick hair, thin lips and an anxious expression;[118] he had come to retrieve Roberto Figueredo's wife and child and send them home. The consul, Manuel Bonilla, was a cousin and an old friend who dutifully ferried himself over to warn Sarita that she and Anita would starve if she persisted in this foolishness. He looked truly distressed, but Sarita just patted his hand. "Manuel," she said consolingly, and in what turned out to be an accurate forecast, "don't worry; in ten years I'll be making more money than you."

When it was Sarita's turn to appear before the half-moon bench with the legal inspectors, and the one who spoke Spanish asked, "How are you going to live?", she invented brazenly, "My family in Costa Rica will send me $300 a month." This great sum, as the inspector certainly knew, was twice the average monthly wage in the United States that year.[119] But, whether out of kindness or expediency, he accepted the statement as fact and cleared mother and daughter for entry.

So at last, on their third afternoon within sight of the United States, Sarita Villegas and Anita Figueredo were let out of the great doors to the ferry and to the brief choppy ride across the river to Manhattan. On the dock, Angela Acuña and her brother Jorge gathered them up with relief and escorted them to their lodging, one tiny single room in east Harlem for three dollars a week.

In 1921 the handsome and hapless Warren G. Harding was President of the United States. The week Sarita and Anita arrived in New York, a new marvel called radio carried the President's voice to Madison Square Garden and to San Francisco's Plaza Hotel simultaneously. National Prohibition was in its second year and had so far succeeded in inventing the night club; and a writer the same age as Sarita Villegas, F. Scott Fitzgerald, had just fired the "opening gun in the pro-youth, pro-freedom, and anti-Puritanism campaign" with the publication of his first novel, *This Side of Paradise*. If Sarita had been able to read English when she got off the boat, she could have picked up a newspaper and read:

> They used to wrap their hair in knobs fantastic high and queer; but now they cut it short in bobs or curl it round their ear. The skirts they wore would scrape the street, and catch the dust and germs; they're now so far above their feet, they're not on speaking terms.[120]

Sarita Villegas was twenty-five, spoke no English, had a child and no visible means of support, but had arrived at a place and time where anything seemed possible.

On the second or third day, she found a nursery school run by Catholic nuns who accepted the children of working mothers for ten cents a day. Angela Acuña recorded in her journal that little Anita was panic-stricken at the separation and cried miserably, but still managed to try to reassure her mother. "I will get used to it, Mami," she sobbed, "I will be good. I know you must work for me."[121]

Sarita Villegas did have to find work, and quickly. Contrary to what she declared on Ellis Island, there was no money at all coming from Costa Rica. She entered the garment trade because she knew how to sew and got her first job stitching leather cobblers' aprons for eight dollars a week. Out of that she sent one dollar every week back to Costa Rica to repay what she had borrowed.

Sarita arrived in what would become the world-famous and fabulously wealthy garment district at a moment of historical change. Half a century after Susan B. Anthony stood up on a platform crying, "Join the union, girls" and "Equal Pay for Equal Work"[122] there were signs of a new order coming. *Our City - Our Union*, a 40th Anniversary review of the International Ladies' Garment Workers' Union (I.L.G.W.U.), described the situation:

> As late as 1920, the mighty garment-center-to-be was a squat, drab district over-built with ancient three- and four-story residences reminiscent of the unsavory tenderloin days...
>
> It was the invention of the sewing machine which made the growth of the ready-to-wear industry inevitable... Out went the call for labor to keep the sewing machines running and immigrants proved a boon to the growing industry. The industry welcomed them with jobs and sweatshops. It was a dark page in the history of the industry. Dawn and midnight found thousands of men and women at their machines in dirty, dismal health-destroying shops, grinding away endlessly to earn enough for bread and little more.[123]

The term "sweatshop" referred to a place other than a regular factory, a small contract shop in somebody's badly-ventilated tenement room, with workers doing piecework as fast as they could for as many hours as they could stay awake. The industry was seasonal, and as soon as the current job was done, there might be a slack time when nobody would earn anything. A sweatshop could be your own cramped apartment,[124] and in Sarita Villegas' case it frequently was. But what was happening just as she entered the industry was the coming-of-age of the I.L.G.W.U.

The union was already two decades old but just beginning to have some clout, in the aftermath of the infamous Triangle Waist Company fire of 1911 when six hundred "women" between thirteen and twenty-three years of age were trapped on the upper floors of a sewing factory tinderbox without sprinklers and with stair doors locked shut. Helpless spectators watched the victims leap to their deaths from flaming windows far above the reach of firemen's ladders. This spectacular tragedy finally ignited a real reform movement in the industry and eventually made a power of the union.[125]   Sarita Villegas, who was a militant by temperament, joined and marched and paid her dues.

Meanwhile she and Anita moved up in the world, by the spring of 1922, to their own small apartment in the house of Julieta McGrigor, a Cuban widow with several children who had lived for a time in Costa Rica and kept a little box of Costa Rican soil. Mrs. McGrigor's house stood on W. 120th Street in what would eventually metamorphose as the center of black Harlem (at Adam Clayton Powell Boulevard), but in 1922 was "Spanish," filled with Cubans, Puerto Ricans, and Central and South Americans.[126]

Mrs. McGrigor's front door had a set of Ionic columns which served as an elegant backdrop for the pictures Sarita sent home, she with frizzed hair curled about her ears, and Anita in short pale dresses and satin bows.   All the photographs from this time give an impression of rightness and happiness: mother and daughter in fashionable clothes and hats, seated on a rock in Central Park; posing with a cloud of balloons; standing arms entwined in a rowboat in baggy black bathing suits; Anita in the cap and doublet of a small prince on a pony. Chola Braun opened these letters and considered the pictures which fell in her lap as visions of another world.

Old General Villegas gathered his strength for this one letter:

> San José, May 27, 1922
>
> My dearest Sarita:
>
> I had the pleasure of receiving your letter and understand from it that you are satisfied with your work in that city, and that Anita is now better-adjusted to her new life, that she understands English which lessens her sense of isolation - give her many loving kisses from me and tell her to write me when she learns how.
>
> My health continues to be very bad - it appears that my doctors can't agree on the diagnosis, and I have

become debilitated to the point that I can do nothing...
In consequence, I cannot write you a longer letter today
- my doctors don't let me write, nor even read -

Many kisses to Anita, and to you my affectionate
embrace

Villegas

Then two weeks later, this from Chola Braun:

...on Saturday your father had 7 hemorrhages of blood
from the mouth and that day he was so gravely ill that
the girls went to keep vigil...On Monday he had another
hemorrhage from 11 at night to 6 in the morning, and
every day since he's had one or more...The doctors say
there is no hope....

Astonishingly enough, General Villegas endured three more months
with this frightful malady (recognizable today as an aorto-duodenal
fistula - an aneurysm eroding into the outlet from his stomach) until
with one final violent burst from his ruptured aorta he "leapt over
the threshold of the Eternal" on the 19th of September 1922. The
newspaper declared,

We are in triple mourning: the nation for the death of
its soldier, the world of letters bereft of the writer with
the incisive pen, and the whole of society for the loss of
a true gentleman.[127]

Chapter 13

Scholar

The week her grandfather Villegas died in Costa Rica, Anita Figueredo began her formal education in the New York public school system. Having turned six in August, she entered Grade 1 at P.S. Model School, Borough of Manhattan. Her teacher, Miss Mary Moorhead, sent home stiff little report cards marked with strings of A's and the slogan "Homework Given EVERY DAY". Ms. Abrahams did the same in Grade 2, marking a single A for each month rather than for any specific achievement; and each month the little cards were signed off by "Sara de Figueredo," who was briefly bowing to American convention by using her daughter's last name.

As it turned out, these were the only school years before college (except for a few months of eighth grade) that mother and daughter would live together. Sarita worked six days a week, formally, but took home piecework at night and, even so, found it necessary to advertise for boarders in the space at Mrs. McGrigor's in 1923:

> **Furnished Accommodations**
> with all modern comforts in the home
> of a Latin Family
> SRA. SARA VILLEGAS

201 West 120th St, Apt 17.

Sarita sent a copy of this classified ad to Chola Braun, and the most remarkable thing about the letter was the unembellished address on the envelope:

Doña Rafaela de Villegas

San José - Costa Rica

There was no "extra" room, and so Sarita gave up her own bed to the boarder, and little Anita often found her mother in the morning asleep in the kitchen over her sewing, head pillowed in the stacks of colored cloth.

It is not clear whether Sarita sent Anita away to school because she was working so hard, or whether she was working that hard in order to be able to send Anita away to school. In either case, Anita's education was the driving force of her mother's life; and somehow or other, in the summer of 1924, the child was enrolled at Mt. St. Joseph Academy for Catholic girls, in the suburb of Chestnut Hill at the northwestern limit of Philadelphia.

The original school building still stands, called the Rotunda. It is a castle-like structure of rough dark stone, very Germanic in keeping with the surrounding community. But inside it is surprising and lovely: a wide atrium rising five stories to a ceiling of stained-glass panels, with a central stairway lifting to a statue of St. Joseph and then dividing and coiling its mahogany balustrades around the four floors above. Today the Rotunda interior is everywhere painted a soft light green and white, and the effect is that of an elegant small opera house. In the corridors, the dormitory rooms look unchanged from sixty years ago with dark walls and heavy dark furniture; but what redeems them is the view from every window of green lawn and old green trees.[128]

Not-quite-eight-year-old Anita was photographed outside the Rotunda in a row of little girls with short bobbed hair and gingham summer dresses, and then in all kinds of poses by herself, all the while smiling cheerfully. But she was too unhappy to appreciate the view when she sat at the big dark desk in her room and wrote this letter home:

July 23, 1924

My dearest little mother:

I got your letter yesterday and it made me very happy...
but never mind about bringing me the Push Mobil,
because it would be better if you just took me home.

Anita

This missive, with a little tooth forlornly stuck to the inside fold, was
put into adult hands for mailing and not post-marked until **one month
later**; it had this added note in adult script on the back:

My very dear Señora:

How is Anita? She is fine, and anxious to see you. It's
true that she's sad...but you know that when little girls
find friends it's impossible to be unhappy. Of course,
Anita wants to see you and leave with you for a few
days as she says. But it would be absurd to take her
now when she's so recently begun to get used to being
away from your affection.

From experience, I will tell you that it would be better
if you didn't come this Saturday...Don't worry about
Anita because she is happy...

But Sarita Villegas did worry about Anita and not about being absurd.
In eight years she had not spent a night apart from her little girl, before
this long summer. The intellectual decision to send her away had been
quite easy. But Sarita's heartache surprised her at work, and at night
when she washed linens for her boarder. She took the train out to
Chestnut Hill and brought Anita home.

Before they chose another school they went hunting a new apartment.
Sarita moved often as Anita grew up, at least seven times, as if she were
sampling New York on every side. She had a door closed in her face just
once, the first time she ventured out of Spanish Harlem. A red-haired
woman with cats cut her off in mid-sentence and declared she didn't
rent to "Puerto Ricans." After that, mother and daughter worked out a

little deception: Anita in her best dress marched up steps to negotiate with landlords and "supers" in her unaccented English, while Sarita pretended to be deaf, standing mute and sweetly smiling behind.

Their first outing of this type got them into a new flat on the upper west side at 93rd Street. They escaped the summer heat in Riverside Park and talked about Anita's education. Sarita asked everyone who might know about boarding schools, including her more affluent friends and her elderly boss at the sewing factory. The boss, Mrs. McFadden, was a bosomy lady with horse sense who approved of clever girls, and it was probably she who recommended The Academy of Our Lady of Good Counsel, in White Plains, New York.

Good Counsel was a boarding academy of the Sisters of the Divine Compassion, a congregation founded in New York City to care for the daughters of destitute Catholic families, of Irish, German and Italian immigrants who were pouring into the great harbor and from there into its slums. The founding women originally opened a house in the Bowery for the ragged girls they found about them on the streets, but by 1890 had moved to the "country" in search of fresh air and space.

The property purchased by the nuns for their Motherhouse was an hour's train ride north from Grand Central Station, and in the early fall of 1924, Anita Figueredo and her mother stepped down from a carriage of the New Haven and Hartford Railway at the station in White Plains. They made their way on foot along Broadway and turned into an estate graced with ancient trees and a handsome old house draped in wisteria vines at the end of an avenue of stately pines. There was a gray stone chapel with an ivy-covered clock tower and, in front of the chapel and the garden on a round of sweeping lawn, stood Anita's new school.

The Academy was five stories of patterned brick with heroic statues of the archangels Gabriel and Michael guarding the door. On the ground floor (actually below ground from the front entry) was the dining room - with tables oddly set for seven - and the kitchen. On the first floor were reception and assembly rooms; classrooms on the second; a wardrobe, sewing room, and dormitories on the third floor; and dormitories and infirmary on the fourth. In early advertisements the upper floors were said to command a magnificent view. All the rooms were "large, cheerful and well-lighted," and the building had been fitted out with steam heat, gas, and the most modern sanitary conveniences.

The house functioned for about a decade as a permanent residence for destitute girls from New York City. By the early twenties, it was a regular elementary school, with only a few orphans, and those mostly wards with income. All the girls, about a hundred when Anita arrived, were boarders who had visitors on Sunday.[129]

So now, in September 1924, Anita Figueredo was one of an orderly line of several dozen young girls filing past the great stone angels into the reception room of Good Counsel Academy. Most of them held at least one parent by the hand and were able to pay a fair tuition. The records show that Anita Figueredo was first admitted to the second grade class of Sister Mary Catherine, no doubt confirming Sarita's low opinion of public school, since Anita has already passed Grade 2 with excellent marks.[130]

After registration, Sarita and Anita were directed up to the top floor dormitory called "Queen of Angels" where the youngest children slept in rows of little iron beds. Together they unpacked Anita's few belongings, and then parted with almost no tears, as Sarita would be back within a week. The trip to Chestnut Hill had been an eighty-mile journey by train plus the transfer from Philadelphia, so that day trips were long and hard. White Plains, by contrast, was a fourth that distance direct, and every Sunday (except the first Sunday of the month, when she had to work), Sarita Villegas could visit her little girl all day long. The most glorious days of the year, almost better than Christmas, were the rare fifth Sundays when Anita could hardly contain her excitement:

> Mami, I'm sending you a little calendar so you can see that Sunday IS NOT the first Sunday, so I want you to write and tell me if you're coming Saturday or Sunday so I can be ready...
>
> I'd like it better if you came Sunday so you didn't have to come after work...but I don't want you to do what

you don't want to do, so if you want to come Saturday, tell me...it's only that I don't want you to work so hard, coming here after work, just tell me...Don't cry when you get this letter, remember what I'm telling you, prettiest Mami, Sunday is the 31st 31st 31st 31st!"

The letters home were different right from the start, quite cheerful and written in a sounded-out Spanish which defies translation unless one reads it aloud. For example,

"Lla me puso la ermana awa-ousijenada en la muela" is actually

"*Ya me puso la hermana agua oxigenada en la muela*", or

"Sister put some hydrogen peroxide on my tooth."

Although English very quickly became Anita's "first" language, her mother insisted they speak Spanish all their lives; and as a result Anita retained her native accent and fluency. But it seemed ridiculous that she "take" Spanish in school, and so she had to teach herself to read and spell it. The arrangement was that Anita write home once a week, and the faithful little letters are a wonderful record of her whole school career and, with the addresses on the envelopes, of her mother's peregrinations around Manhattan.

The plan for the pupils of Good Counsel was still much as mapped out by the foundress:

> Girls are to be cared for, given the elements of a good education and fitted for the practical duties of life. It is Mother Mary Veronica's purpose to make the school as little like an institution and as much like a home as was possible. Tender sympathy united to firm discipline is to be the basic keynote of the girls' training...The Sisters' attitude toward the children is to be motherly.
>
> The girls rise at six and file in twos across to Mass in the grey stone chapel; upon entering, they say the aspiration: "Good Morning, dear Jesus, give us your blessing. And

before leaving, they kneel and say: "Good-bye, dear
Jesus, make me a good girl for the rest of the day."

After breakfast, they make their beds and do the little
household tasks assigned to them. School begins at 8:45.
In addition to the usual grammar-school subjects, they
are offered vocal music, cooking, sewing, and typing.
All are taught to be gentle and well-mannered.

The garden, with its white lattices and rosebushes, was a lovely backdrop
for pictures of little Anita and her classmates in winter uniform: long-
sleeved navy dresses with hip sash and side pleats and large white
rounded collars and cuffs; what with their chopped-off hair and bangs
and full-length dark stockings and shoes, the effect is that of a flock of
little Pilgrims assembled for a Thanksgiving play. The long black habits
of the Sisters, Mary Anselm, Mary Catherine, Mary Agnes, portly
Mary Consilio, Mary Clement and Mary Ethelburge, are distinguished
by a short square yoke called a *guimpe* bordered on three sides with
crimson braid; an impressively large black crucifix hung against the
breast between the guimpe and a wide black belt.

On Monday, December 8, 1924 (a "holy day" in honor of the Blessed
Virgin Mary) Anita in white dress and veil made her First Communion.
Sarita took the day off from work at her daughter's impassioned
request: "You made a mistake, you thought it was Sunday, but it's
really Monday, so come Monday, for sure, for sure, for sure!" She came,
bearing statuettes of the Virgin and a little angel which Anita placed at
the head and the foot of her bed to watch over her as she slept.

After Christmas vacation (which Sarita casually extended for an extra
week), the hill behind the school was covered with snow and Anita
wrote home that Sister said she might have a sled. Next Sunday she
was happily sailing down and trudging up the hill in a heavy long coat
with fur collar and white knit cap, along with Sarita and all the other
sledders and mothers.

By the end of January 1925, after one semester at Good Counsel, Anita
had been promoted back up out of second into third grade, and beyond
into fourth; she was eight years old. In line with her new maturity, she
began to worry in her letters about her mother's work, as in:

Pretty little mother, I ask the Lord often to let you repair a lot of lacework and earn a lot of money. And I hope you have a lot of old ladies working for you who don't bother you much.

But mostly she wrote:

I'm very happy, and I feel fine. I can't wait until Sunday so I can see you. I am behaving myself and studying hard. A thousand kisses and hugs from your little daughter who loves you so much and never stops thinking of you. Don't cry over this letter, Mami. Millions and millions of kisses and hugs from your daughter who adores you. My dearest, enchanting, divine little mother. DON'T CRY

By spring Anita's name was on the Honor Roll posted on the classroom wall for all the world to see, with "three stars after it" for especially good behavior.

Summer came and the letters stopped. Anita was cared for somehow or other during the week, at times by the landlady's family, now and again by boarders. Some days she was on her own. Once the doorbell rang at their third-floor apartment, and Anita opened it to find a strange man who asked, "Is your mother home?"

"No," said Anita, frankly, "I'm all alone."

"I'm hungry," said the man.

"Come right in," she said, in a manner that never changed the rest of her life. And the stranger sat down in the kitchen, while Anita searched around for a box of Uneeda biscuits and water, which she served to her guest with the pious apology that "Jesus said: 'A glass of water given in His name will be appreciated.'" The stranger, no doubt eyeing her curiously, ate and drank and took his leave.

Another day she was leaning out her window watching the world hurry by. An organ-grinder and his monkey seemed unable to stop the flow; the monkey's outstretched palm was mostly empty, and his little face seemed mournful. But Anita knew where her mother hid a five-dollar bill. She dangled the unimaginable riches out the window, and the creature in the scarlet coat scaled the building with lightning speed to snatch it and vanish with his master before any adult could make it down the stairs.

But on Sundays, at least, mother and daughter were together, and they escaped the humid city at the beach. They piled into the subway car with crowds of their friends (including the Costa Rican consul from Ellis Island) and traveled across the East River to Brooklyn and Long Beach. The old photo album is a documentary of changing styles in swimwear: long and baggy in 1923, mid-thigh and quite curvaceous by 1927.

The first letter home from school in the new September term was a birthday letter for Sarita, and Anita's present to her mother was a prodigious number of prayers, as follows:

Our Fathers	300
Hail Marys	500
Blessings	500
Rosaries	30
Creeds	300
Lord Jesus Christs	400
Masses	5
Communions	3
Glory be to the Fathers	700
Obediences	1000
Acts of Contrition	100
Acts of Charity	109
total	4297

Much of the available space on Anita's little folded letters was devoted to assuring her mother that she was happy, as in "I am happy and I have always been very happy, so don't worry about me because I've been fine and my teacher likes me a lot, and almost all the nuns love me." And "I am having so much fun I feel as if I were in the house of happiness." And "I'm much happier than I was before because I have about three more friends, which makes ten friends altogether."

At Christmas in her second year at Good Counsel, Anita went home for vacation to a new apartment on the upper west side, the fourth in four years. All their homes in Manhattan, with one exception, are still standing; this one on W. 88th St. is five stories of brown brick a few steps off Broadway. Sarita walked out her door into the bustle of that wide avenue and looked across it to the Hudson River before descending to the subway for the ride downtown to the garment district, fifty blocks south. Halfway between her apartment and the garment district was the famous theater section of Broadway, ablaze again with color and light after a brief setback at the start of Prohibition when its elegant restaurants and hotel dining rooms closed for loss of liquor revenue. The 1924-25 season was called by at least one critic the "best" theater season of all time, with 228 new shows displaying the talents of Eugene O'Neill, Maxwell Anderson and George S. Kaufman, Alfred Lunt, Lynn Fontanne, Fred Astaire and Katharine Cornell, George and Ira Gershwin, Cole Porter, and Richard Rodgers and Lorenz Hart.[131]

Sarita's life had its own color and light. She worked hard, but she was proud of herself and, when her work could wait, she liked going out on the town. She moved in a large, lively, affectionate crowd of Latins, temporary or permanent exiles like herself, from Cuba and the Dominican Republic, Central and South America, who were all accepted on equal terms provided they were *gente decente,* which is to say, educated, and from a genteel background. It mattered not at all that some were seamstresses now, and others physicians or diplomats or the heirs to family wealth. Sarita dragged herself home on Saturday night, put on her makeup and pretty clothes and walked across Central Park for dinner and poker with Amalia Bacardí, who lived in elegant rooms supported by the best Cuban rum.

She also dated, and the principal man in her life while Anita was at Good Counsel was one Luis Greñas, a man whose real occupation was something prosaic, but who was so handsome with his chiseled features and slicked-back hair that little Anita dreamed about him as her father and, in her imagination, made him into an "author," which was the most romantic work she could imagine. She told the other girls at school that he wrote Tarzan.

Back at Good Counsel after Christmas, Anita made rapid progress. By February she was in fifth grade, and when school began again in September of 1926 she was is in sixth, a month after turning ten. It was a rather peculiar progression up and down the educational ladder, beginning a half-year behind and now a year ahead, with a only a few months here and there in any one class. All in all, the Sisters of Divine Compassion seemed to display remarkable flexibility in allowing a bright and determined child to move along at her own pace. It appears they respected the pact between mother and child that this expensive education be acquired and filed away as quickly as possible. The pace also brought out Anita's interpersonal gifts; she had friends of all ages who failed to be annoyed as she collected her medals and passed them by.

Anita was relatively tall in fifth and sixth grade, for the only time in her life; she entered adolescence very early, at around eight or so, and now at ten was physically mature and near her adult height (although at the end of this year she was requesting size 1½ shoes). In her first letter home this term she wrote: "Mama, they finally changed my little bed for a big one and I slept like a dormouse - last night I didn't wake up a single time."

This winter of 1926-27 had early snows, and Anita was able to ice-skate after recovering from a badly sprained ankle. She dutifully reported applying "camphor ice" as instructed every night before bed and every morning before going outside, to ward off colds; she always wore her new "goolashes" and coat, and was further fortified by boxes of chocolates from home, and "thus it is that I am always warm and happy."

The letters from Good Counsel end in the spring of 1928. Anita had been there four years and arrived at the end of seventh grade. She wrote of having the most important part in the Mardi Gras morality play; originally supposed to perform "Experience", she was promoted to "Love" at the last moment when Sister discovered she was "a born actress." There is also this poignant note, accidentally in English (which Anita never used when writing, as her mother warned she would return the letter unread): "Darling, last Sunday I got dressed thinking you might come up on account of the snow and you didn't come but I was playing all the time in the snow, so I didn't mind…"

At the end of this term, Sarita arrived to collect Anita from the good-hearted Sisters in White Plains for what turned out to be the last time. Graduation would occur the following year, but neither mother nor daughter was sentimental about such things, and it was time, Sarita said, for a long and leisurely visit to Costa Rica.

They set out in August 1928. In their passport picture - still Costa Rican citizens - they look more alike than at any other time in their lives, both with sleek bobbed hair waved just to the tips of their ears, exposing the perfect ovals of their faces. Their mouths, which were not alike in life, are painted in identical Cupid-bows. Sarita is thirty-one and Anita on the verge of twelve.

The trip was a brilliant success lasting several months. They lodged as before with Chola Braun who treated her *palomita* ("little dove") Anita with a tenderness which was practically unprecedented and dumbfounded her daughters and her other granddaughters. Anita had her picture taken alone and in pairs and crowds, in ordinary dress and in every imaginable costume including that of a woodland nymph. She and her mother were honored at teas and young people's parties of all kinds, and excursions to the provinces. They were petted and lionized as returning heroines.

Sarita renewed a discreet romance with an old friend named Santiago Chamberlain,[132] a mining engineer who lived in the field but seemed to find business in the capital so long as Sarita was there. (Although she was officially still a separated wife, it was widely known in Costa Rica that Roberto Figueredo remarried in Guatemala at the end of 1926[133], giving Sarita a *de facto*, if not a precisely legal, divorce.) There is a picture of Mr. Chamberlain with his head of prematurely white hair and his handsome face, standing with his arms around Anita and her favorite cousin; Anita, who claimed never to miss her real father, labeled the photo: "Gladys, **Dad** and myself".

It was hard to leave all this cumulative affection but, after six months, Anita's education was languishing; it was time to go back to New York, and in early February 1929 the newspaper reported a farewell picnic in the countryside for thirty-eight friends and relations. This time the voyagers boarded ship at the western port of Puntarenas. The *S.S. Virginia* was en route from San Francisco to New York, and they had their pictures taken in life preservers on deck as the ship made its way through the locks of the Panama Canal.[134]

The boat trip was, as always, via Cuba; ashore in Havana, Sarita telephoned Santiago to her beloved mother-in-law, doña Anita Lora, who had fallen ill in Costa Rica and returned to the remnants of her Cuban family. Her sister informed Sarita sadly that doña Anita was dying as they spoke.[135]

A number of the little letters from school in Sarita's collection mention arriving a week or two after the other students; Sarita was always casual about this sort of thing, taking it for granted that Anita would catch up. This time, however, Anita returned to a new school, St. Gregory's parochial, near their 88th St. apartment, **five months** into eighth grade. But years later, after Anita's picture appeared in a national magazine, she got a letter from a classmate reminiscing about everything they'd done at St. Gregory's, about walking home together and sitting on the steps planning the future, about their friends, about Anita playing the role of Buttercup in Gilbert & Sullivan's "Pinafore," and it was as if they had started together in kindergarten.[136] And of course she graduated, in top form, with the Class of 1929. From then on it appears that Anita took charge of her own education.

CHAPTER 14

Southern Seminary

Though not yet a teenager, Anita had become necessarily self-sufficient. Her mother was still working at the latest of several dress factories, still bringing home piecework and distributing it to others, and running her boarding-house, and they still saw each other principally on Sundays. Anita earned her lunch on weekdays at St. Gregory's by walking a neighbor child to and from school and sharing the hot meal his mother made. A responsible child could still move safely around New York on her own. This last summer after grammar school Anita walked alone nearly every day to a big public swimming pool several blocks away, and while she walked she thought about high school.

There seemed to be no question of a day school nearby; St. Gregory's was alright as an interim, but Anita was not to spend her high school years studying at the kitchen table until the lodger retired and vacated the living room couch. She was to have the best private boarding school to be found, and it was up to her to find it.

One day she saw an advertisement in a magazine for Southern Seminary, "A School of Character for Girls and Young Women," in Buena Vista, Virginia. She wrote off for a catalog, which arrived decorated with line cuts of riding to hounds and the mounted noble figure of Robert E. Lee. Inside, Anita read that "character" was to be nurtured by the healthfulness of the school's location (since disease is an ally of sin), and that there was an abundant supply of steaming-hot water with which the Seminary students at all times fought the battle of personal cleanliness. Most important of all was the home life on campus: "From the cheer and comradeship radiating from the great open fire in the front hall…to the spiritual restfulness of family prayers at evening, every student feels and visitors seldom fail to remark upon the home atmosphere of the school."[137]

Anita's already well-developed character was looking for a home away from home, and Southern Seminary sounded exactly right. She showed her mother the pictures in the catalog, which Sarita agreed were attractive. They were all that Sarita would ever see of the school until the day of her daughter's graduation. Anita filled out her own application, arranged for the transfer of her grades and testimonials of her good moral character; and then, a few days after her 13th birthday, put on her best pink party dress with ribbons at the sleeveless shoulders. She kissed her mother goodbye at Grand Central Station - easier now after years of partings - and joined her escort and a handful of girls (in pleated skirts, middy blouses and V-neck sweaters) for the train ride south: 350 miles through Philadelphia, which she had seen as a little girl, and then the unknown country of Baltimore and Washington to Virginia and the Blue Ridge Mountains.

What Anita encountered when she arrived at Southern Seminary was a converted resort hotel on the brow of its own hill, over-looking the town and river and surrounded by "rank on rank of mountains with their myriad shades of blue," as the catalog said. The main building was an extraordinary red structure of pressed brick, stone and ornamental shingles dreamily assembled into turrets and gables and wide verandas and balconies, all set on expanses of green lawn dotted with white swing chairs and great oaks. And then there was an indoor swimming pool, gymnasium, hard-surface tennis courts, golf course, acres of playing fields and stables with the heads of gorgeous horses at the doors. The campus included both high school and junior college and was run by a family of four: the tough-minded President, Dr. Robert

Lee "Daddy" Durham, who was both an intellectual and an ex-football player and once cleared off unwelcome company with a shotgun; the deeply kind and religious "Mother" Mary Durham; their daughter Margaret Durham Robey, who was principal of the high school; and Margaret's husband H. Russell Robey who, as financial officer, would keep Southern Seminary soundly afloat through the depression which rapidly followed there on the heels of Anita Figueredo. [138] [139] [140]

Within a week of her arrival at Southern Seminary, Anita sent her mother this telegram (to the 88th St. apartment Sarita occupied nearly four years, in a record of domestic stability):

> Today is your 33rd birthday, and I wish you all the happiness in the world - may God bless you and let us be together always - I promise to be the best a daughter can be and to study hard so that someday I can make you happy.

When Anita enrolled, the Durham family had owned and managed Southern Seminary for exactly a decade and continued its Methodist tradition. A girl of any religious background might attend, but all were expected at Sunday evening vespers and at "family" prayers, and all were asked to honor the Sabbath by refraining from work or play more strenuous than strolling about the quiet campus or reading in an overstuffed chair in front of the fire.

The curriculum was designed to suit girls with varying aspirations. There were six classes: freshman, sophomore and junior (which was officially the high school); and then junior middle, senior middle and senior (which was officially the junior college.) The "twelfth grade" did not precisely exist in Southern schools at this time, but its equivalent was the "junior middle class." The era was that of the finishing school; and Southern Seminary's elegant quarterly reports list on the left the rigorous "solids" of English and History and Math, and on the right such things as Story Telling, Dancing and Piano, Cooking, Sewing and Interior Decoration. Anita's report was always dense with A's on the left, and utterly blank on the right. Her favorite teacher, Miss Annie Moore, would write of her sixty years later:

There are three, maybe four, of us living who remember the vibrant Anita Figueredo when she arrived at Southern Seminary campus early one September morn in 1929....When classes met on the first day, I knew I had a challenge before me - a mind that would demand the best I could give her....All of Anita's teachers were captivated by her pure aspiring mind and sought to nurture it....We all let Anita take over the specific class from time to time. She was a born teacher and shared herself with her classmates....Anita endeared herself to all of us and amazed us with her eagerness to absorb all that this school of <u>her</u> choice had to offer....In your biography just say: Southern Seminary fell in love with the electrifying Anita Figueredo. They couldn't help it.[141]

Annie Parks Moore was twenty-four in the fall of 1929, a gentle young woman from North Carolina who had also just arrived at Southern Seminary; she was the newest member of the faculty, assigned to Latin and Algebra.

The faculty in general, or at least Anita's teachers in her full slate of "solids," seemed quite good: the white-haired and beautiful Elizabeth Baker in English; in History, Mary Louise Israel, a tall, cool intellectual who made herself Anita's mentor; Mary Alice Price in Chemistry and Civics; Ernestine Landrum in Biology, who respected Anita's refusal to kill any living thing for dissection, and allowed her to study from books and her neighbor's specimens; and Laura Sheppe, the Dean who taught Geometry. But it was Annie Moore who was Anita's instant friend. Miss Moore was the faculty sponsor of the freshman class, thirteen girls in all, and she wrote:

Maybe because I was nearer to her age and understood boarding school life inside and out, and was chosen often to chaperone her group on mountain trails, to movies and on Monday day trips, we had a splendid chance to get acquainted.

Within a month of Anita's arrival the stock market crashed, and a few of the girls from good families were discreetly recalled from Southern Seminary. But Sarita Villegas, who had nothing to lose in the stock market, continued to work steadily.

As the depression settled in, there were leaner times. Annual charges for: "(1) Room with bath on hall, board, heat, light and servants' attendance; (2) Bible; (3) Library and reading-room fee; (4) Fee for medical attention; (5) Lyceum fee; and (6) Instruction" is $650.00, or $65/month. Anita was not on scholarship to begin with; but the administration was very kind to her when it came to payment. Sarita was allowed to send money when she could, and then as Anita's intellectual gifts became obvious, there were partial scholarships for whatever was still owing at the end of term. There were added charges for extra-curricular activities; but Anita, temperamentally, was suited to her limited means. She rarely aspired to things she could not have, although for some reason she longed to take archery, and Mr. Robey himself arranged, very discreetly, that she should have the class for free. He was very protective of her dignity, and her mother's, and never even mentioned that the archery was not included with tuition." Still Anita had to watch her pennies, and her letters often mention her expenses:

> Mami, I have $7 left, because what with paying 75¢ for laundry every week, the money just goes. Today we went to Lexington to Mass and we had to have breakfast and it cost me 50¢ and you know with putting a nickel or dime in the plate at Mass it ends up being about 95¢ a week and there goes the money. I got your dollar, Mami, thank you a million. I promise to spend as little as possible.

Lexington, one of the most beautiful towns in the Shenandoah Valley, was five miles west of school; Anita went to church there and nearly lost her faith. Although Southern Seminary tried to provide honorably for the religious needs of all its students, this was the South which had just sunk the Presidential campaign of Alfred E. Smith in a tidal wave of anti-Catholic anxiety.[142] The town of Buena Vista had at least a dozen churches, but none for the tiny Catholic minority at Southern Sem - perhaps four or five girls in a student body of ninety-five - who

105

took a car and a (Protestant) chaperone every second Sunday to Mass in Lexington. The itinerant priests were a grim lot who flailed away in a decomposing church about the evils of Protestantism, while Anita sat and squirmed beside the patient chaperone. By contrast, Sunday evening vespers back at school were filled with the relative gentility and light and sweet hymns of Methodist chapel, and mild homilies by Mother Durham on loving one's neighbor.

At Thanksgiving her first year, Anita had the exquisite pleasure of being invited to a Prom, "me, 13 years old!" It was a very formal affair, with some girls even "coming down" from New York:

> What do you think, pretty mother? Since you can't take me I would have to take a chaperone (here they don't let us go anywhere alone.) I would **love** to go because it would be my first "Prom," but it would cost a lot because I would have to pay for the chaperone and stay in a hotel...maybe I should wait until next year, or later this year?

(Anita could never remember if she went.)

As time passed, she was invited to more and more dances at the boys' schools in the area: Virginia Military Institute in Lexington (where General "Stonewall" Jackson once taught Confederate cadets)[143], and Staunton Military Academy which was about thirty-five miles north and required an overnight stay. Eventually Anita was asking her mother to help her choose by Special Delivery whether to go with Adolfo Ponzanelli, the son of a Mexican sculptor and "the only Latin at V.M.I."; or with Bill Baker, "an American and very nice," to the Easter ball at S.M.A.

At the end of Anita's first year she was voted into the section of the yearbook called "Who's Who at Southern Seminary" as "Most Intellectual" girl. With her dark hair parted severely down the middle and bobbed behind her ears, she was photographed in a borrowed crepe dress with a fancy dipping hem, and a big straw hat.[144] The Costa Rican papers were thrilled:

> Honor to the princess of intelligence and knowledge,
> and congratulations to the mother of such a scholarly
> and distinguished daughter.[145]

The summer after ninth grade Anita rode the train home from Virginia to another new apartment, this one a stone's throw from Riverside Drive in the hilly neighborhood west of Harlem called Hamilton Heights. (Decades later, this house and the ones around it are badly deteriorated, with old paint flaking from their Grecian columns and graffiti covering the walls. But the area is still attractive because of the nearness of the river and the trees and hills, and must have been very appealing in 1930.) It was much farther north than before, at W. 137th Street, so the ride downtown for Sarita was now a hundred blocks. But neither she nor Anita minded traveling around Manhattan. This summer again, Anita walked nearly daily to the swimming pool on the roof and began lifetime friendships with three teenage boys: Jimmy Sazani, who was Greek and came swimming from somewhere out in the boroughs; Jackie Berutich, whose family had rooms in a building way uptown; and Tommy Bennett who lived with his divorced mother in California and drove his own car to see his dad in New York the summer he turned sixteen.

This summer also, Sarita Villegas had a new gentleman friend, a Colombian physician, Dr. Francisco Marulanda, who was a well-to-do bachelor perhaps twenty years older than she. Dr. Marulanda began to appear in pictures at the beach, a dignified balding man with short gray hair at the temples and a gray moustache; beside him Sarita looks young and pretty in longer dark hair and her customary black wool swimsuit, now cut to show the entire length of her shapely legs. "The Doctor" took her dining and dancing and won her affection but not her heart. He referred ruefully, in a letter dated November 1930, to the May-December nature of their romance:

> Remember our outing of the second of November
> when we so much admired the snowy water fountains,
> diaphanous and pure like the sentiments of your soul,
> and we contemplated by twilight the autumn leaves
> with their withered red-hued leaves?

> I seemed to myself like one of those poor trees which,
> in the midst of its decay, will still dream of spring.[146]

But Sarita would not marry "Francis," nor anyone else, for fear of jeopardizing Anita's education; she did not want to consider a husband's opinion on the matter. (And she remained legally married to Roberto Figueredo, as a deliberate impediment.)

It was at the start of her second year at Southern Sem that Anita conceived the idea of finishing high school in three years because she had time on her hands:

> Since I'm only taking 5 courses it seems to me that I don't have much to do...and I am thinking that if it's going to be like this I could go to summer school to take an English course or maybe two. I'm sure you're going to say no, that I have to rest, but there are only 4 hours of school and they don't give homework, and so it turns out I only study in the morning five days a week. So next year I could take not only the three courses I'll have left but also chemistry and whatever other science I need for medicine....I would graduate in three years with two credits more than I need....Tell me what you think.

Anita was president of her sophomore class, and this was also the year she came into her own athletically. She was a starting center, at all of five feet, on the basketball team that beat the college freshmen. She became a champion archer, a tennis player "charged with teaching <u>six</u> other girls how to play," and she even dared to mention her father in a letter home: "I'm also practicing the high jump and the long jump (that is where the <u>Figueredo</u> comes in...)"

She also, despite her brave self-sufficiency, wrote this after a bad sunburn during an April heat wave:

> Oh mother, last night I missed you as never before. You know I'm so burned, and last night there wasn't even anybody around to put any Mentholatum on me. You can't imagine how much I wished you were here.

> Today I hurt all over. I tell you that in these 7 years
> that I've been living without you, most of the time I
> still need you for absolutely everything!

But, usually, Anita at fourteen felt there was nothing she couldn't do, and she wrote her mother this about her future plans for them both:

> We are studying the World War and I just discovered
> that Costa Rica fought against Germany. I didn't know
> that! It's a grand country, and one day I am going to
> make it as rich and great as the United States. Don't
> laugh, I'm serious -
>
> I have it all planned out. I don't know if "society" will
> like my method much, but they are going to have to
> swallow it because in the end it will do them good.
>
> I have it planned with pure Civics and Social Science,
> so it's not craziness. Don't be shocked, Mami, I'm not
> crazy, but very serious - when I see you I'll tell you
> everything and I want you to help me.

This theme, of returning to Costa Rica with her mother and doing something wonderful together for the rest of their lives, is one that recurs through the next twelve years, up to and including the early months after Anita's marriage. It seemed to be a notion that they both accepted as right and inevitable, and implied that Sarita Villegas viewed her whole sojourn in New York as the time in which to get a certain job done and then go home where they belonged.

Anita's last year at Southern Seminary turned out to be the double bill she dreamed up the year before, "junior" and "junior middle class" together. The administration may have been dubious - Anita refers to wanting to "show these people that I am capable of more than they imagine" - but they were ultimately supportive, and Anita did such things as English III and IV simultaneously.

The grinding-on of the Depression was reflected in the census at the school: eighty-eight girls altogether with only six in the freshman class. Anita was business manager of her class and also of Kappa Sigma Phi sorority, her exploits in tennis and basketball earned her election to the Athletic Hall of Fame, and she was once again voted "Most Intellectual" girl. This time the photographer posed her in a swing, which was possibly more appropriate to her age than to the sophisticated image they may have been after.

On Mother's Day of 1932, just prior to graduation, Anita wrote Sarita this remarkable letter:

> You are my ideal - everything I do with my life, every act however small, I do with the hope of being someday like you - as noble and admirable as you.
>
> Jesus said that the love of God is like that of a mother... and that is why I have such faith because if He loves me as you do, then I have nothing more to do than put my life in His hands, knowing He will care for me. When I think what kind of God has given me a mother such as you - I love Him indescribably - and I am not afraid, because He must be so good!
>
> I hope that some day, with the help of God, I can repay in some part the happiness you have given me. I will never be able to make you see what you have been to me: mother, father, brothers, sisters, uncles, aunts, friends...in sum, everything - an angel of God, really, who has taught me the mysteries of heaven and the truths of this world - and from you I have truly learned to know the good in both.
>
> The influence of your life on mine will never be erased and will always be the guiding force in everything I do. Judge me always as you have done up to now, with gentleness, because though I may fall many times short of your expectations, you know that while I have strength I will pick myself up anew and continue trying.
>
> May you spend this day and every day until eternity happy, knowing that you are adored by your Anita

Sarita Villegas folded this love letter into her purse and a few days later made her first and last journey to Southern Seminary, escorted by Dr. Marulanda, to attend her daughter's high school graduation. She wore a stylish cloche hat and slim, silky dress and looked young and beautiful. On graduation day Anita stood on the great lawn among fifteen girls in gored and flounced white ankle-length frocks and T-strap shoes, holding armfuls of long pink roses. In view of her superb academic record, she was offered a full scholarship to Southern Seminary Junior College; but Anita was single-minded about her academic path. It so happened that Barnard, the women's college of Columbia University, was not far from her mother's apartment in Hamilton Heights, and she applied there and was accepted. Thus, in May of 1932, Anita Figueredo and her mother took their leave of Virginia for the train to New York, and college. Anita was fifteen years old.

CHAPTER 15

Manhattanville

In 1932, much of the country had sunk into a long misery. One of every four American workers was unemployed, and in New York itself half the males were out of jobs or working part time. A killing drought had settled over the southwest which would last for eight years and turn the exhausted Great Plains into the Dust Bowl. The governor of New York, Franklin Roosevelt, was a man whose legs were paralyzed but whose will was not, and that summer he was running for President of the United States with the pledge of a "new deal" for the American people.[147]

In 1932 also, the Polish-born David Dubinsky came up through the ranks to the presidency of the International Ladies' Garment Workers' Union and gradually brought it back to power, after a long "Communist" strike nearly flattened it in 1926.[148] Sarita Villegas had been making ladies' dresses in New York for eleven years; she accepted praise for her work but never the bosses' suggestion that she keep a dress or coat she made for herself. Her reputation for incorruptibility made her friends, though, on both sides of the aisle, and there are pictures of little Anita holding hands with one factory owner and another. About the time her daughter left school and came to live with her again in New York,

Sarita was union chairlady (or, as she always pronounced it, "cher-lái-thy") who one day pulled the main plug on all the sewing machines in her shop when the bosses refused to come to terms.

At this time also, Sarita was a sort of unofficial Costa Rican consul in New York, caring for a steady stream of friends, and friends of friends, who needed doctors or lodging or clothes or just company. She visited the sick and fed and housed worried families, often for weeks on end. She arranged for hotels in New York, and excursions to Niagara Falls where she posed with her guests in raingear and shower caps. And she began taking fashion-conscious women to the garment district, introducing buyers to sellers and arranging good deals on both sides. These casual favors evolved into a formal clothing export business -- New York to Costa Rica -- as the Depression finally waned.

Anita was now home in New York to stay, a nearly-grown-up girl who was happy with her mother's company but could manage on her own. In July, she appeared at Barnard College as directed, to take a scholarship exam. Sometime later she was called in to see the dean of admissions, a thin woman who looked down at her over her glasses and informed Anita that she had indeed won a scholarship - much to the dean's surprise since "those Southern schools" were so inferior, and so rarely turned out qualified graduates. Whereupon, Anita drew herself up to her five feet and told the dean with great indignation that, if she was going to insult her beloved Southern Sem, she could **keep** her scholarship, and stomped out never to return.

When she arrived home, still angry, she realized she had no idea what to do next. Sixty years later, it is hard to see why she did not take herself down to one of the public universities of New York and just sign up. But that seemed to be no more an option than a city high school had been. A private school was still wanted, undoubtedly an expensive private school that would have to give her financial aid, that knew nothing about her, and would be opening for the fall semester in less than a month. The closest one to her house, six blocks away at 133rd Street and Convent Avenue, was Manhattanville College.[149]

Manhattanville was founded by the Religious of the Sacred Heart, one of a network of highly-regarded Sacred Heart colleges and schools around the world, and was in the 1930s "dedicated to providing young women with a liberal education in the Catholic tradition." Things have changed since then. Manhattanville has moved upstate, leaving its urban campus to the City College of New York; it serves men and women both, young or mature, and "of diverse religious beliefs." But when Anita Figueredo first approached the heavy front door, it was a Catholic women's college run by semi-cloistered nuns. This, Anita thought, was a serious disadvantage.

She had been embarrassed and disillusioned by the chilly Catholicism of Lexington, Virginia. Her mother Sarita was nominally Catholic but irreverent and anti-clerical, and attended Mass partly to read along audibly in her Spanish missal and drown out the Irish priests. They never belonged to a parish in New York, and not only because they moved so much. Sarita believed she was excommunicated for having married outside the church. No one informed her that according to church law she had corrected her situation by leaving her husband; she thought that compounded her sin, and consequently never received communion because she felt herself to be outside a state of grace.

Anita, though, was naturally religious. She had a strong sense of a personal God to Whom she owed everything, Who was lavishly generous to her, and to Whom she had to account for the proper use of her gifts. The piety of her childhood had been nurtured through the years at Good Counsel, and then flowered at Southern Seminary into a more mature and intense spirituality. At the same time she became increasingly disenchanted with traditional Catholicism because of what she saw as its rigid form and intolerance of other paths to God, its insistence that it was the only way. Methodism had attracted her by its relative simplicity and spontaneous prayer during services, which she thought was like a dialogue with God. The Methodism at Southern Seminary didn't seem to be anti-anything, only pro-good works and prayer. What Anita wanted in her life was a strong working relationship with God, and she did not care much for rules and regulations which got in her way.

At Manhattanville, Anita stood in the dark foyer of the main hall and asked to speak to the person in charge. After a time a nun appeared in the ancient French habit of the Religious of the Sacred Heart, which was the ordinary dress of a widow at the time of the French Revolution. Over the typical nun's black gown she wore a cape called the *pèlerine*, buttoned and short to the waist in front, and long to the ground in back; her floor-length veil fell in transparent folds from a white widow's cap, which was starched and baked to an extraordinary frill worn flat against the sides of the face and fastened under the chin. What with this and a wide bandeau of grosgrain ribbon tight across the forehead, only the midface could be seen head-on, and not even the tip of a nose from the side. As the binding served to smooth out wrinkles and there was not a wisp of hair to be seen, and the swaying, long gown hid the feet and gave the impression of angelic gliding, it was impossible to guess the age or station of the nun who introduced herself to Anita as "Mother Dammann" and asked what she required.[150] [151]

Anita explained herself: although she was as young as she looked, she was a high school graduate who needed admission to the college in three weeks time; she was an excellent student whose transcripts lay in the admissions office at Barnard College which she would not attend because the dean had disparaged her high school; she was a religious skeptic and did not want Catholic dogma forced upon her; she intended to do a pre-medical course; **and** she would need a scholarship. Mother Grace Cowardin Dammann (who was president of the college) interviewed this small, forceful person very seriously for a time, and then informed her that by pure chance the scholarship exam would be given the very next day.

Anita returned as instructed and found herself completely alone in the room where the scholarship exam was administered. Within a day or so she was awarded the financial aid she required, which was basically whatever her mother was unable to pay, and this arrangement endured throughout her college career. Only years later did she discover that Mother Dammann invented an exam and a scholarship for her which had never existed at Manhattanville. As to "pre-med," there was only one upper-division girl actually taking such a course; Mother Dammann had it repeated for Anita and one other freshman, a tall, slender Russian émigré by the name of Catherine "Katusha" Illyne, who had a general interest in science and was happy to keep Anita company. As regards religion, Anita's attendance was expected at the required courses, but she was free to discuss and argue, accept and reject as she chose.

Thus, in September of 1932, Anita formally entered the campus life of Manhattanville. The college stood on the seventeen-acre island of green grass and trees which had been its home since 1847, though then it was a country estate in a village eight miles north of the city limits of New York. It had been a boarding Academy through the Civil War (when it sheltered a number of girls from Confederate states) and up to World War I, at which time it was chartered as an urban college. The buildings Anita knew dated from the post-fire reconstruction of 1890.

The great main building was of ivy-covered brown stone in a sort of Romanesque-French Gothic, with a face of rounded arches and turrets rising first to a black-faced clock which could be read across the campus, and then to the "high, gleaming tower" of the College Song. There were statues of saints in niches in the face, a rose window and cross, and a tall arched entryway with a long flight of steps leading up into the foyer. This building was four stories of nearly everything: administration, classrooms, dormitory, dining halls and chapel. Like Southern Seminary, it stood at the crest of a rise, and falling away on all sides was its own lovely park, dotted here and there with shrines and grottoes.

Anita walked to school, and was one of a small minority of commuters who sat together for lunch at assigned tables, where they were served as in a restaurant, and who after four years of such togetherness were very close friends. The college on the whole was an intimate place, but the demands of her pre-medical course prevented Anita's enjoyment of certain French-convent traditions such as *goûter,* which was tea in the afternoon. Her schedule was too full for tea. She wanted no breaks in her day, no study halls or free periods, and when one threatened she wandered about looking for courses to take, such as *The Divine Comedy* in Italian. Her advisor warned her that the Dante would be rough going without some Italian, and indeed she had to drop the course when her Spanish was not "close enough" to get her through; but the small blue leather-bound books are on her end table decades later, a tribute to her energy and intellectual curiosity.

There was an excellent faculty at Manhattanville in those years, though the Religious of the Sacred Heart followed a rule of cloister which was among the strictest in the world. The nun who lived her life deep in the great city would never see more of New York than could be glimpsed through the bars of the high college gates. While a teacher she lectured, of course, and spoke in a comfortable way with her students. Among her sister nuns she never spoke - not at meals, not at "recreation" (which consisted of darning black socks to the accompaniment of an inspirational reading), not ever except in matters of great urgency, and then in a few words. She also never had a day off; never an hour off. Her entire life was devoted to prayer and the education of herself and her students.

But as regards education, the Religious of the Sacred Heart had the most liberal view and, in striking counterpoint to their rigid daily rule, required all of their teaching nuns to obtain their advanced degrees at the great institutions of the outside world. Anita's first-year history professor, Mother Eleanor O'Byrne, held a fresh Oxford M.A. and was a brilliant, attractive young nun who was made dean before Anita left the college, and later a dynamic president. (The yearbook tells us there were a half-dozen others with Oxford degrees; and the lay faculty were drawn from universities all over the United States and Europe.)[152]

The science professors were nearly all men, including the Jesuit priest Joseph Assmuth who commuted from Fordham College to teach biology; he became fond of Anita, and would later officiate at her wedding. An odd figure on campus was the German Baron Hermann von Walde Waldegg, who invented a new method for language instruction and who sold himself to the administration by conducting an experiment as follows: six top students (including Anita Figueredo) who were new to German, were given half a semester of his instruction, and then were to go to any city summer school and take the highest upper-division course in German for which they could qualify, and report their results in September. Anita had already fulfilled all language requirements for her degree with her Spanish; still she took German on top of everything else in the last three months of her junior year, in a little seminar conducted on a park bench, and then enrolled for a summer of *Goethe* in the evenings at CCNY, passed the course, and contributed to the permanent hiring of Baron von Waldegg.

Anita worked very full days at Manhattanville, with the long "labs" of the pre-medical major as well as the required readings for a philosophy minor. She took her religion courses reluctantly at first, arguing and belaboring every point while the other girls sat quietly by because "to question is to doubt" and doubting might be a sin. Nearly all of Anita's classmates were graduates of Catholic high schools, mostly other Convents of the Sacred Heart, and these students presumably chose to continue in a religious tradition they already accepted. Anita was a curiosity in religion class, with her hand waving in the air to debate what her classmates took for granted. But eventually she became an intellectual convert to Catholicism, and asked to be confirmed in her junior year. Years later she was invited by President Mother O'Byrne to respond in print to the question, "What did you get from Manhattanville?", and she replied:

> The expected answer, no doubt, is: an excellent training in the basic sciences which prepared me for medicine. And yet that is not my answer. The pre- medical course was good, and essential to my further training, but, to my mind, it was of little consequence compared to the really important matter of the way of life I learned there. Manhattanville taught me basic Catholic philosophy, and thereby gave me an insight into the tremendous system of truths which has since helped to clarify my thinking no matter what the problem. I shudder to think how bleak might have been my life had I attended a purely scientific institution.[153]

Anita re-found the structure for her innate spirituality and it became the deep center of her life, although she went on ignoring accretions which she thought unhelpful, and she never had much use for the notion of sin except as a failure to love God and one's fellow man.

Weekday evenings during college she spent with Sarita, writing papers while her mother packed her boxes of clothes for export. As they lived together now, there were no regular letters exposing Anita's state of mind, but Mother's Day always opened a well of tenderness:

13 May 1934

My soul's dear little Mother:

This day, your day, I would like to give you everything you want - but it is not possible...**yet**. One day it will be, because I am working as hard as a student **can** work with the intention of someday - soon - being able to do it. It wouldn't be proper to say here that you deserve it, first because it's so obvious, and secondly because words fail me in trying to express your goodness. At least I can make you see that your dear affection and all your efforts have not been lost on me - that with all my soul, my life and my heart I thank you, and that for me you will always be the most <u>magnificent</u> mother in the world...

Sarita evidently felt secure enough in her daughter's affections to allow her to date young men without any of the supervision that would have been the rule in a Latin society. So on weekends Anita dated a series of interesting college boys; one was the manager of the Columbia football team, and another a pianist who introduced her to the music of George Gershwin in the penthouse apartment on Riverside Drive his family kept for him, his piano and his records. From the time she began dating, Anita attracted many and various admirers; and, partly because she made it clear from the outset that there was no question of getting "serious" as she was going to be a doctor, most of these old boyfriends remained friends for life.

There were always summer jobs. In 1933 after freshman year, Anita spent her mornings as personal secretary to a wealthy man who lived on Park Avenue, and afternoons she returned to the old swimming pool on the roof. In 1935, while doing the infamous *Goethe* at night, she worked days at Metro-Goldwyn-Mayer in New York, writing Spanish subtitles for a film of *Romeo and Juliet,* using a volume of Spanish

Shakespeare and working the snatches of poetry into the allowable rectangles for a princely $25 a week.

The summer of 1934, Anita was nearly eighteen, and she and her mother returned to Costa Rica together for the second time. It had been six years, and Anita had changed from a pretty adolescent into a truly beautiful young woman. Sarita herself was lovelier than ever at thirty-seven, wearing the graceful long knit dresses of the era, long earrings, and wonderful wide-brimmed hats at an angle like Ingrid Bergman. The voyage down was a great adventure in itself, with more than a little shipboard romance for Anita.

When the boat finally docked in Costa Rica, they returned as before to the house of Sarita's mother, Chola Braun, who was now an ancient-looking seventy-six, bent and thoroughly wrinkled and peering at the world through enormous round lenses which magnified her nearly-blind eyes. She wore the long black skirts and blouses of a turn-of-the-century widow. Resisting all modern contraptions, she called for a horse and carriage when she absolutely could not walk. She still lived with her second daughter Tita, the nurse/midwife who delivered "everybody's" babies. Separated from her husband many years before his death, Chola Braun was nevertheless honored nationally as his widow on the first Costa Rican Mother's Day (15 Aug 1932) with a large formal photograph published in the paper as representing Costa Rican motherhood.[154]

Now, two years later, Chola was pleased to see her youngest daughter, and uncritically approving of Anita. With her other granddaughters she was rigid and puritanical, fussing with them about their modern "immodest" clothes and manners. But, to her, Anita looked *preciosa,* even in the white shorts she wore nearly daily to play tennis.

Roberto Figueredo was back in town, and he meant to see his first daughter and first wife. He was thirty-nine, had been married again seven years (after almost a decade of separation from Sarita Villegas) and was restoring a dilapidated old house in Alajuela for his new family, including a son Roberto and daughters Julieta and María Luz. (The fateful choice of this particular house, next door to a family with an unruly boy named José León Sánchez who loved Julieta, would lead to catastrophe when the children grew up. But that is a later story.)

In Guatemala, Roberto had been a journalist, most notably a sportswriter with a popular column on soccer (for which he had "invented a new lexicon.") He was also the star center of the most formidable Guatemalan soccer team, author of the definitive rulebook, and a widely-respected coach whose players called him "The Little Master."[155] That summer of 1934, Roberto brought from Guatemala a superb Mayan Indian dress as a homecoming gift for Anita, a museum-quality costume in four pieces, of indigo cotton heavily embroidered in brilliant silk, intricate woven bands and blue and green tie-dye. The teenage Anita was photographed in this dress, posed like an Indian maiden with long dark braids and a jug on her shoulder. This was the second gift Anita received from her father since her parents' separation. The first was a $20 gold piece he one day sent her in New York, a similarly dramatic and romantic gesture which constituted the sum of his child support.

It is perhaps curious that Sarita permitted Roberto to spend the summer with their daughter, but it appears that she was even feeling successful and confident enough to entertain him herself. At least they had dinner together, and he came to Chola Braun's house to visit. He and Anita played tennis and swam, and picnicked with all the college-age cousins and their friends. In one photograph, six of them stretch out in the grass of a tropical garden, Anita deeply tanned, and Roberto reclines on an elbow with an enigmatic smile. Describing this prolonged reunion with her father in later years, Anita said only, "He was a delightful friend; we enjoyed the present, and I learned nothing of the past." When they separated that September there were no mutual pledges to keep in touch, and Anita heard of Roberto only rarely and indirectly for the next thirty-five years.

Her closest friends that summer were, as always, her cousin Gladys, who was a beautiful young woman herself, and a remarkably handsome law student named Mario Leiva,[156] whose tanned and muscular chest was bared by his topless swimsuit, and with whom Anita was photographed all over the Costa Rican landscape. (Pried from her album years later, one of these photos was found to be inscribed on the back: "If you could be with me always, smiling in just this way, I could have no greater happiness. Mario. 18 Sep 1934") Sophisticated pictures of Anita Figueredo Villegas with eye makeup and dangling earrings appeared in all the papers over prose like this:

> Lovely, beautiful, delicate like the blossom of a lily, Anita Figueredo is a dream, a smile, white with all virtues. She is justly admired in our society, and takes her place in the elegant assembly of distinguished maids of honor at the great anniversary ball of the San José Athletic Club...[157]

and in poetry which loses its intricate rhyme, and no doubt something of its sense, in translation:

HER GAZE

Like the soft caress
of a limpid ray of sun
which tints the red sky
of the dawn it brings,
her gaze engenders
a protective tribute
which her eyes cause to flower
with their sweet excellence.
Her gaze is the fragrance
of an enchanting life.
-José M. Zeledon

(This particular poem went on into second and third verses entitled "HER VOICE" and "HER SMILE.")

Much more quickly than the leisured visit of 1928, this particular triumphant return was over with the end of summer, and it was time to return to school and work. Sarita celebrated her thirty-eighth birthday on board the *S.S. Virginia* of the Panama Pacific Line,[158] and Anita wrote her a note on ship's stationery regretting that she had nothing to give her but a little money for silk stockings, and the wish that she could give her the whole world.

Junior and senior years at Manhattanville passed in the same intense way as the prior terms. Anita somehow found the hours to play basketball, at left forward for the varsity team. As senior year got underway, it was time to apply to medical school. There were still not many choices for women, although it had been nearly ninety years since the first woman, Elizabeth Blackwell, was admitted to an American medical school in 1847. In 1934, a questionnaire sent out to all the hospitals in the United States revealed that nearly half had never employed a woman doctor; and 28% of the medical schools had never graduated a woman. It was generally held - once the admissions committees quit fretting about women looking at naked bodies - that a woman would not stay the course, that she would "just get married."

Anita Figueredo earned excellent grades throughout her career at Manhattanville, for which she was admitted at graduation to Kappa Gamma Pi, the National Scholastic and Activity Honor Society of Catholic Women's Colleges. These grades could be discounted by admissions' committees, however, for the very reason that they were achieved at a "Catholic girls' school." It was because she also scored in the top 5% on the nationwide medical college admissions test (MCAT) that she was granted several interviews, although most of the interviewers dismissed her as certain to marry. The primary reason she was given a place in the freshman class of 1936 at Long Island College of Medicine seemed to be that that school had previously "taken a chance" on a Manhattanville girl who had "turned out alright." (The quiet and studious Christine Heffernan had pioneered pre-med at Manhattanville two years before Anita requested the course from Mother Dammann and, fortunately for Anita, Christine was proving to be an excellent medical student at Long Island.)

The Manhattanville senior yearbook, *The Tower*, shows us the unlikely pair who spent four years of their lives together huddled among the basement beakers and Bunsen burners - small, bouncy Anita and the elegant Katusha Illyne. Under her Greta Garbo-like picture, Katusha is described as:

> the epitome of aristocratic calm. Regal in bearing, classic as to features, she is the possessor of a matchless poise. Her very definite opinions and thoughts are

protected by a cool and almost diffident outlook on life...

Katusha, who always claimed that she did science semi-accidentally, to keep Anita company, went on to a long career as director of the hematology laboratory at Columbia Physicians and Surgeons Hospital. She wrote of her little lab partner many years later:

> If anyone should be brought to the attention of today's public it is she. In all those   years we shared the many classes and labs I never saw or heard a word of discontent. She always had that sunny disposition. I remember her working away at some lab exercise and singing: "I'm a Latin from Manhattan" or "Yo te quiero mucho." I also remember our professor Dr. Fair explaining some organic chemistry theorem and Anita interrupting him to say, "but if you do this, such and such will happen." "Yes, Miss Figueredo," he'd say, "I'm getting there." That is how fast her brain worked.[159]

The text under Anita's picture would be apt in any decade of her life:

> The harder Anita works, the bigger is her smile. She may have a thirty-hour schedule, but no one would ever know it from her expression. And it isn't because she loves work, but simply because nothing ever seems to get her down. She is an ardent person with a keen interest in all that goes on around her, and her perseverance carries her through all things with ease. Anita is staunch in her beliefs and upholds them with strong conviction and determination. Her lively mind is   always searching for new fields, and all this boundless energy is contained in a small and utterly charming person.

Graduation from Manhattanville in June of 1936 was a happy affair attended by many dear old friends, including Sarita's first landlady in Spanish Harlem, doña Julieta McGrigor. The Costa Rican papers printed a picture of the nineteen-year-old graduate in her robes and mortarboard, under the half-inch headline:

COSTA RICAN ANITA FIGUEREDO AWARDED A GOLD MEDAL, TO BE A DOCTOR OF MEDICINE

and "José M. Zeledon," the author of "Her Gaze, Her Voice and Her Smile," outdid himself with a rhapsody on "Doctor, little Doctor of rare gentility...", losing sight of the fact that she was so far just a Bachelor of Arts.[160]

That summer of 1936 Anita was presented with an extraordinary invitation. Her great-aunt, Guarina Lora (baby sister of her dead grandmother doña Anita) was married to the Dominican Max Henriquez Ureña; and Max was then, in the 1930s and '40s, ambassador plenipotentiary from the Dominican Republic to all of Europe. Guarina was deaf from some childhood illness but she spoke four languages and used an ear horn. Max and Guarina had two eligible sons but no daughters, and they invited their niece Anita to spend the year after college graduation living and traveling with them, and being "presented" at all the courts of Europe. This was to be a re-creation of Angela Acuña's "season" of 1908. But Anita declined, in order to go on to medical school.

Where she went that summer, instead of to London and Paris, was to Girl Scout camp in the Adirondacks; and there, because of her language instruction from the Baron at Manhattanville, she was assigned as counselor and archery instructor to a group of German Jewish girls who were refugees from a strange and hostile new regime. The girls told Anita she didn't speak German like an American - which pleased her until she realized they meant she spoke it like a Spaniard.

CHAPTER 16

Medicine and Love

In September 1936, Anita Figueredo entered The Long Island College of Medicine in downtown Brooklyn. Franklin and Eleanor Roosevelt were lifting the country's collective spirit. Governor Herbert H. Lehman was guiding New York with such skill as to make the " horrendous task seem almost effortless"; and the mayor of New York City was a multilingual magician named Fiorella La Guardia who, on his first day in office, read a pledge on the radio which ended with these words: "We will strive to transmit this city not less but greater, better, and more beautiful than it was transmitted to us."[161] It was possibly the most competent administrative team for New York since the Iroquois governed themselves.

Sarita Villegas had moved some twenty blocks south from Hamilton Heights to 105th Street on the upper west side; but for Anita it was still a subway ride of nearly an hour down to the tip of Manhattan Island and under the East River to Borough Hall Station in Brooklyn, and from there a walk of six or eight blocks to the medical school.

The Long Island College of Medicine was founded in 1860 as a hospital and medical school under one roof, on the progressive principle that medical students should learn to care for patients. Before that, according to *Medical Education in Brooklyn: The First Hundred Years:*

> Medicine was taught almost entirely from the pit of a lecture hall. Except for a variable amount of dissection, no laboratory work was offered. Most schools provided little or no contact with patients....To obtain a diploma, students were required only to attend two courses of lectures of at least four months each...[and] almost anybody could obtain a charter to start a medical school.[162]

But Anita's new school inaugurated the hospital-college system of medical instruction in the United States, and for more than thirty years was the only institution in the country providing what has since become the central feature of modern medical education.

The building first approached by Anita and her classmates was Polhemus Memorial, which dated from 1897, the same vintage as Manhattanville. It was eight stories of distinguished brown stone with restrained ornaments and pediments including the motto "SALUS POPULI SUPREMA LEX" ("The Health of the People is the Highest Law") displayed prominently inside over the door. It housed the lecture halls, the chemistry labs, the top-floor dissecting rooms, and was the primary home of first year students. Across the street was a smaller, older building with a peculiar serrated facade at the ends of its peaked roof; this was the famous Hoagland Laboratory which, when completed in 1888, was generally regarded as one of the finest and best- equipped buildings for medical teaching and research in the country. Here were the labs for the second year courses: bacteriology, physiology, histology and pathology.[163]

On the day Anita Figueredo began medical school, the whole class assembled on a tall staircase in Polhemus, waiting to register. There was a long line, and she was on a middle stair against the rail; she turned and looked down, and her gaze was arrested by a young man on the landing. He stood with his hands in the pockets of his striped suit, head down, appearing shy and apprehensive, and as Anita looked at the back of his head, she suddenly heard an inner voice tell her, "This is the man." The words were so clear that she was jolted to attention. The two had no eye contact and did not speak.

No matter how skeptical the listener, Anita never modified this story. She would maintain all her life that she didn't really plan to marry, that she had plenty of male friends and, as other women didn't seem to view her as threatening, she thought she could have been happy just dating casually or going out as part of a threesome when she wanted company. Before her attention was riveted by this stranger, she was not particularly sensual, and she never had any specific desire for children. Yet she recognized her future husband from the back of his head.

When pressed for an explanation, she said it was an act of God.

Not long after this fateful assembly on the stairs, the students were assigned cadavers for dissection, in groups of four arranged alphabetically. The galvanizing young man was named Doyle and was at one table with his college roommate Jack Cooke and two other D's. Miss Figueredo's table was next with three difficult E's and F's. Her dissecting partner was a blustering fellow named Earl, who had failed from the freshman class of 1935 into this one of 1936; he knew everything already, and slashed through the work before them, impatient with Anita's fruitless attempts to slow the pace long enough to glimpse the muscles or nerves or ligaments assigned for the day. The pair across the cadaver were another F who was bright enough but a snickering ally of the unpleasant Earl; and a quiet F who was pleasant enough to Anita, but sticky-fingered and ultimately expelled for stealing a microscope. Mr. Doyle did the elegant dissections of a trained artist and paid no attention to the small girl one table down; but his friend and partner, Mr. Cooke, did. (In fact, as the weeks and months of the first semester wore on, Anita interested most of the boys in her section of the alphabet except for Bill Doyle.)

Jack Cooke and Bill Doyle had been at Georgetown University together as undergraduates, and they shared an apartment in a skinny five-floor brownstone, about fifteen feet wide, near the medical school. They had a room on the fifth floor, "like Mt. Everest at the top of a narrow stairwell." Jack and Anita began walking home together, as the apartment was on the way to the subway station, and they naturally ran into Bill Doyle. Before long the three of them were often eating or studying together in the second story common living room and Anita, who was acutely interested, learned quite a lot about Bill.

He was six feet tall, thin as a poet, with lustrously thick, dark wavy hair and a broad upper lip which was bare of the fox-red moustache he would cultivate later on. He was from Utica, New York, a younger son of a prosperous Irish mercantile family which was almost unaffected by the Depression. To Bill, the difficult times meant chiefly that his closest high school friends were unable to go on to college, and he himself was a member of the smallest class at Georgetown in the modern era (the college having lost nearly half its students between 1929 and 1933). Yet Bill had a brand-new car as a senior in 1935.

Bill had been to art school, and seriously thought of a career as a painter until he decided his talent was not first-rank, and he had better learn a more practical profession. He was quiet and chivalrous and wrote sonnets, and - despite having been close to a girl named "Pat," who was now studying in Italy - had made up his mind not to get involved romantically until he finished his training.

This was a matter of intellectual discipline, because Bill Doyle was keenly attuned to the messages from all his senses: to words and music, to paintings, photographs and the whole visual world, to food and wine and the draw of a good pipe, to the feel of fine clothes. His favorite attire at college was "white tie," tails and a silk top hat, with a long white scarf artistically draped at the neck of his cashmere coat. A deeply religious Catholic, he reveled in the beauty of the ancient ceremony, all the ritual and pageantry, incense and golden vessels and Gregorian chant, and might have been a priest, and an excellent bishop, except for wanting a wife. He certainly wanted a wife, though not at the moment he was chosen by Anita Figueredo, and not one like her in any case.

Bill Doyle expected to have a marriage like his parents', and the senior William Doyles of Utica were a most traditional family. Bill's father, William Edward, had begun life in some prosperity as the youngest son of an innkeeper on the Erie Canal. But the boy was orphaned early,[164] and then had to suffer the charity of relatives until he could make his own way. Luckily, Will was both smart and industrious, and ultimately, with a grade-school education, owned stores in several New York counties selling "ladies' requirements."[165] He had a contingency fund for hard times, and he did not speculate; because of this old-fashioned stance, he had one of the best businesses in Utica in the 1930s.

The orphaned Will Doyle longed, one supposes, for a real family; and he made himself one, eloping with an Irish Protestant "typewriter" named Elizabeth Carroll[166] and persuading her to abandon her work and her uneasiness about Catholics and make him a safe and orderly home. Young Billy was the fifth of their six children; and he and his baby brother were "the little boys," beautifully dressed, wonderfully fed, and pleasantly spoiled by their mother. Elizabeth Doyle was a gentle woman, a reader of books and arranger of flowers, whose husband was the head of the household she managed at his request. This was the sort of wife Bill Doyle envisioned for himself.

By the spring of her freshman year, Anita learned the essence of this about Bill and, against all logic, remained convinced he was "the one." She was not, at this stage, in love. She was, in fact, enjoying the attentions of the other young men in class; and Bill Doyle confessed later that even he mused a bit about Anita when he was assigned the chair behind her in physiology class. The coming of spring meant sunbathing on the roof of the Brooklyn apartment and one day, when Bill encountered Anita there alone, it suddenly penetrated his consciousness that she was a "beautiful little person" and he was strongly attracted to her for the first time. But she was Jack's girl (he thought), and he would not consider intruding.

Anita gives this account of what happened next:

> It was time to stir something up. I knew a good Southern accent from my days at Southern Sem, and I decided to put it to use.
>
> Bill had just gotten a letter from his old girlfriend, Pat, with a picture of her in North Africa. He showed it to Jack and me at lunch, and gave us all kinds of details about her Mediterranean tour - itinerary, highlights,

weather and so on. That night I put on my best fake drawl and called Bill up at home. I said I was "Jane", a friend of Pat's from the tour; I said I was just passing through New York and Pat had told me to be *sure to* look him up. Then I threw in a few details about the tour, and Bill was hooked.

Over the next two weeks, I called him up about three times to chat and flirt; and every time at lunch the next day I listened innocently to Bill's reports about his phone calls from the charming stranger. He was obviously getting more and more eager to meet his Southern belle.

It was really the most fun thing I've ever done in my life

Finally Bill made a date with "Jane" for dinner at the Hotel Roosevelt in mid-town Manhattan. We were at school together that day, and as we walked home to the apartment Bill was very talkative and excited - so much so that he insisted that I wait while he dressed for dinner so that we could take the subway into the city together. I was caught between my strong wish to spend the time with him alone and my need to get home to my own house, change into my dinner clothes, and be back at the hotel by 6:30. It seemed simplest just to go with Bill, and all the way in on the subway he talked about his exciting date. Meanwhile, he got out about 40th Street, right on time, and I went on sixty more blocks, changed clothes without even *trying* to explain to Mother, and returned at least an hour late.

When Bill entered the hotel and found that "Jane" had not yet arrived, he sat down at the bar to wait, telling the headwaiter to let him know when she came in. After cooling his heels for about thirty minutes, he decided to go in to his table where he could at least hear the band. By the time an hour passed he was really beginning to think he'd been stood up, and was feeling irritable and foolish, when all of a sudden he looked up to see Anita walking up to the table. His first reaction was pleasure, although he couldn't imagine what she was doing there.

Then Anita said, in her telephone drawl, "Hi, y'all, Ah'm Jane."

Bill was furious. He had been made a fool of, and wanted to rush away. But Anita spent about a half-hour calming him down, and then they danced together. Another hour later they were riding on top of the Fifth Avenue bus in the moonlight, and they kissed. They walked through Central Park after midnight, Bill took Anita home, and then fell into his own bed about two in the morning. A few hours later he woke to hear Jack Cooke observing that his date must have been a good time, what with the lipstick on his handkerchief; and later, when Anita called Jack to tell him she was in love with Bill, the old friendship was badly strained. But fortunately it was near the end of term, and the three of them soon went their separate ways for the summer.

Bill went home to Utica, and before long realized that there was "no future" in this romance with Anita and that it had to stop. They were too different. She was small, Latin, pragmatic, sweetly iconoclastic, extroverted, impoverished, boundlessly energetic and indifferent to her surroundings. He was tall, Anglo, romantic, intensely conservative, introverted, affluent, contemplative, and exquisitely aesthetic. What could come of such a union? So Bill wrote Anita a letter telling her that he couldn't be "involved" during medical school. And Anita ignored the letter, a technique she would use to advantage all her life.

In September they just took up where they left off; and by mid-year Bill ceased fighting it. Here was somebody who really loved him, the first person besides his parents in whose love he could really believe and it was one of the most powerful maturing forces of his life.

Except for the winning of Bill Doyle, the first year of medical school was notably difficult for Anita. She had never before **not** excelled in an academic situation. But here she found herself struggling to survive. On that first day in 1936 when the new class gathered together to be greeted by the dean, there were few pleasantries; they actually heard the hackneyed warning: "Look to your right and left, because statistically one of the three of you will not be with us at graduation." Anita was always a highly serious student but self-directed, with different goals from the girls around her, and she set her own pace. Here at medical school she was pushed and jostled from all sides by students from big universities jockeying for top positions in the class.

The worst feature of the first year was that it was virtually all anatomy - endless dissections in the cavernous eighth floor cadaver room with the reek of formaldehyde - and that the four students at each table cooperated or sank together. The dissections on the halves of the body were supposed to go on simultaneously, with one member of each pair reading instructions and the other cutting; but disease or injury or normal variation often obscured the anatomy on one side, so that inept work on either side was a serious disadvantage. Nor could any such ineptness be made up by simply studying the pictures in the text: much of the student's grade was determined by the weekly "bedside" demonstrations before the professor, in which each was asked to show off his dissection and point out the exposed course of a specific vein or nerve. This looked easy enough in the book, where nerves were bright yellow, arteries scarlet and veins royal blue, but was harder when everything was puce.

Still, Anita Figueredo had good hands and might have gotten on well enough with a different crew. But things went from bad to worse. There were final exams, Earl the slasher failed out for good, the nice young man who stole the microscope vanished overnight, and Anita was called into the office of the professor, Dr. Congdon.

Edgar D. Congdon was a small, neat gentleman with colorless hair who gave crystal-clear lectures and had a fatherly manner with the students. On this day, he explained to Anita that she was failing anatomy, but that he understood the difficulties under which she was laboring, that he believed in her, and had given her a conditional passing grade based on completion of a special "make-up" project. This was to be done at home over the weekend and returned directly to him.

What Dr. Congdon gave Anita to take home to her apartment was a man's head severed at the neck. The lips and eyelids were sewn roughly shut with thread like thick black wire. Lacking any other conveyance, she stuffed the head in a brown paper bag, and rode the crowded, jerking subway with the thing in her lap, all the while imagining it rolling out in a grisly, slow-motion tumble down the aisle. At home, she sagged in relief inside her door, plucked the head from the bag and - as it was summer in New York - stowed it in the refrigerator. She was napping when her mother dragged up the stairs from work, and went in search of a cold glass of water.

With "the head," Anita passed the first year in good standing, and after that her fortunes rose steadily. The second-year labs at Hoagland did not excite her particularly, but she worked diligently, Bill Doyle enhanced the drawings in her laboratory notebook a bit, and she got through creditably enough. But in the first clinical year, the third, she began to shine.

Anita had from the beginning an empathic manner with patients, and an excellent sense of the components of wellness and illness. She was an accurate diagnostician, she was compassionate, and she understood the mind-body connection so that she was careful to treat the whole patient, as good doctors have always done, but as most medical students must struggle to learn. In general, the junior and senior students divided their time between the relatively refined Long Island College Hospital where private patients were attended by the medical school professors, and the vast wards of King's County Hospital which served the indigent of the borough of Brooklyn in more than three thousand beds.

Anita's work was generally admired by the attending physicians, but there was one professor - a Prussian-type with steel-rimmed glasses and thick moustache named Alfred Beck - who taught obstetrics and resented women physicians. They belonged at home with babies, he believed, refusing to allow them on his service at Long Island College Hospital, though he accommodated all the men. The administration accepted this, but did arrange a substitute obstetrical service at King's County for the four women in the class. At the County Hospital the deliveries were continuous and simultaneous, and the house staff eager for any extra pair of hands. Anita was sent out in November, and the first night on duty discovered that, since there were no sleeping accommodations for women, a bed had been placed for her on the open balcony of the seventh floor. She dutifully went outside to bed, but froze; then got up and wandered through darkened halls until she found a door labeled "Doctors" which led to a room full of beds with sleeping forms. She crept around until she found an empty one, climbed in and collapsed to sleep. The next morning she awoke to the silent stares of the men. When they grasped the situation they were disconcerted but agreed she couldn't sleep outside; and, since she didn't make an official issue of it, didn't use their bathroom and so on, she was allowed to go on sleeping there all year. (Many years later, in the early sixties, Anita was invited to give a talk on cancer to the Connecticut Medical Society and was introduced by the program chairman, who said, "It's obvious Dr. Figueredo doesn't remember me, but I'm one of the boys she used to sleep with in Brooklyn.")

Anita's obstetrical experience at King's County was much superior to what her fellow students had at the quiet college hospital. She handled at least three hundred deliveries herself and stayed on there the whole fourth year, though even at King's County there were certain frontiers that could not be crossed by women; she was barred from male urology, and also from ambulance duty, which at that time required some brute strength since there were no paramedics, just the intern and the driver. Her clinical work was consistently of the highest quality, and this was recognized at graduation.

The tenth annual commencement of the Long Island College of Medicine was held in the Brooklyn Academy of Music on June 6, 1940. Anita Figueredo was awarded the medal "For the member of the class whose scholastic average in the fourth year has shown the greatest improvement over that of previous years."[167] The class as a whole had lost a quarter of its men, but its four women were all present at commencement and each went on to a long and successful career. The headlines in Costa Rica read:

ANITA FIGUEREDO GRADUATED IN USA AS
DOCTOR OF MEDICINE

The 6th of this month in New York she received the diploma brilliantly won after long years of study, and she is now preparing to return to Costa Rica to practice her profession.

There was no poetry underneath but a long article by Angela Acuña which began:

> It was the fifth of November 1921 when Sarita Villegas and her little daughter abandoned their homeland and set out for the United States of America. Handkerchiefs waved like the sea in an endless, sorrowful goodbye...

and ended:

> Anita Figueredo Villegas is the sweetest compensation for the unflagging tenacity of her mother - who not only inspired her with confidence, but also taught her by example.[168]

This article, in turn, inspired letters of the following sort from the founder in San José of a "Center for Social Religious Culture" in which school age girls met weekly to discuss improving society:

> We were reading religious poetry, fragments of the Bible, and the account of a young doctor of medicine recently graduated in the great City of the North. 'Who is she?', they asked excitedly, 'Who is she?'...so, as the girls sat perfectly still, I read what was written of them, mother and daughter; and then they passed the photograph from hand to hand and talked of the self-sacrifice of the mother and her iron will, of the noble girl who has so elevated the position of Costa Rican women, who will forever be a model for feminine youth, and who has touched the little hearts of her tender sisters here.
>
> Glory to God, to the tiny great Doctor, and to her great mother!

The summer before graduation, Bill Doyle took Anita home to meet his family in Utica. His father, the elder William Doyle, was first-generation American and unsettled by the notion that his son had taken up with a "foreigner," especially a Latin one. (Mr. Doyle had already had the experience of buying off a "Cuban adventurer" who blew through town and nearly eloped with his youngest daughter, Mary.) He assured Bill that there was no need to bring "that girl" home as it surely couldn't amount to anything; but his tolerant and perceptive wife Elizabeth insisted that Anita come up and, by Friday evening of a long weekend, William Doyle, Sr. was captured for life.

Sarita Villegas, for her part, was less enthusiastic. In essence, she shared Mr. Doyle's initial view that this particular romance of Anita's surely could not amount to anything, as the principals had completely incompatible goals.

There they are in the *Lichonian,* the 1940 yearbook of the Long Island College of Medicine (with its astonishing front cover of a naked white boy issuing forth from a pair of naked black breasts):

WILLIAM JAMES DOYLE

expects to engage in general practice in Utica, New York

ANITA VILLEGAS FIGUEREDO

intends to return to Costa Rica to practice medicine

What was to be done? Ordinarily charming and even mildly flirtatious with Anita's gentleman callers, Sarita was cool with Bill Doyle from the start, and her reserve became icy as she began to hear talk of marriage. However, such talk revolved around the distant future, and Anita went casually on dating surgical residents and others, so that her mother relaxed again for a time, though she always managed to be "out" when Bill Doyle came around to visit.

Bill, for his part, was a fish out of water in the Latin community that was Sarita's world and, peripherally, Anita's as well. It so happened that Sarita's friends accepted Anita's choice of a *novio* before her mother did, and began to invite them together to important parties. At one of these elegant affairs, Anita was whisked away to dance with another man, leaving Bill stranded at a table of jeweled and hatted matrons chattering rapidly in Spanish. Miserably self-conscious, he struggled to work out a sentence from the few Spanish words he knew, and then blurted it out. Whereupon, a ghastly silence fell over the table and the ladies stared at him without a shred of comprehension. Bill's face burned, at the sight of which his companions politely looked away, and resumed their impenetrable conversation.

CHAPTER 17

The Path to Memorial, Marriage and War

In 1940, there were no advisors for planning post-graduate training, no "matching programs" for medical students and likely hospitals. One theoretically worked this out with one's parents, and, of course, Sarita Villegas was unable to help; but as Anita had to stay on in New York, the reality was that a female medical graduate had one choice there: New York Infirmary for Women and Children. This was the hospital founded in 1857 by Elizabeth Blackwell, the first American woman physician,[169] and it was still staffed entirely by women. Anita was accepted at New York Infirmary for a rotating internship beginning in July of 1940, and continued on there as a senior intern in obstetrics and in surgery-gynecology through June of 1942.

Meanwhile, Bill Doyle completed one pediatric internship at Long Island College Hospital and was in the middle of another in medicine and surgery at King's County, when Pearl Harbor was bombed by the Japanese on December 7, 1941. Up until this moment the young doctors of their class had not been much concerned with the troubles in Europe and Asia. They believed with most of their countrymen that the United

States could avoid war, and they made their postgraduate plans assuming they would not be interrupted. Now everything changed.

Within two weeks of the declaration of war, Bill applied for a commission in the Navy Medical Corps; however he heard nothing about his application for several months. He and Anita began living from day to day, and the question of when to get married became yet more complicated. Bill kept a diary, and on February 17 wrote that he had pretty well decided not to get married before leaving for the war even though "Anita and I kid about it a lot." But he wrote her a Valentine letter that week from vacation at his parents' home in Utica, full of love and eight lines of an old sonnet he'd written for her and fished out of a drawer:

> I long for you - and more because I know
> Your heart is mine, than from some vain desire
> To capture one who lures me with a low
> Dark look, designed to light and fan my fire
> Of love. I long for you - and yet, no sense
> Of aching or despair need mark my part
> Of solitude, for this is my defense...
> The full and shining armor of your heart.

and then three days later, when he got a telegraphically short note in return, he wrote this:

> I received your communication yesterday. I don't feel I can honestly dignify it with the title of letter. However it brought me assurance that you are alive and kicking (especially kicking) and for that reason it was welcome.
>
> I suppose you are off this weekend, carousing around and garnering a few more proposals of marriage. I don't really know why everyone wants to marry you. I don't know why I want to myself and I'm sure if I were anyone else I wouldn't. No one but myself as

individually constituted could possibly complement adequately your devious personality....

But somehow on March 31 they were looking at diamond rings together, on April 1 he bought the one she liked best, and on April 2, 1942 they were officially engaged when they took Sarita out for dinner, and Bill asked her for Anita's hand. Sitting in the padded booth across from her daughter and her beloved, Sarita Villegas bowed to the inevitable. Soon after that Anita was also wearing a heart-shaped gold pin set with matched pearls, her engagement present from "Dad and Mother" Doyle.

Then on May 2 Bill suddenly received his Naval commission - with a special waiver for thinness - and four days later left his internship, bought his uniforms, and reported to the Naval Yard at Portsmouth, New Hampshire as LT(jg) W.J. Doyle. For the rest of May he learned how to be a Naval officer and provided what little medical care was needed by the civilian ship workers in the area. On the first of June he was ordered to report in Boston to the newly-commissioned destroyer *U.S.S. Nicholas.* He spent much of the summer on a "shakedown cruise" in the coastal Atlantic between Maine and Philadelphia, partly to train the crew, and partly to chase German submarines which were harassing U.S. shipping lanes. During that cruise it became obvious that any time now their ship would be sent to the war zone, presumably to the South Pacific.

On July 26, the ship sailed down to a submarine base at New London, Connecticut to pick up torpedoes, huge things which looked like submarines themselves. Bill asked the skipper for leave, took the three-hour train trip to New York, and went to see Anita who - since July first - had suddenly become one of the first two women residents ever accepted at the splendid new Memorial Hospital for Cancer and Allied Diseases.

The chief pathologist at New York Infirmary while Anita was there was Dr. Elise L'Esperance, a woman who was independently wealthy, single and single-minded. Her mission was to advance the cause of women in medicine. Elise L'Esperance was the "faithful associate" of Dr. James Ewing, the famous director and pathologist at Memorial called "Mr. Cancer"; and she was also a member of Memorial Hospital's

Board of Managers. Toward the end of Anita's second year at New York Infirmary, Dr. L'Esperance became aware that Memorial was losing its male residents to the war, and that the hospital was willing to consider taking on females for the first time in its history. Anita was summoned to Dr. L'Esperance's office along with one other resident, a big Nebraska farm girl named Lucile Loseke. Lucile was a stern Lutheran at a time when Catholics were thought to be practically satanic, and she and Anita were not close friends, though they came to appreciate one another. Evidently Elise L'Esperance decided that Anita and Lucile had the best chance (among perhaps fifteen or twenty house staff) of succeeding at Memorial. Dr. L'Esperance was not a mentor; she was cold and impersonal, pursuing her own agenda, and this was Anita's first meeting with her in the two years she'd been at New York Infirmary. She told the two women of the opportunity which existed at Memorial, and advised them to seize it. In Costa Rica this cool proposition was reported as:

DR. ANITA FIGUEREDO VILLEGAS CALLED TO MEMORIAL HOSPITAL

A famous physician of the United States has discovered in her a special ability for surgery and has said to her colleagues: **"We have to do something for the hands of Dr. Figueredo."**

Anita's simultaneous engagement to Bill Doyle was also of great romantic interest to the readers back "home." The May 1942 issue of a journal called *Revista Costarricense (Costa Rican Review)* had Anita's picture on its cover and inside a feature story on her career to date, observing that "She is the first Costa Rican woman ever graduated as a Doctor of Medicine and has been accepted as a resident at a world-famous Hospital." The article recounts the sacrifices made by Sarita Villegas, and their happy conclusion:

How many sleepless nights! How many hard hours of sewing on the machine which was her only companion when her little girl was still too young to understand the sacrifices of her poor mother. Another woman would have thought of remarriage - outside the Church - for help in educating her daughter; but, faithful to God, she did not consider this for a moment....

And now Sarita Villegas has God's reward in seeing her daughter crowned with glory and with the prospect of a marriage which undoubtedly will be brilliant - because when Doctor Doyle selected her for his future wife, it was because he understood the treasure which is Dr. Figueredo.

Now Anita had no particular interest in cancer. She and Bill Doyle were going to be married, and their plan was that he would do pediatrics, she obstetrics and gynecology, and they would work together (in Utica/ Costa Rica). However, Anita did want to do surgery and had already received good training under such professors as Isabelle Knowlton, a superb gynecologic surgeon. This operating experience was very significant to the Memorial job because the treatment of cancer at that time was primarily surgical. Radiation therapy was more advanced at Memorial than anywhere else, and all the surgical oncologists were forced by James Ewing to learn and use it, but the field was really still in its infancy; and similarly, it was while Anita was at Memorial that the first chemotherapeutic agent, nitrogen mustard, was introduced. Almost always, cancer was "cut out." This was the era of immense, mutilating operations, hemi-pelvectomies, even hemi-face-ectomies, after which survivors rode the bus into follow-up clinic with gauze sheets taped over gaping holes in their heads.

In any event, Anita always liked a challenge, and she did what she was told. The interview at Memorial went well, and she was accepted to the resident staff, along with Lucile Loseke. They were quite a pair - large, staid Lucile and little, cheerful Anita, looking about sixteen years old - but fortunately they were absorbed almost naturally into the program.

Anita Figueredo rarely dwelt on obstacles in her life, rarely saw them, in fact. Even so, her scaling of the all-male heights at Memorial could have been a bruising endeavor, with subtle or all-out resistance at every level, except for the war. The four years from 1941-45 were suspended time when women might not only operate for cancer, but also rivet ships and play major-league baseball.

Memorial Hospital for Cancer and Allied Diseases was the first true cancer center in the United States, and was world-famous.[170] It was born as *The New York Cancer Hospital* in 1887, a place for patients with cancers of the breast and uterus who had nowhere else to go after the Board of Lady Supervisors barred them from New York Woman's Hospital. The disease had a frightening stigma - so much so, that after eleven years even this new institution had to change its name to the *General Memorial Hospital* and to hide its cancer patients away on two back wards. Finally again before the first World War, the Board of Managers was persuaded - with an offer of considerable money and several grams of ultra-precious radium - to resume the exclusive care of cancer patients. James Ewing, author of the classic text, *Neoplastic Diseases,* was the man who knew more about cancer than any other of his time; and it was he who became director (1919-1939) and chief pathologist of the re-named *Memorial Hospital for the Study of Cancer and Allied Diseases.* Anita Figueredo arrived there one year before the death of James Ewing (of cancer), but the old man was still consulting pathologist, and a legendary presence.

Memorial had been "forever" in an old castle at W. 106th Street and Eighth Avenue, but just at this time moved into large modern quarters on the other side of town, on York Avenue at E. 68th Street; and it was there that Anita's Naval officer fiancé found her on July 26, 1942.

He came up softly behind her at the nurses' station where she was writing orders. "May I take you to dinner, Doctor?" he asked, "to some secluded spot where I can feast my eyes upon you?" They dined and danced at the elegant Clermont, overlooking the Hudson River. Then they climbed up, arms entwined, to the hospital roof, and stood there in the warm night air gazing out over the lights of New York.

Bill said, nuzzling her hair, "I might get three whole days of leave soon."

Anita said, "I want to get married."

It was so abrupt after nearly six years of courtship, that Bill, the born conservative, was taken aback considerably and "talked her out of it." Then he took the midnight train back to New London and crawled into his bunk at daylight.

The next day he phoned Anita. "O.K.," he said, "O.K."

But he was still nervous. By the 29th he asked the executive officer for six days' leave, and it was all settled. They were to be married in St. Patrick's Cathedral in Manhattan (about a mile from Sarita's latest apartment on E. 70th Street, which was quite a "good" address, with an attractive courtyard entry and an ornate lintel with brightly-painted, Moorish-looking carvings.) Anita kept working up to the last minute in order to have a few days' honeymoon, and it was left to Sarita Villegas to put on a wedding in ten days' time.

Sarita was fundamentally apprehensive and unhappy about the marriage. She and Anita were on the verge of complete triumph, of returning home to Costa Rica to live out their lives, and she could not see how Bill Doyle fit into this scheme. He was learning a little Spanish, but he was a Yankee, pure and simple. Sarita's father, the sophisticated and well-traveled General Villegas, once published an essay entitled "The Yankee Peril" in which he contrasted the North Americans "enlisted like soldiers in the army of work" with the Latins like himself who wished to live "the romantic life of the troubadours of ages past, with a sword at the waist and a poem on the lips, withdrawn from the furnace of labor." Ironically, Bill Doyle was very much like General Villegas in some ways, particularly in their mutual sympathy for the art and literature and chivalry of earlier centuries. Nonetheless, Sarita Villegas was correct in her assumption that her son-in-law would not easily embrace a life of permanent exile from the United States.

Still, she gave Anita an almost miraculously lovely wedding. Anita secured the church and the services of the priest; Bill went ashore in Boston and bought the wedding rings and a pair of white silk pajamas and, two nights before the wedding, met Anita in New York for the marriage license and a happy evening with his family at the St. Moritz opening wedding presents.

Sarita managed everything else herself: invitations, flowers, photographer, dresses and shoes and trousseau, and the reception at the New Weston Hotel (with the help of her influential friends, the Bacardís.) Anita did not even try on her own gown before the ceremony, but her mother's business was dresses, and she knew her daughter's measurements. Sarita's

147

taste was impeccable, and not only was Anita as perfectly dressed as it was possible to be, but Sarita herself was strikingly attractive in long, rose-colored crêpe chiffon with a draped and fitted lace bodice and a triple strand of pearls at her graceful neck. At forty-five, she looked like an older sister of the matron of honor, Bill's sister Dorothy who, as a buyer for her father's stores, also knew fine women's clothes and had independently chosen the identical dress in gold.

Anita entered the intimate stained-glass space of Our Lady's Chapel (at one end of the vaulted enormity of St. Patrick's) on her mother's arm. No one in the church had ever seen a mother walk her daughter down the aisle, but this departure from convention was only congruent with all that had gone before, and a statement before God and man that Sarita Villegas alone had the right to give this lovely girl away. Anita wore white satin with long, tight delicately-pointed sleeves and a fitted bodice encrusted with seed-pearls; her knee-length veil fell from a pearl tiara in her short dark hair, and as she stood at the altar her shimmering train cascaded down the steps behind her. Her groom stood beside her in the white dress uniform of a Naval officer, attended by his oldest brother Edward as best man. They were married at noon in a Nuptial Mass performed by Anita's old friend and professor, Father Joseph Assmuth. Afterwards the wedding party and guests paraded down the street on foot to the champagne reception; and then finally there was a private family luncheon among the flowers and green of the roof garden.

The newlyweds set out on their honeymoon by train from Grand Central Station north to Lake Champlain on the New York-Vermont border. Their destination was the Allenwood Inn in Burlington, Vermont; but as the train arrived at five in the morning, they first went to breakfast and then 6:30 Mass, before summoning the hotel car. They were delighted with the inn, a three-hundred-acre estate where they had a fine large separate bungalow with French windows looking down through a birch forest to the shimmering lake. They had a "perfect" three days there, talking, strolling through the sunken garden and along the shore, and slipping away from the other guests in the dining room with the huge cobblestone fireplace. They breakfasted before the open windows of their bedroom, served by a discreet and gracious staff. On the second day, Anita sat in a little glass house perched high up on the very edge of the lake and wrote her "Adored little mother," describing all this loveliness, and then saying,

> We are perfectly happy - we live in a mental, spiritual and physical harmony that only a direct act of God could have created. The past years of intimacy have molded us to one another such that we don't have any differences. You can see in Bill's every glance and movement his love and happiness and I am the same. You don't know how happy I am about the years we waited - they served as a test, a training ground. I'm certain that we have already passed through the difficult adjustments which always occur the first years of a marriage, and I only feel sorry for those who marry without having known and understood each other over years, as we have.

The newlyweds did not think or talk much of the war. They just thought that if they were not destined to live their lives together, at least they had had the best.

On the morning of the fourth day they rode the train again from Vermont down to Boston, where Anita took a room at the deluxe Ritz-Carlton Hotel, and Bill joined her in the evening after reporting back to his ship. They dined in the rooftop nightclub (where the Mills Brothers were the featured attraction), and the bill survived for this whole elegant Boston interlude: $19.76.

When the ship finally sailed on the 14th of August, six days after the wedding, Mrs. William Doyle, Jr. rode home to New York alone. But their luck held, and the ship put in at New York overnight; so that they had two more days and a night together before the *Nicholas* and its young "assistant surgeon" sailed for the South Pacific at last on August 23, 1942, the day before Anita's twenty-sixth birthday.

News of "THE DOYLE-FIGUEREDO WEDDING PERFORMED IN NEW YORK" took up half a page of "Social World" in the Costa Rican *Tribune* and introduced the groom to its readership as a suave, rather Latin-looking fellow with a fine moustache and a smoldering cigarette.[171] Not long afterward Sarita Villegas returned to Costa Rica alone "to enjoy a much-needed rest" as it said in an interview published under her wonderfully lovely picture from the wedding.

"I am satisfied," she was quoted as saying. "I have fulfilled the mission of a loving mother. The difficulties overcome, the effort expended, are happy memories.

> "To educate my daughter was my joy, the best motivation of my life - I trod the path I had to follow, and I have achieved my goal; the effort bore fruit; I had a clear vision of the end for which I was striving and for that reason I found the battle sweet and obeyed the impulse of love itself...."

After three months (and a farewell party attended by her old friend Santiago Chamberlain), Sarita returned to New York to wait and watch. Anita was still saying that they would yet live in Costa Rica, and meanwhile she had resumed her residency at Memorial Hospital.

At Memorial, the anatomical approach to cancer surgery was brought to perfection, and the great men there were masters of certain areas: Hayes Martin of "head and neck," George Pack of "gastric and soft tissue," and Frank Adair of "breast." Heads of state and dignitaries of all kinds came to Memorial to be treated. George Pack, especially, was sought out by the rich and famous of the world; one was Evita Perón, for whom he flew to Argentina. Dr. Pack was a dapper, gentlemanly, gracious man who treated everyone with interest and kindness, and he was completely accepting of Anita as his resident, although a few of his patients were taken aback. One man, a VIP who came a considerable distance to consult the great Dr. Pack, flatly refused to have this "little girl" as his doctor, which Anita understood as rather reasonable. But when she reported it to Dr. Pack, he appeared at the man's bedside and told him, "Dr. Figueredo is my choice as your physician, and if you don't wish to accept my judgment, you may leave the hospital." The man stayed, with Anita as his doctor.

Hayes Martin was a different type altogether, a tyrant who browbeat everyone around him, but he was astonishingly mild with Anita. She became his favorite assistant, and he asked for her on important cases. He had been a "mean old bachelor," and it was said that Anita Figueredo mellowed him enough to let him get married, soon after she left Memorial.

Meanwhile, the United States was getting on with the World War, and Bill Doyle steamed into the midst of it in the South Pacific.[172] When the *Nicholas* and her crew left New York, they sailed south past Puerto Rico to the Panama Canal, on a course for Tongatapu, southwest of Samoa. They were escorting the new battleship *Washington* to the campaigns for Guadalcanal and the Solomon Islands. They reached the Tonga Islands on September 15, after three weeks at sea, and were then constantly on the move on a triangular course between New Caledonia, Guadalcanal and the New Hebrides, under frequent air attack. (In fact, for a while the ritualistic war machine of the Japanese sent in every day at noon a squadron of twin-engine bombers called "Betties", which flew at 22,000 feet, just above the maximum straight-up range of American guns. The time was so exact, that after a few of these forays the Marine bombers anticipated the runs, and forced the Betties down into the range of the guns on the ground and on the *Nicholas*. The captain rescheduled mess from 1200 to 1130 hours so that the men didn't have to miss lunch.)

Meanwhile, Bill Doyle and the rest of the crew of the *Nicholas* were wondering where all the other ships were that they saw being built on the East Coast. On November 9 1942 they learned what Bill called in his journal "the best-kept secret of the war" when 800 ships and 140,000 men suddenly converged for the invasion of North Africa, the turning point of the European war. After this brilliant maneuver, all the ships which had carried men into Africa then poured into the South Pacific and the forward progress of the Japanese was stopped at Guadalcanal, although it took the American forces six months to secure these islands and begin the roll-back.

All this time, Bill was writing regularly to Anita and dreaming about their nine days of married life; but it was nearly three months before he first heard from his wife. The *Nicholas* was briefly anchored at Auckland, New Zealand the first week of November when Bill got eleven letters all written after October 5 - which meant that six weeks of earlier letters were sitting in a bag on some other island. A week later they were found in the New Hebrides, and after that the crew got mail every week or two when they made port in New Caledonia after skirmishes around Guadalcanal. In one of the earliest letters from this time, Anita - who knew only that the ship was due to sail through the Panama Canal and hoped that Bill might get leave to fly the short distance to San José - gave two clues about her thoughts of their future:

> This is the first of my letters addressed to San Francisco [the actual location of the ship is top secret]; I only hope you will soon be there. Tell me whether you like it out there, for just as soon after I'm finished here as you want me, I'll go to join you wherever you are...to stay! Won't it be wonderful, darling --a home together.. you always at my side, I always at yours?

and then this:

> Did you, my love, get a chance to see or at least speak to the family in Costa Rica? It is my desire to have them love you as I do; to have them compliment my superb choice; to have them write me news of you. Also, I wished to know your reaction to a place you've heard so much about....I had always wanted to show it to you, but that being impossible for so long, I wanted you to see it so that another basic thing would be added to the myriad we have in common....

One day shortly before Christmas, a crew member on the *Nicholas* showed Bill a copy of the December 1, 1942 issue of *Look* magazine: there on pages 24-26 was a photo-essay entitled "WOMAN SURGEON" and featuring Resident Surgeon Dr. Anita Figueredo of "New York Memorial Hospital." The gist of the article was that

> Wartime reduces the odds against her in a field rife with anti-feminine prejudice... [and] By the end of 1942, some 35,000 of the nation's 160,000 men doctors will have been called - and Dr. Figueredo and her 7500

women colleagues so far barred from the Army will get
a crack at the home posts.

There were eight photographs of Anita: scrubbing for surgery, operating (showing "no signs of the emotional instability or nervousness which are stock arguments against women in medicine"), putting her feet up after surgery and having a glass of milk, carrying a child patient in her arms, marrying Bill Doyle, and answering the phone in bed with very heavy eyes. The text under this last picture said:

> A resident surgeon's day doesn't end when the operating room closes. On call three nights each week, she makes "evening rounds" - visits to some 50 private and ward patients - laboriously writes up charts, then sleeps in the hospital with a telephone next to her pillow. For the many responsibilities of an assistant resident, she receives the standard monthly stipend of $15, plus her room, board and laundry.

Christmas that year for Bill was in New Caledonia and "about as pleasant as it could be out there," with an excellent turkey dinner on the ship, followed by a cigar and a movie on the fantail under the stars. His present from Anita arrived on time: a beautiful oil miniature of his bride in her wedding dress.

Near the end of the Guadalcanal campaign when the Marines had taken the south end of the island, Bill Doyle had his baptism by fire as a wartime physician. All these months, as the only doctor on a small tin can (as the agile little destroyers were called) he had been running what amounted to an infirmary for a shipload of able-bodied men. There were some minor casualties but little infectious disease on the *Nicholas*, as they started out with a healthy crew and had been at sea most of the time. Dr. Doyle spent most of his time instructing rotating groups of officers and petty officers in military first aid, triage, bandaging and the judicious use of morphine. [173]

Then on February 1, 1943, their sister ship, the destroyer *DeHaven*, was sunk off their portside bow. The *Nicholas* and *DeHaven* had carried Army troops to the fighting at the north end of Guadalcanal, and were returning with their empty landing craft, when the lookout on the *Nicholas* spotted Japanese bombers through broken clouds overhead. The *Nicholas* went to flank speed, turning in a great continuous circle, and took no direct hits, though she had ugly holes in her side and three of the crew were killed by huge chunks of exploded shrapnel.

The *DeHaven,* still sailing in a straight line, took a bomb between the stacks and sunk within five minutes dragging more than half her crew with her to the bottom of the Coral Sea. One hundred ten men were picked out of the burning debris, and the wounded spread over the splattered deck of the *Nicholas.* Bill Doyle and his medics treated penetrating wounds, fractures and partly severed limbs with their limited stores of splints, pillows, heavy bandages and morphine until the injured were put ashore behind friendly lines to be taken out by hospital ship next day.[174]

A few weeks later, in April 1943, Bill went ashore in the New Hebrides, and soon afterward developed pneumonia, the first case on his ship. There were no antibiotics - the first vial of penicillin he would have for use as a medical officer was sent him in 1945 - and his condition rapidly deteriorated during the week that he was treated by his own corpsman. Transfer was arranged to the flagship of the task force, the cruiser *Montpelier*, where there were at least oxygen and I.V. solutions; but his condition became so critical that there was an entry in the ship's log stating that he was "expected to die," and the captain came to pay his last respects to an officer. The *Montpelier* went through several battles in the Solomons before she made port in the New Hebrides and the semi-conscious Bill Doyle could be off-loaded to a jungle hospital; there he recovered somewhat before being transferred again by hospital ship to a base hospital in Auckland, New Zealand. At the time of his transfer to Auckland he was still a "stretcher case," unable to walk or feed himself, skinny and pale with a scraggly, matted red beard, and with his labored breathing now complicated by horrible boils on his back, festering sores acquired in the jungle hospital when he couldn't breathe well enough to turn over in bed.

Bill got good care in Auckland. A device was rigged up to apply hot packs to his back while he still lay face up, and then the boils were drained by the ward surgeon. During this phase a "Gray Lady" volunteered to write his wife for him. Because of the erratic flow of mail from the war zone, Anita never learned that her husband was ill until this letter arrived informing her that he was on the road to recovery. In fact, during the time that he was so critically ill, Anita got the letters from previous weeks; and ironically, because of the unpredictable mail delivery and strict censorship of any identifying news of the war, she was most worried about Bill **before** he got ill. On April 1 she wrote him saying that she finally got a letter - the first since Valentine's Day, and

> I don't know yet what was wrong with you - I'm beginning to believe you were wounded but have recovered sufficiently to write - is that it? Whatever it was or is, you're better and that's all that matters....I am a little disappointed, though - because until this morning I was certain you would soon be sent home to me, and now I don't think you will be!

But in reality Anita's letter was a forecast of imminent events, and was returned to her unread, so that Bill never saw this unique and kindly postscript in Spanish at the end:

> My dear Bill: You can't imagine how worried we've been, but now, thank God, we know you are better, which we celebrate immensely.
>
> Much affection from Sarita.

In any event, Anita knew she would be notified if Bill were dead; she was, above all, an optimist and all her life too busy to worry much about what she could not control.

Around the end of May, a troop transport ship put in at Auckland to carry ambulatory sick and wounded officers back to the United States. Bill Doyle was carried on a stretcher up the gangway of a converted ocean liner, the *S.S. Washington* of the United States Line, and given a large cabin on A-deck for the non-stop, 6000-mile voyage to San Diego, California. By the end of the twelve-day trip he was walking a mile a day around the deck, though still short of breath. For two more weeks he was confined in sick officers' quarters at Balboa Naval Hospital in San Diego. But then he was finally well enough to take the train to New York; and there he moved in with his wife and mother-in-law in June of 1943, ten months after his wedding and departure for the war.

His little wife was overjoyed to have him safely home, but the lovers had only scraps of intense reunions as Anita worked and lived-in at Memorial. Sarita also worked all day and made it a point to be out most nights with friends. Thus Bill, who was orderly even in a weakened state, kept house and was astonished to discover that there is no defense against the black soot of New York City.

Sarita, meanwhile, discovered a lump in her breast. Anita examined her and found a small, vague mass which could almost be disregarded except for recent family history. Sarita's mother Chola Braun had died of breast cancer the summer Anita graduated from Manhattanville. Chola had told no one what was growing under her pleated blouses, never saw a doctor, and only gave in to her weakness and emaciation by going to bed two weeks or so before her death. It was then that her nurse-daughter Tita undressed her and found the huge, fungating growth which had replaced half her chest. So now Anita took her mother to Memorial to see Dr. Frank Adair, the world-famous breast surgeon. Dr. Adair thought as Anita did that cancer was unlikely, but the family history - and the fact that this was Anita's mother - pushed him to do an excisional biopsy, with Anita at his side. While Sarita lay anesthetized on the operating table, the lump was sent to Dr. Fred Stewart who was, with the death of James Ewing, the pre-eminent cancer pathologist of his day; and Dr. Stewart found "three or four" malignant cells on frozen section. Sarita awoke some hours later to Anita's voice telling her she had had a radical mastectomy. She was cured of breast cancer almost before it began, in the greatest cancer center of the mid-20th century - primarily because her mother died a 19th-century death seven years before.

CHAPTER 18

Washington and Motherhood

In the summer of 1943, Anita was nearing the end of her residency at Memorial; it would officially end July 31, and she was offered a Special Fellowship there to begin August 1. Sarita recovered rapidly from her surgery, and Bill was also well enough for a brief second honeymoon with Anita in Myrtle Beach, South Carolina. Then in August Bill was called back to active duty in Washington, D.C. - a pediatrician assigned by military logic to the care of 600 WAVES (women sailors), a rotation of general medicine, gynecology and a good deal of psychiatry.

Anita meanwhile, still in New York, discovered that she was pregnant. Her delight filled a letter to Bill in Washington. Sarita postponed a visit to Costa Rica and began hovering around her "like a brooding hen" (though a few months later Sarita did go on to San José, where she took the trouble to divorce Roberto Figueredo, twenty-seven years after she walked away from his parents' house.)

Anita's pregnancy dovetailed nicely with the end of her residency and she decided that the thing to do, what with the vagaries of war, was to "take a year off" from medicine. Thus in August 1943 she followed

Bill down to Washington, to an apartment in Anacostia overlooking a military landing field.

Their new home was scarcely in the heart of the capital. The young Drs. Doyle and Figueredo - Anita kept her own surname, in the Spanish fashion - were among the first tenants in a fresh, clean apartment complex, three-story yellow brick buildings arranged in a friendly fashion around central lawns. The setting was picturesque, a quiet hillside with a view across the Potomac River through a forest of tulip trees. But it was definitely on the other side of the Potomac, and that year off turned out to be "a little bit miserable" for Anita, though not because she pined for the galleries and monuments and libraries of downtown Washington. She had not been married to Bill Doyle long enough to miss those things.

She left the intense physical and intellectual activity of Memorial to have a baby, but she needed something to do in the meanwhile, and decided to learn to drive a car, to cook, to sew and to play the piano. It is hard to know why she wanted to play the piano, as the Sisters of Divine Compassion had long ago gently suggested to Sarita that her money could better be spent on something other than piano lessons for Anita; but a friend taught her a single piano piece at New York Infirmary, and somehow Anita thought it was a skill she should pursue. She never arranged any lessons in Washington, however, for lack of transportation, and even though she did learn to drive their big Pontiac, Bill took the car to work.

The cooking was self-taught, from cookbooks, and only modestly successful. The problem, which endured for several decades, was that she was too pragmatic, more attuned to getting something on the table than to lingering over presentation and the correction of seasonings. She took some sewing lessons, and at this she excelled though the teacher was somewhat disapproving of her surgical ties. Home arts did not come easily to her, and she was steadily more frustrated. She was less and less able to suppress the knowledge that there was something else she did very well, and she began to feel resentment - an unheard of emotion for her - when Bill came home with stories of complicated cases from his clinic.

Their first son, Billy - William James, Jr. - was born on April 16, 1944 after an uncomplicated pregnancy and delivery at Georgetown University Hospital. As there were no physician charges with professional courtesy, and nurses were paid next to nothing, the total hospital bill for ten days was $60 - $4.50 per day for the room, plus $15 for the operating room and anesthesia. Billy was a physically beautiful, intense and colicky baby, who was difficult to hold and feed, and Anita was defeated at breast-feeding. She became very emotional, crying while she changed him, and unable to reconcile her joy at the miracle of her son with a relentless undercurrent of discontent. There were other young mothers in her building, and Anita's natural friendliness drew them to her, but her heart was not in it. She started reading women's magazines, and when she realized that she was looking forward to the next issues so she could continue her serialized stories, suddenly she could not stand it. She thought she was losing her mind, and she had to go back to work.

The house staff of the major hospitals had nearly all gone to war. But a young neurosurgeon named Harvey Ammerman lived in their building and still worked at Sibley Memorial Hospital, about ten miles across the river and northwest across town to the border with Maryland. Dr. Ammerman suggested that Anita approach Sibley about a job; and another neighbor, a childless woman named Helen Wiker, offered to care for Billy. So Anita approached Sibley Hospital and, as they were short-handed in the operating room, they hired her on as a "special surgical assistant" beginning in July 1944. Her chief duty was assisting the staff on their private cases, and she soon made the acquaintance of Oliver "Buttonhole" Cox. He, before long, asked that she be assigned to his cases exclusively.

Oliver Cox was a funny, wiry, skinny little man in his late sixties who worked seven days a week. An intense man who was very curt with residents and staff, a "Napoleon" whose mind had to be read, he treated Anita with great kindness. Before long, he called her his alter ego, his other hands, very like Anita's relationship with the feared Hayes Martin at Memorial, who wrote to her in December 1944:

It was nice to have your Christmas letter and to know that you have not fallen from grace. I am tremendously pleased to learn that you are getting a solid and basic surgical training and, speaking for myself, I can assure you that I would like very much to see you back on the Fellowship Staff at Memorial.

When Anita started at Sibley, ten weeks after Billy's birth, she joined a carpool. Gas was rationed, and in any case she and Bill had only one car. The carpool rendezvous, where a different vehicle picked her up every day, was a long downhill block away on a main road, full of traffic. Surgery began at 7:00 A.M., which was all right during the summer, but in winter was pitch dark. One day, as Anita stood there in the gloom at the appointed spot, a car stopped and opened the door, and she got in. The car contained five men, and as they drove Anita realized gradually that she had never seen any of them before. She remembers saying, "Are you going to Sibley?" and their saying, "No." She spent about a quarter of an hour talking them into letting her out of their car. They could not believe she really thought they were her carpool. Finally they pulled over and unloaded her somewhere in the middle of the city; she eventually made her way back to Sibley Hospital about an hour after surgery began. When Anita explained to Dr. Cox what happened, he was beside himself with dismay. From that day on, he sent his own car for her. Dr. Cox had a chauffeur named Gene who brought him in the morning, sat all day waiting, and then took him home, and now Gene did the same very happily for little Dr. Figueredo, "in her condition."

Anita worked with Dr. Cox for just about the nine months of her second pregnancy, and perhaps the adjustments at the operating table for her growing belly contributed to his solicitousness. (It was during this time that an ad agency photographed Anita offering a cracker to ten-month-old Billy; the picture appeared in a national magazine campaign under the slogan, "Their **fathers** are DOCTORS - Their cereal is CLAPP'S!")

Although Anita "felt wonderful" and wanted to continue working until the last possible moment, Mrs. Wiker next door said that much baby-sitting was more than she could handle; and thus Anita left Sibley

Hospital and Dr. Cox a few weeks before I was born at Georgetown Hospital in April, 1945 just one year after Billy. I was named for both grandmothers, Sarita Elizabeth; and Sarita Sr. descended from New York to help out.

Anita began casting around for another day-nurse, but then Bill was abruptly called up to sea duty and sent to Mobile, Alabama to join the *Bellerophon*, a converted tank lander refitted to repair landing craft for the invasion of mainland Japan. Although Adolph Hitler had committed suicide on April 30 and brought an end to the war in Europe, three months later the Pacific war was still raging.

The separation within six weeks of the birth of their second baby was hard on all of them, and the letters this time around between the lovers were even more mournful than when they parted a few days after their wedding. Anita was unable to return to work, and would be housebound again for more than nine months. Meanwhile, Bill sat for two months "in the middle of a dry, flat, sun baked, absolutely treeless island in Mobile Bay" with "heat, dust, glare and humidity and swarms of avaricious mosquitoes from nearby swamps" which made him think with relative affection of the South Pacific. He diverted himself by writing "The Story of Bellerophon" for the crew (about the mythical Greek warrior who rode the winged horse Pegasus and destroyed the Chimera), by studying Spanish, and by trying to figure a way for Anita to join him. Even he was a bit taken aback, however, when Anita suggested leaving the babies with their grandmother **for a month;** he wrote, "I really feel that two weeks would be maximal..." He wondered how Anita was sleeping without him, and hoped that she was not "clutching on" to her poor mother. They finally managed a two-week rendezvous in Mobile and Biloxi, where Anita swam happily in the warm waters of the Gulf of Mexico - and then Bill was gone to sea.

The *Bellerophon* steamed toward Japan and was just west of the Panama Canal on August 6, 1945 when the atom bomb was dropped on Hiroshima. Eight days later the Pacific war was over, and Anita wrote Bill an ecstatic letter; her mother was in downtown Manhattan with "the maddest crowd she'd ever seen" and was coming down to Washington on the next morning train to celebrate with her and the babies. And Anita ended, "Our little ones will be so happy to have you home again!"

But the *Bellerophon* was ordered north to San Diego to await orders, and the crew waited nearly another two months anchored off Harbor Island without specific instructions. Anita was furious at the Navy for keeping them separated; but this time at least Bill was well enough to do some exploring. One day in late September he boarded a bus marked "La Jolla" and rode to the end of the line, and that evening wrote Anita this long letter:

> I went back out to La Jolla, the town I spoke of...and covered the whole place in detail, I was that interested. I walked literally miles, from a high hill in back of town for a panoramic view, down thru residential districts, looking closely at houses, yards, trees, flowers & lawns, down thru the business district and then for a mile or more along the sea.
>
> Main facts gleaned are: La Jolla is a town of about 8,000 people situated directly on the sea coast, 14 miles north of San Diego. The climate, yesterday and today, consisted of warm sun in the afternoon ideal for swimming, with a quick drop in temperature after sunset to topcoat weather. Yearly mean high is 75° and mean low 56°...the shore line is cliffy and rocky with small curved sandy beaches at frequent intervals, very picturesque, with the unlimited blue expanse of the Pacific as a backdrop for the whole town. Three very nice hotels & several small ones, as the place is a semi-resort...or rather a haven for artists...One hotel (Casa de Mañana) would be an ideal spot for a 3rd honeymoon. The business section is very smart & modern-looking. There's a modern hospital (I would estimate about 100 beds) and an adjoining Metabolic Clinic which is supposed to be nationally famous....
>
> The predominating architecture is heavily Spanish in flavor (white and cream stucco, red tiles, patios, garden

walls) with a good deal of modern. Most houses look small, as they're mostly one story but ramble. Average prices seem to be $9-10,000 for a 3-bedroom house, $950- 2,000 for a lot in a good location. There's a moderate boom on, I guess.

The foliage in town is a combination of those heavy-trunked palm trees, pine trees and abundant flowering vines around the houses.. I noted 3 doctor's offices all in little one-story separate buildings. There's a nice little Catholic Church, "Mary, Star of the Sea", which appears to be brand new, and in which I lit a candle and said a prayer for us.

Well, that's La Jolla. As you can see I was very favorably impressed...every time you turn a corner it makes a picture, and I think that's what I really like best.

Bill walked through a town of one and two-story Spanish colonial buildings, all whitewashed stucco and red tile roofs along the central avenues, to the beach and the Casa de Mañana, which was already then a wonderful old hotel, dripping with bougainvillea like a Spanish inn, and there he had a meal on the patio and looked out over the sea. He noticed that September was warm with brilliant sun, but not hot, that the ocean breeze was light and cool, the sand white and mostly unblanketed, and the sea azure blue. It was nothing like New York; it was possibly something like Costa Rica.

Bill and Anita talked a lot about where they would settle down permanently. As recently as the year before, Anita told an interviewer for a Spanish-language periodical (which was picking up the *Look* story) that "after the war I intend to return with my family to Costa Rica to live. At the present time my country is undertaking a vast public health program, and my husband and I wish to contribute our efforts to this work for the public good."[175]

Certainly Sarita had planned all along on their permanent return to Costa Rica; but it appears that Bill never imagined that he could be happy living as an expatriate, and - despite what Anita told the press

- never felt that she seriously expected him to go. Furthermore Anita was nearly as "American" as Bill. She had been brought up on a wide stage, and the lovely Costa Rican interludes were like a step back in time. Her real life was dynamic and modern and on the literal cutting edge of high technology.

On the other hand, Dad Doyle took it for granted they would settle in Utica where Bill was offered an excellent position at the locally prestigious Slocum-Dickson Clinic. At the time the war ended, he was promised a pediatric job there at an annual **starting** salary of $20,000, a tremendous sum. (Twenty years earlier, Bill's father was one of the wealthiest men in Utica with an annual income of $25,000.) But Anita always hated the cold, was exquisitely uncomfortable in drafts, and really did not want to cope with New York winters all her life. So that when they talked about other places to live, the musings revolved around Florida and Southern California. The desert did not appeal. Bill loved the sea.

Having discovered La Jolla, Bill explored several more times and learned from the Chamber of Commerce that there were six doctors, all general practitioners. He was encouraged to think that he and Anita could establish their medical practices, though up to this time all the specialists were in downtown San Diego. When Anita received his letter extolling the virtues of La Jolla, she went to see some Hollywood people in her building complex (at work in the Navy photo lab in Washington) who gave her glowing reports of La Jolla's climate and beauty, but told her one "couldn't actually live there because there's no way to make a living." Anita, relying on her usual optimistic instinct, wrote back saying La Jolla sounded fine.

CHAPTER 19

Cancer Detection and the Call of the West

Not long after the armistice, in the winter of 1945, Dr. Lucile Loseke (Anita's co-pioneer at Memorial) wrote to say that the hospital had opened a new department of Cancer Detection at what was called the Strang Clinic, and was looking for a doctor to perform cancer detection exams. The job had regular hours and paid the incredible wage of $20 a day. (Her residency had paid less than $20 a month.) Anita applied and was accepted in an instant, but she needed a home in New York for her family.

Her mother's apartment on West End Avenue was not large enough for three adults and two toddlers, but rentals of the size the family needed went for some $400-800/month furnished (with "awful stuff", as Anita writes Bill) and were hard to find at that. Costa Rican friends who owned a house in nearby Jackson Heights convinced them they could buy. This was the very beginning of the long-term mortgage with small down payments and monthly installments. Still, none of Bill Doyle's older married siblings ever owned a house, despite well-paying jobs. But Anita, together with her mother, put $3000 down, and moved to the old community of Flushing on Long Island; just after Thanksgiving 1945, they installed themselves and their babies in a new attached row house, with three bedrooms and finished basement for $43/month. It was here that Sarita Sr. was renamed Lita.

Just at this time, *Mademoiselle* magazine ran an article featuring "Latin Americans to the North." The copy, under a picture of Anita in a velvet-collared jacket, reads:

> Dr. Anita Figueredo uses her maiden name professionally, but she's married to a former classmate at the Long Island College of Medicine. She's waiting now for his return from Navy sea duty, and looking for a Spanish-speaking nurse for her two children so she can go back to work.[176]

In the text is a review of her career, and Anita is quoted as saying that "she expects to have more children, and to continue with more hospital work and surgery"; there is also a description of "Sarita Villegas, a most youthful-looking grandmother who has made her own way for years as an exporter to Costa Rica of women's clothes" and the following comments:

> It runs in the family to pioneer, for [Sarita's] sister was the first society woman to become a trained nurse, and her cousin was the first woman lawyer. There may be a reason why Costa Rican girls, though they do not have the vote, appear to lead all others in achieving brilliant careers. Costa Rica has the largest per capita budget for education in Central America, the highest per capita wealth, and is regarded as the most advanced and democratic of all the American republics.

From October 1945 to January 1946, Bill was in San Francisco with the *Bellerophon* fitting out ships to bring American troops back home. The Navy officially released him to inactive Reserve on January 10, 1946, and he then had three months terminal leave at home in Flushing, enjoying his little family and puttering around building a maid's room in the basement. In April he started a pediatric residency at Long Island

College Hospital. It was every other night and every other weekend in the hospital for Bill, and Anita commuted an hour each way to E. 68th Street in Manhattan across the Queensboro Bridge; nevertheless their son John Carroll was conceived in June and born the following March.

Anita was becoming accustomed to pregnancy as a natural state of affairs. Having decided to marry Bill Doyle she cemented forever her commitment to traditional Catholicism, and this meant a willingness to bear as many children as God might send. However she did not again assume that God insisted she stay home. She found a housekeeper (a Costa Rican woman sent by a cousin) and continued on very happily for two full years at Memorial, learning all the tools of early cancer detection - regular breast exams, selective excision of moles, Pap smears, sigmoidoscopy - and this training was the model for what she would do ever after in private practice. Had they stayed in New York, Anita would likely have worked indefinitely at Memorial. But Bill would finish his residency in July 1947, and they now talked "endlessly" about La Jolla.

Finally in September, when it was particularly hot and humid in New York, they took a child-free reconnaissance trip. They had a beautiful room at the Casa de Mañana overlooking the ocean, and while they were sitting on a corner of the "Casa beach" they decided to look at houses. They asked for a five-bedroom house, which didn't exist then in La Jolla except in the beautiful villas which were out of their price range (such as the elegant home at 417 Coast Boulevard which enchanted Anita on that trip.)

When a realtor couldn't find them *any* house they liked and could afford, they boarded a bus going south on La Jolla Boulevard and happened to see a man hammering in a "For Sale" sign at 6114. They pulled the buzzer, jumped off the bus, ran over and bought the house that day (for $17,000, 50% down). It was a two-bed-room, ranch-style bungalow with a huge living room and separate dining room, and was brand new.

Then, having become official residents of the town, they investigated their professional opportunities. Bill spotted a shingle with the word

"Pediatrics" outside a small office on Ivanhoe Street. He entered the little building and found it entirely empty except for the doctor himself, who was packing boxes and who responded, when Bill asked about the practice of pediatrics in La Jolla, "There isn't any. I'm just leaving town."

Anita, for her part, brought a letter of introduction from Hayes Martin to Dr. Hall Holder, a surgeon he had worked with during the war. Dr. Holder was one of the best-regarded surgeons in the county; at his downtown San Diego office he read Dr. Martin's glowing letter about Anita and listened to Bill's description of his own training, and then said kindly, "Dr. Doyle, I have no doubt but what, in time, you can build up a pediatric practice. But as for you, Dr. Figueredo, no woman has ever opened a belly in San Diego County, and I do not expect to see it in my lifetime."

Back home in New York they encountered a similar lack of enthusiasm. Lita was formally invited to go west with the family, but was appalled at the idea of leaving Manhattan. She had already made a significant concession in moving across the East River. Even then she traveled back to the city most days on shopping expeditions for her export business, and often stayed into the night to party with friends. She could not imagine that there was life in California, and Dad Doyle was similarly doubtful when he heard the news.

In addition Anita, taking leave of her teachers, encountered the wrath of Dr. Elise L'Esperance. Oddly enough, the woman who had hand-picked Anita Figueredo for greatness had not followed her career closely enough to learn the details of her personal life. Now when she heard that her protégé had three babies and was moving to the west coast, Dr. L'Esperance ejected Anita from her office, saying that she had let her down and wasted her superb training.

In this somewhat gloomy atmosphere the Flushing house was sold for $12,000, a one-third profit which funded both the La Jolla house and a new house for Lita on Long Island. Lita was very attached to her three *chacalínes* (literally "shrimps", her babies), and found it hard to let them and their mother go and to advertise for roomers again, but still harder to imagine dislocating herself from everything else she knew and loved.

New York was a magical place to Lita, "the most wonderful city in the world," and she could not leave it for a village in the hinterland.

At the end of October, Bill and Billy set out for California in their 1946 Chevrolet. They arrived at the empty house in La Jolla the day before Halloween, bought bunk beds and a refrigerator and settled in to wait for their furniture. When it materialized a few days later, Bill called Anita in New York, and she and the two babies flew thirteen hours cross-country to La Jolla.

It was November 1947. Anita Figueredo Doyle was thirty-one years old and Bill Doyle thirty-two, and they had settled themselves down in a romantic, unrealistically small garden of a place, a continent away from all their family and friends and sterling professional connections. Billy Doyle was three, I was two, and John eight months; and within a week or two Tommy was conceived as part of the general and continuing celebration.

In New York: Pictures sent home to the family in Costa Rica emphasize prosperity and good times with other Latin friends. Sarita and Anita in Central Park soon after their arrival and at Long Beach in 1924.

Anita (8) waves goodbye to her mother from her first boarding
school in Chestnut Hill, PA. Passport photo of Sarita (31) and
Anita (11) for their first return visit to Costa Rica, 1928.

Anita's high school, Southern Seminary, Buena Vista, VA. Graduation Day 1932 with her favorite teacher, Annie Parks Moore.

Manhattanville College of the Sacred Heart, NYC. Graduation 1936: with her mother [far right] and their first landlady and close friend, Julieta McGrigor.

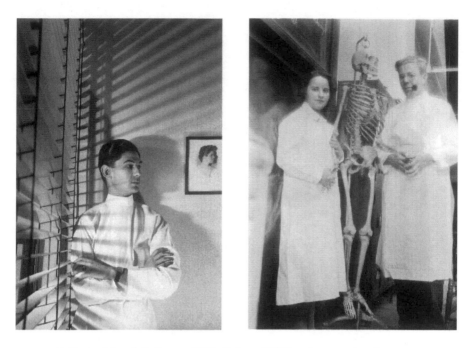

At Long Island College of Medicine: Bill Doyle as Anita first saw him in 1936. Anita with classmate and skeletal friend. Costa Rican front page news of Anita's appointment as first female surgical resident, Memorial Hospital for Cancer, NYC.

August 8, 1942 Anita marries William James Doyle at St. Patrick's Cathedral. Sarita Villegas (45) gives the bride away. Four months later, December 1, 1942, *Look Magazine* features the bride in a three-page photo essay.

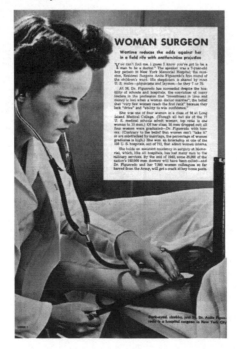

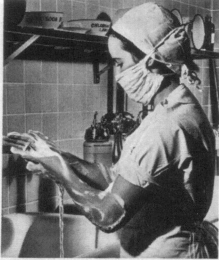

Her small, deft hands are scrubbed in soap and alcohol for 10 minutes before each operation. Actually, surgery is essentially woman's work. It is a delicate manual process, demanding skill with scissors and needle.

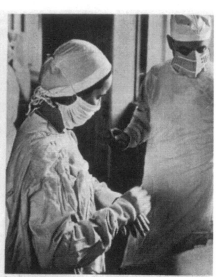

Steady and intent on the problems of the operation ahead, Dr. Figueredo shows no signs of the "emotional instability," "nervousness" or "lack of detachment" which are stock arguments against women in medicine.

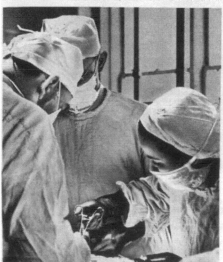

Teamed with men in an operation upon a male patient, Dr. Figueredo refutes the charge that women doctors can't work on equal terms with men, proves their work should not be restricted to gynecology and child care.

"A little pale but all there" is a senior surgeon's description of Dr. Figueredo after a grueling 10-hour session in the operating room. Men used to working with women doctors testify to their stamina under strain.

Continuation of 1942 *Look Magazine* photo essay.

A favorite in the children's ward, Dr. Figueredo calls her young patients "Butch." In addition to work with children, her routine includes admission of new patients, X-ray therapy, blood transfusions.

Her marriage to a medical-school classmate, Lt. (j.g.) Bill Doyle, M.D., won't end her career. They crammed wedding and honeymoon into his three-day leave last August. Then Bill returned to duty.

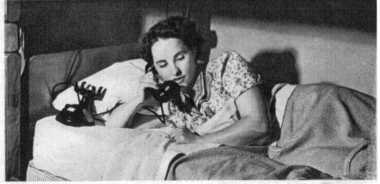

A resident surgeon's day doesn't end when the operating room closes. On call three nights each week, she makes "evening rounds"—visits to some 50 private and ward patients—laboriously writes up charts, then sleeps in the hospital with a telephone next to her pillow. For the many responsibilities of an assistant resident, she receives the standard monthly stipend of $15 plus her room, board and laundry.

Last page of 1942 *Look Magazine* photo essay.

PART THREE

A Heaven of Blackred Roses
California, 1947-1993

if there are any heavens my mother will(all by herself)have
one. It will not be a pansy heaven nor
a fragile heaven of lilies-of-the-valley but
it will be a heaven of blackred roses

my father will be(deep like a rose
tall like a rose)...

(suddenly in sunlight he will bow,
& the whole garden will bow)

e.e.cummings[177]
"XLIII"

CHAPTER 20

The New Frontier

My first memory is of flying to California.

My mother made a bed for me across her airplane seat and mine so that I mostly slept through the noise and shudder of the great propellers as we rose and fell in the sky. She stroked my cheek, and I was aware that my sweet baby brother, with his silky long lashes and his big ears, was smiling at me from inside her arms. Our big brother, she said, was waiting for us somewhere with our father; and I have a hazy recollection of waking when the wheels jolted down, and of stumbling, clutching her hand, into the twilight of Lindbergh Field and San Diego.

San Diego in 1947 was a sprawling, big, waterfront town of about 350,000 people which had doubled in size from the years just before, to just after the Second World War. The most inspired of its buildings were the lovely residue of a 1915 Panama-California Exposition, a cluster of Spanish Renaissance towers, domes and cloister-walks across a high graceful bridge in Balboa Park. For the rest, the "old town" left by the Mexican settlers was a dusty ruin, and the new-style buildings closer to the water ran to the low and drab. But the natural setting was spectacular, with nearly perfect Mediterranean weather, seventy miles of shoreline, and air kept clear by the gentle prevailing winds. Development was concentrated in the old downtown bay front and hills, and along the coastal highway; cows grazed in Mission Valley near the newly-restored remains of Padre Junipero Serra's church; and vast stretches of the city and county were left in sagebrush and chaparral, although water from the Colorado River had just arrived in great clay pipes and would transform everything it touched.[178]

The suburb of La Jolla itself, protruding into the sea at the northwestern edge of the city, had once been nothing more than a grey-green coastal blanket of sage and chaparral. But now there were thousands of sixty-year-old trees, half of them palms, the rest mostly cedar and eucalyptus; and the village had come into the beauty foretold by the earliest entrepreneurs. La Jolla's population also grew by half during the war[179], and it seemed there should be enough work for two new physicians to do. But six months after moving to California, Drs. Anita Figueredo and William J. Doyle had just enough money in the bank to give up and go home, to get their growing family back to New York and jobs with steady salaries in Utica. They debated. The words between our parents swirled above our heads at dinner, then while they soaped us in our triple bath, and later on the other side of our wall, as we lay awake in our bunks while the headlights of the boulevard flashed around our room. But finally it was settled that we should stay.

The community of La Jolla had an excellent 56-bed hospital, Scripps Memorial, built in 1924 on a hill overlooking the sea. Sickrooms had windows opened to the salt air and were furnished with mahogany bedsteads and dressers and bentwood rockers like a fine hotel. Next door was the Metabolic Clinic, a research institution, with specialists who were theoretically pleased to have an oncologist in town, and might be expected to refer the occasional patient to Anita Figueredo.

She arrived in La Jolla in November with a letter from the eminent George Pack to his friend Dr. E.F.F. Copp at Scripps Metabolic Clinic. Dr. Copp was a specialist in diabetes who trained in the laboratories of Banting and Best, the discoverers of insulin. He was a thoughtful man, impressed with what George Pack had to say about Anita Figueredo, and he invited Anita and Bill to the next combined staff meeting of the

Scripps Institutions (perhaps ten physicians altogether) where he gave them a gracious introduction and assured their hospital privileges.

Anita Figueredo's training as a surgical oncologist required some explanation. It had been in many ways the best training available in the world at that time for the treatment of cancer. But the war had made a peculiar impact, first admitting her to a previously closed field and then, with her marriage to a naval officer, disrupting her orderly progress up the educational ladder.

Until the summer of 1943, Anita and her fellow-pioneer at Memorial, Lucile Loseke, had comparable training experience. They were interns and junior residents at New York Infirmary where they rotated through all the medical and surgical wards and encountered Dr. George Papanicolau, the developer of the "Pap smear" for early detection of cancer of the uterine cervix. Before they were called to Memorial, the two young women planned to enter a traditional three or four-year residency in the specialty field of their choice, in Anita's case, probably obstetrics and gynecology.

However they were invited, suddenly, into the young field of surgical oncology, and after a year, their paths diverged. Lucile Loseke, who never married, entered into a general surgical residency at Bellevue Hospital lasting several years, became a colon and rectal surgeon, and eventually chief of surgery at New York Infirmary. Anita's surgical education was first and last an apprenticeship to great technicians, first to Pack, Martin, Adair and others at Memorial where she learned the principles of radical procedures, huge incisions and careful inspection of all the contents of the exposed body cavities for cancer cells which might be left behind; then to Oliver Cox, who taught her the contrasting skills of the smallest possible incision, the neatest and quickest repair, and the least disturbance of adjacent body organs, which is to say, minimal exposure and minimal trauma.

After Oliver Cox, her career further invented itself when she entered the new world of the cancer detection clinic. Here she stopped operating altogether for a time, except for limited outpatient procedures. She used her hands and eyes instead on the seemingly well, seeking the earliest signs of malignant disease. The revolutionary idea was that small, young cancers might be curable with less mutilating treatment; and to that end Anita worked to perfect the Cancer Detection Exam (C.D.E.), which came to include the most rigorous inspection of the outside and inside of apparently healthy people -- the whole skin surface, head and neck, breasts, and every orifice. Patients submitted to the new techniques of proctoscopy and Pap smear, and then laboratory evaluation including chest X-ray and certain screening blood tests. Suspicious lumps and lesions were excised without delay and sent to the pathologist, and any wider treatment arranged posthaste. A corollary of this approach was that a certain number of specimens sent to the pathologist were inevitably "benign." The idea was, after all, to find the very earliest cancers, and the earliest cancer was only one cell beyond the benign. This concept is taken for granted today. But it was new and would create some trouble for Anita in the early years of her practice in La Jolla.

In addition to her surgical skills and the C.D.E., Anita was knowledgeable in the use of the few chemotherapeutic drugs then known (basically *thiotepa*, radioactive iodine for thyroid cancer, and radium implants for the uterus); and finally she had training in radiotherapy (at the insistence of James Ewing, who had no patience with cancer surgeons who did not use and understand radiation) and this means that she not only planned the radiation her patients received but also designed and made the lead shields which protected their healthy organs.

Soon after she arrived in La Jolla, Anita set out her credentials in a letter to the general physicians in town and offered to perform the C.D.E. as a service to their patients, by referral only. The letter was met by silence. There was no tradition of specialization in private practice in the village. Specialists worked downtown in San Diego, and the generalists were satisfied with that arrangement. They specifically handled their own cancer patients, which most of the time in 1947 meant predictions as to how much time was left to the sufferer on earth.

At a Christmas party given by a new doctor friend, Anita described again her *curriculum vitae* and her aspirations. Soon after the party she was called by Dr. Frank Hankins, a general surgeon with special interest and training in oncology who practiced at Mercy and at

Paradise Valley Hospital in the fields of National City, not far from the Mexican border.

Frank Hankins was intrigued enough by the idea of a Memorial-trained oncologist in town to assess Anita's competence himself. He invited her down to his office, and there she walked into an impromptu examination of her abilities. A patient with a huge mass on the side of his face presented himself to Dr. Hankins for treatment, and now Anita was asked for her own opinion of the case. When she recommended a "Commando procedure" (a radical dissection of the face including disarticulation and removal of half the jaw) Dr. Hankins took her on as his surgical assistant.

He did not hire her, in the sense of paying her a regular salary. Rather, he allowed her to see patients in his San Diego office, to assist him in surgery and to make rounds on hospitalized patients before and after surgery (in at least three hospitals, Mercy and Quintard downtown, as well as Paradise Valley in National City, which was twenty miles of two-lane roads south of La Jolla.) As Dr. Hankins and Paradise Valley Hospital were Seventh-day Adventist, their day of rest was Saturday, and the regular Sunday operating schedule began at 7:30 AM. Anita rose before dawn, made her way to National City in time for 6:00 AM Mass, prayed for strength in the simple yellow mission-style church of St. Mary, and then got on with her day. Winter Sundays she got up long before daylight, arranging her pregnant self and then the babies with her husband, who in turn dealt with the sitter when she came; and weekdays she slept an extra hour if nobody woke in the night. Her pay for all this was what she made assisting at surgery only, as the cases were all Dr. Hankins'. One month she earned seventy-five dollars.

It was only after our move to a larger house that Anita had live-in help. During our two years on La Jolla Boulevard, she made do with day help, some of it good and reliable and some not. One unhappy woman actually hit us (probably a single slap, although our collective outrage enlarged it to a general and bloody whipping) but we were truly afraid, as our parents saw, and the woman vanished without a trace. We were not used to being handled roughly. It is true that Billy was headstrong, but as Johnny and I were pacifists absorbed in one another, there was relatively little in-fighting in the early days and certainly nothing like what would come with the strong personalities who followed.

Meanwhile Bill Doyle opened a pediatric office in La Jolla at the junction of Fay and Kline Streets, and Anita shared his single consulting room a few hours a week. The photo sent to Lita shows a squat white building with a top deck and shiny chrome trim, like a cabin cruiser berthed on its corner under big La Jolla trees. (Also in the packet sent to wintry New York were strategic photos of mother and children on the beach in the February sun.)

At home, we three "older" children slept in double bunks in the larger of the two bedrooms, leaving one space free for Thomas Alan, who was born at Scripps Hospital (where Anita had yet to operate) in August 1948. Lita flew out in September for the baptism, and sat looking slim and happy and stylish, pearl earrings and pearl combs in her short waved hair, at the center of a formal portrait with Anita. As our father was excluded, this was essentially an update of their life series of dual portraits: baby Tommy in long baptismal gown on Lita's lap, Billy and I seated to one side and our mother to the other (her hair now drawn back in the classic bun she wore for the next twenty years) with toddler John nestled up to her chin. This time Lita stayed several weeks, partly because she was suddenly disabled by Ménière's disease (a disorder of the middle ear causing ringing, dizziness, nausea and vomiting) which came on so abruptly that she toppled out of a chair while lunching with Anita in a restaurant. She was flat in bed for a month or so in the living room, where even the mild fluttering of the blinds triggered off waves of distress. Just about the time the family portrait was mailed off to Costa Rica and Lita recovered enough to return home to New York, Anita was pregnant again.

At the end of 1948 Anita Figueredo Doyle, mother of four and a half Americans, appeared in San Diego Superior Court and formally relinquished her Costa Rican citizenship.[180] Although she had won appointment to the medical staff of Scripps Hospital in May, there was some discussion as to whether an "alien" should have full operating privileges. In any case it seemed time for Anita to minimize the oddities of her position and to declare her "intention to reside permanently in the United States."

By the beginning of 1949, Anita told Dr. Hankins that she must have a regular salary, that she could not make ends meet with assisting fees, and they agreed on the sum of two hundred dollars a month. Bill's practice as the only pediatrician north of San Diego and south of Newport Beach was steadily growing. He made house and hospital calls to Ocean Beach and Pt. Loma, Oceanside and Escondido. They could afford to look for a house with more bedrooms.

There were still beautiful open lots, west of La Jolla Boulevard toward the sea, scattered in among the existing houses of the section called Hermosa Terrace. (East of the boulevard were mostly fields of Black-eyed Susans, and hills of brush and foxtails growing into the gun sites of cement bunkers left over from the war.) On the corner of Avenida Cresta and Mesa Way was the beginning of a large-enough house, a cement slab and parts of a frame, and construction was halted for a month or so while the rest was redesigned to fit the Doyles. Billy and I could ride our tricycles the three blocks down to supervise, and in August of 1949 the local paper announced "The William Doyles Now in New Home":

> The 5-bedroom Kesling modern is designed for gracious living. A striking feature of the living room is the enormous picture window that commands a sweeping view of the water from three directions. A walled garden affords privacy for entertaining and outdoor living, while the couple's five small children have their play yard. The children are William, Jr., Sarita, Johnny, Tommy and Charlie.

Charlie was Charles Edward (July 1949), an angelic-looking, curly-haired blonde at the end of a line of four dark little heads, who was christened in October when Sarita Villegas reappeared. This time Lita stayed a block or so away at the pink home of Florence Miller, a small, brisk, tennis-playing widow in her sixties who was pleased to rent out her former maid's quarters to a woman with the same sort of no-nonsense style as her own. In this enhanced privacy and comfort, Lita stayed on through the fall, and before she left she apparently surveyed her clutch of grandchildren and convinced herself that their destiny was not in Costa Rica. Sarita Villegas too became an American citizen in San Diego Superior Court (taking three years off her age in her declaration.)[181] She was actually just turning fifty-three, and had lived more than half her life in the United States.

No sooner did her mother fly away again than Anita, with five children under six, went three months without steady help. The Avenida Cresta house had a maid's room and bath and, as soon as we were settled, Anita filed a formal request with the State Employment Office for a live-in housekeeper-sitter. The pleasant clerk assured her the position would be promptly filled. But for all that, not a single applicant ever inquired, though the agency did keep the request on file, and ten years later called to see if Anita was still interested. Startled, she said, "Yes." But the call was evidently just a bookkeeping maneuver, as nothing more was ever heard from the agency again. A few families Anita knew employed women from Mexico, and eventually she too found excellent, long-term help this way, single women or mother-and-daughter pairs who stayed with us several years at a time. But this was a hit-or-miss, grapevine sort of source and, around Christmas of 1949, it ran dry.

I was four and did not understand, in the weeks that followed, what had happened to our mother, who now found herself trying to care for five little children and a big new house and to practice medicine all over San Diego County. She had always been fully occupied, cooking, feeding, diapering, speaking thoughtfully into the telephone, laughing with our father, writing to our grandmother, dressing for work and driving away, hugging us on her return. So that when she was overwhelmed she did not look busier -- how could she? -- only different.   I only saw that she stopped hearing what I ran to tell her, and even spoke to me sharply when I pulled at her. My brothers quarreled, and whatever my mother did seemed to make it worse. And strangest of all, she stopped smiling at my father and even spoke to him now and then in a voice I had never heard. After his own long work day, Bill measured and poured the home-made infant formulas, and bathed pink bodies and put them to bed. Different babysitters came for fractions of the day, so that my mother could run to her office or on to the hospital, but it was she who changed the sheets before she left and washed the clothes on her return. It so happened that at this time Mary, Star of the Sea Catholic Church got a new young curate, good-hearted but "FBI" which meant Foreign-

Born Irish and more conservative than God; and one Sunday Father Creaton dropped in on the Doyles. He was dismayed to see Anita on her hands and knees, on this Day of Rest, scrubbing the kitchen floor; but she assured him the Lord knew she had no other time, and went on scrubbing. Ordinarily invigorated by challenge, Anita was now beaten down and exhausted. She confronted the fact that she was not being a good mother or wife or doctor, that there was no way to continue, and that the only thing she could give up was medicine.

There has probably never been a time in this century when a woman doctor could reasonably take a decade or so "off" to raise a family, because her education would be hopelessly out-of-date when she tried to return to practice. Certainly this was true of the field of cancer therapy in 1949; and, in any case, Anita was still having babies ten and twelve years later, so there never would have been any "good" time to return to work, had she ever left. The frustration of the situation kept building until one day Anita's big Chevrolet broke down, and she found herself on La Jolla Boulevard, waiting for a city bus to haul her to an office full of patients. She was weak with fatigue and a sense of helplessness, and that night she announced to Bill that she was quitting medicine.

It was a logical solution, but one which Bill refused to accept. Neither one of them could ever really explain why Bill refused - or, indeed, how this deeply conservative man, raised in so traditional a household, so meticulous and so religious, somehow became exactly the husband Anita needed. Bill said that falling in love with Anita was "complete and utter capitulation" and from that moment on he wanted whatever she was and whatever she had to be. Now, in this crisis of will and spirit, he insisted that Anita's medical career was no more negotiable than anything else of importance in their world, and that giving it up would obliterate all the bright promise of her life before their marriage. And in fact soon after this they found reliable help, and Anita continued on. Decades later, after she was awarded an honorary doctorate, Anita received a reminiscing letter from a long-time patient which began: "My earliest memory was in the late '40s when you made house calls with children in the back of your car...."

There now ensued a year, 1950, when Anita was not pregnant. For Mother's Day, *The San Diego Union* commissioned a formal portrait of Anita and her five children at home, and published it under the banner "San Diego Mother of the Year." (This was a famous picture around our house as we grew up; and many years later we re-staged it, as a 25th-wedding anniversary gift for our parents: five young adults in the original poses and costumes, complete in every detail down to Tommy's big body scrunched into his little red rocker, holding his xylophone, and Charlie's rubber ducky.)

The family settled down with relatively stable domestic help, and the first two children went to school, to Stella Maris Academy, each of us a year early because Anita decided we were ready, the only criterion she found useful for placing a child in the "proper" grade.

She also found a close woman friend. Betty Stirnkorb moved to town with her husband, Bob, who was a builder. The Stirnkorbs were Catholic and were sent to see the Doyles by the pastor when they asked about a pediatrician. The two couples found they had much in common, including at least two children the same age, and a shared (male) interest in sailing. Betty herself, at twenty-nine, was nearly five years younger than Anita. She was a tall, blonde housewife whose husband, as fascinated as he came to be by Anita, did not approve of wives working outside the home. But the chemistry was right, and the two women became good friends, partly because Betty was willing to accept the unconventional terms of such a friendship. She even accepted the fact that Anita was always late and that she always did two things at once; when the couples went out to dinner or the theater, Betty knew she would sit in the car with Bob and Bill in the dark street outside a patient's house, while Anita ran in for a "just a minute." Bob might squirm with impatience, but Betty and Bill knew that this was the way it was with Anita, and were allied in their acceptance and support.

The medical practices of both Anita and Bill flourished to the extent that they needed larger quarters. Anita was determined to found a real La Jolla practice, and by now she understood that it would have to be primary care. The novelty of this was that a surgeon customarily treats patients by referral. But the very nature of the cancer detection exam, to which she was committed, required the regular evaluation of apparently healthy people. Before long, most of the women in her parish chose her as their physician. But the general physicians, perhaps understandably, were not willing to refer their own patients. A few were openly hostile to her eagerness to educate the village about cancer. At a time when the doctors' lounge of any hospital was filled with a blue haze of smoke, a story appeared in the paper about "No Smoking" cards over the ashtrays in Anita Figueredo's office. Angry letters erupted in the Medical Society Bulletin, accusing her of "advertising."

After two years in San Diego, Anita built the nucleus of a surgical practice, first with patients whom she cared for when Dr. Hankins was not available, and then with others who were increasingly self-referred. Some were transplanted New Yorkers, referred by the staff at Memorial. A few of these were actually former patients of Anita's at the Strang Clinic who were committed to the idea of an annual C.D.E. for the rest of their lives. Anita operated in whatever hospital was closest to the patient's home, mostly still in downtown San Diego and National City.

Anita Figueredo was the first woman to "open a belly" in San Diego County, much to the pleasure of Dr. Hall Holder who predicted he would not live to see it, but was delighted to find he had, and she continued as the lone female surgeon for the next fifteen years. She was the most unlikely figure in the operating room. There was the matter of her overall size and the number of stacking stools required to bring the top of her into view over the table. And then once the accommodations were made for her height, she nestled her current pregnancy into the patient's side. She wore size 6 gloves when she could get them, which were child-size next to the typical 7½s and 8s the other surgeons wear. And she was feminine and pretty. But above all, she had only the better attributes of the so-called "surgical temperament": decisive and quick and self-confident, but without a hint of arrogance or abuse of the O.R. staff. The nurses and the operating room supervisors loved her, and many became devoted patients.

Anita's surgical privileges (the list of operations a hospital agrees a surgeon is competent to perform) were all related to oncology, the detection and treatment of tumors. She was unique in this as well. Even

Frank Hankins, who had a large oncology practice, also did general surgery much of the time. Anita's medical-staff file at Scripps Hospital listed full privileges in "head and face, thyroid and neck, breast, and major gynecological surgery, as well as minor surgery including the removal of lesions of the skin." She did big procedures.

One of the earliest at Scripps, in December 1948, was an operation on a forty-seven-year-old woman for cancer of the tongue. Anita resected about two-thirds of the tongue as well as a number of malignant lymph nodes in the neck on the same side as the cancer, and then several months later on the opposite side of the neck when the patient had recurrent metastatic disease. This is called bilateral radical neck dissection, and was an aggressive surgical attempt to control an already-advanced cancer; but the patient did well and was still alive and cancer-free as a very old lady in 1993.

A second early case involved a cancerous node in front of a patient's right ear. This was removed, and the tumor found to be "amelanotic melanoma," the type of cancer usually found in black moles on the skin, but without the black pigment. The tumor was metastatic from somewhere else, but the "primary" lesion was not known. Anita removed the few small visible lesions, on the lip, the inner angle of the mouth, a pinpoint black spot of the right temple, the scalp and the back, and was informed that they were all benign. Then she asked the pathologist at Scripps to send the slides of the tumor to Fred Stewart, her pathologist friend at Memorial, and Dr. Stewart wrote back:

> I would make an unequivocal diagnosis of metastatic melanoma. Where this started, of course I cannot say, but I will inform you that on two occasions I have had melanomas that were seemingly actually primary in the parotid.[182]

Now this was an extraordinary situation for Anita. She had tremendous faith in Fred Stewart, who was the most experienced cancer pathologist in the world; and the lump had indeed overlain the parotid gland, which sits in a horseshoe shape in front of the ear and under most of the cheek. However, a melanoma in this gland was so rare that no one but Fred Stewart had ever seen it; and through the parotid runs the nerve which controls the muscles of half the face. Anita thus had to convince her patient that she must remove his parotid on the **chance** that the tumor was there, knowing she would likely have to sacrifice the facial nerve. Her judgment was accepted, the tumor was indeed found in the resected parotid duct, to Anita's considerable relief, and the patient lived on with his partially paralyzed face, very grateful to be alive – and able to contribute in a lovely and unexpected way to the happiness of the entire Doyle family a few years later.

Because of her special expertise, in addition to her own operating schedule, Anita attended "tumor boards" in virtually all the city hospitals. These were a new idea in cancer care, sessions at which any physician could present a patient with malignant disease and get a state-of-the-art treatment plan, at no cost to the patient or physician.

From the beginning Anita inspired devotion in her patients and was written long, grateful letters and even poems such as this one from 1950 called "Pattern":

> How can a hand that rocks a cradle
> so skillfully guide a surgeon's knife?
> How can a face so like an angel's
> take such a serious view of life?
> All are met with interest kind
> and understanding heart,
> There's something in her attitude
> that eases all at start.
> To have a doctor so endowed
> gives more than health to many,
> One gains a faith, a lasting thought,
> I'd not trade mine for any.[183]

Early in 1951 Anita found that she was going to have another baby; she was also elected chairman of the education committee of the local American Cancer Society. Always a gifted public speaker, she now began lecturing around the county on the "Insidious Enemy," and her small pregnant persona became a fixture on the luncheon and dinner circuit. In April of 1951 she was featured on a television show called

"People in the News" (just as she finished paying off a loan for our first little black and white TV), and the event was covered with a vaguely carnival air by *The San Diego Union:*

> One of the leading cancer authorities in the country, Dr. Figueredo is as attractive as she is brilliant. An additional feature of the show will be a cancer patient who has been cured - a person who suffered from cancer but who is living proof of the fact that cancer can be cured by scientific treatment...[184]

Toward the end of 1951, Anita and Bill and a dentist friend[185] bought and remodeled a former restaurant in La Jolla wrapped around the corner of Girard Avenue and Torrey Pines Road, and turned it into a medical-dental building complete with laboratory, operating room and two recovery rooms. And just about the time Bill hung her diplomas in her new office, Anita gave birth in October 1951 to their sixth child, Anita Maria.

She had not told her mother she was pregnant. The last two times she divulged this news, Lita's response was, *"Mi hija, ¿estás loca?"* ("Daughter, are you crazy?") But as the actual arrival of the new babies always mollified her, Anita thought it best this time to just skip to the event itself. Now she telephoned Lita with the news of the baby's birth, interrupting a card game and taking her completely by surprise. Anita was gratified to hear the amazed pride on the other end of the line as word of her latest accomplishment -- "A girl!" -- spread around the poker table.

Then, the day after giving birth, Anita drove away with Bill and the Stirnkorbs for a week's rest at a homely place called Warner Hot Springs Resort, leaving their little daughter behind in the hospital nursery. There was not, forty years ago, quite the emphasis on mother-infant bonding that exists today, but this was still an unorthodox move. As much as Anita loved her children, and as willing as she was to have more and more of us, she mostly viewed infancy as a trying stage to be got through until an interesting, talking person emerged, like a butterfly, at the end.

The December 1951 issue of *The Virginia Reel*, the alumnae magazine of Southern Seminary, lists her achievements this way:

> Anita Villegas Figueredo is a physician specializing in oncology. She is the first and only woman in San Diego County doing major surgery. She and her husband, who is a pediatrician, have built modern offices which they share. Both are active in Church and Civic affairs. **Among other things**, Anita has found time to have six children, four boys and two girls.

And this is no doubt an accurate reflection of the way Anita managed her life. The having of babies was not her primary business; she was good at it, as she was at most things. She had babies very gracefully, with little bother to herself and none to anyone else. She just carried on, pregnant or no, and other people considered this quite marvelous. In the fall of 1952, when she was eight months pregnant yet again, she was the keynote speaker for a huge conference of Business and Professional Women[186]; the title of her talk was "The Complete Woman in Modern Society." "It's time women stopped trying to be men," she declared.

> There is great need in the world for the talents of women as women. Women, since the beginning, have been a source of love and stability and gentleness... We must again be the peacemakers. We must make our wishes known to the legislators and stick by them. We must use organized clubdom to feed the hungry and succor the displaced. In order to do this, we have a national obligation to be well-informed.
>
> If we start in the home and educate our children for peace, proceed to the community level, and take an active part as citizens in influencing the domestic and foreign policy-making of our government, we can accomplish a great deal.
>
> I don't mean we should restrict ourselves to the so-called womanly pursuits. Medicine has been called a

man's field, but taking care of the sick has always been woman's work.

When the seventh child, Richard Anthony, was born (December 1952), his oldest brother was eight-and-a-half. Anita was pregnant nearly continuously for most of the first five years she lived in La Jolla, and had infants and pre-schoolers always. Just now there were five at home all day. Anita was absolutely accepting of this state of affairs. She had seven thoroughly healthy babies, carried and delivered without injury to herself or them. This is statistically something of a miracle - which is the way Anita viewed it, and our father cherished her for that. She was always calm and happy when she told him she was pregnant.

Not long after Ricky's birth, a journalist named Alice Dutton wrote a long story about Dr. Anita Villegas Figueredo, saying

> Few would guess the work of the dainty, petite, twinkling-eyed young woman seen daily, driving her green station wagon to and from crowded schedules as a cancer specialist at famous Scripps Hospital, her private practice in La Jolla, and her work at Mercy, Quintard and County Hospitals in San Diego, as well as donating much of her time as cancer consultant at Guadalupe's medical center in National City. Yes, it is the same woman featured in *Look* magazine ten years ago as a rising cancer specialist working for $15 a month at Memorial Hospital in New York. Only now seven children have been added...

The "green station wagon" was a 1952 woody, a classical surf wagon which was a fixture around La Jolla for the decade or so that Anita drove it, and a collector's item forever afterwards. It was just large enough for a family of nine without seat belts, and was frequently parked full of children in the Scripps Hospital parking lot while their mother ran in "for a minute to see one patient." (To this day I am alarmed at the thought of sitting in a hospital parking lot.)

Once an organization saw what Anita could do, there was no end to the jobs she was offered. It was as much her style as her ability; she was fun to be around, and she motivated people by her own effervescence. And, of course, if Anita Figueredo "had the time," it was hard for anyone else to refuse to pitch in.

The way she chose and mastered her outside commitments was a study in time management. The children had bedtimes so fixed that nothing short of fire or an act of God could change them: the youngest two went down at 7:00 P.M. and the oldest at 8:30, with the four in the middle retiring on the half-hours in between. Our father might be out making house calls into the night, injecting adrenaline or phenobarbital into wheezing or convulsing children, but cancer is rarely an emergency, and the next three hours were Anita's own. She did not settle into a book or a hot bath nor crawl between her own white sheets. She was not even sleepy, which is perhaps more remarkable than anything else. She just sat at the refectory table in the dining room with telephone at hand and did community projects, usually two at a time and, when one was finished, she took on another. It did not really matter much what the job was, because Anita was vastly curious and generous; and she assumed, like any good executive, that she could learn what she needed to know (which is how she came to found, later on, an orchestra chorus and a bank).

Further notes on getting things done: Anita had no "leisure activities," no bridge, tennis or golf. She and Bill did no entertaining and almost no socializing except as associated with charity, Church and professional obligations (leading one frustrated friend to make the famous comment, "The trouble with you, Anita, is you're only a friend in need.") When they did have occasional gatherings in their home, Bible Study, work groups for the Charity Ball, and so on - no matter what it was, Anita served the same refreshment: instant coffee, and pound cake from Safeway under vanilla ice cream with frozen strawberries drizzled over the top. Her friends remembered it all their lives.

Anita was self-employed and arranged for herself a dependable, flexible schedule; in total control of her practice hours, she did not have to consider the wishes of a partner, and simply scheduled in her committee meetings, family activities, speaking engagements and so on. She always attended the children's special things, the piano recitals and nursery school plays, and was more than once the only mother there. (Wondering about this early on, she came to the conclusion that the housebound mothers probably didn't have babysitters, and the working mothers couldn't leave their jobs.) And then there were two nearly absolute rules: she and Bill were home for dinner with all the children at exactly 6:00 P.M.; and lunch was a daily restaurant tryst for the two of them alone.

CHAPTER 21

The Second Coming

By now, Sarita Villegas had lived for six years in her own house in Flushing, taking in a series of genteel Latin women as roomers. She was, however, no longer running a boarding house; her paying guests were on their own in terms of meals and housekeeping, and only shared the rent and a little company. Lita herself was at the height of her career in the export trade, arranging for the transfer of all kinds of American goods -- stoves and refrigerators as well as dresses and shoes -- to Costa Rica, the Dominican Republic and Argentina. People sent her their wish lists, and she spent the day in Manhattan visiting her suppliers and arranging deals. The furniture and appliances were sent off directly from the warehouses; but the smaller goods Lita wrapped and mailed herself, and the dining room of her house was usually covered with cardboard boxes sealed with twine in her intricate knots.

She had money, and in the evenings she dressed up for dinners and parties at the homes of friends or at the Casa de Costa Rica, a club for "friends of that republic" which sponsored supper dances at places like the Hotel Pierre. Lita was an officer of the Casa de Costa Rica for a time, and was always available, as she had been for thirty years, to anyone from "home" who needed a friend in New York City.

Adventure still beckoned, and she learned to drive a car when she was fifty years old. An automobile on Manhattan Island is the worst sort of liability; but out in the suburbs one can actually park and drive without much threat to life. It is an exaggeration to say that Lita ever learned to drive well. She was taught by Johnny Martinez, the friend from Costa Rica[187] who sold Lita and Anita and Bill on the suburbs in the first place, and he was a man of some courage. The principal misunderstanding was the meaning of the dotted line down the middle of the road; Lita seemed to use it to center herself in traffic, so as not to get too close to the shoulder on either side.

She was more comfortable, in an economic sense, than she had ever been in her life. She had good health, good looks and good clothes. She was still admired by men, as well as by women friends of several decades. But she was distracted by the thought of Anita in California, with all those children.

It is not, really, that Lita was lonely without us. After all, she and our mother had shared the same house very little in twenty-five years. Through nearly all of grade school and high school they lived apart, and even during the holidays Anita mostly looked after herself while her mother worked. During college and the first half of medical school, when the two did live together, they were both so busy that they rarely shared more than a few affectionate words at a hurried meal. And as soon as Anita's clinical work began, the hospital claimed her nights.

Nor was it circumstance alone that kept them apart. They were not very much alike. Lita was a cynic sometimes, with a shameless way of rolling her eyes and pursing her lips to one side. She was a clever woman, but never an intellectual, and she had strong opinions about God, marriage and our father which were hard for Anita to take. What held our mother and grandmother together spiritually, besides love, was Anita's quest to be a doctor. And when that was accomplished, there was not much else to talk about when they found themselves alone.

Except the children. We were simultaneously the best and the most distressing children alive. When Lita came to visit, we shied out of her clutches as she swooped down upon us like a Spanish-speaking eagle on a pack of startled mice; but then our mother urged us soothingly forward, and we nervously endured the hugs to the smoky breast. (Our soft-spoken Doyle grandmother visited us once or twice, smelling of violets and patting us gently on the hands. It was hard to imagine that this daunting figure was the same sort of relation as Nana Doyle.)

Lita told us she was ninety-three and had come to eat us up beginning with our *fondos*, our little bottoms. We shrieked with horror and delight, and a day or two into every visit it seemed to us that our mother's mother had always been a part of our household. She sat on the patio, smoking and watching us play, the horde of us swinging nearly upside down on the gym set and piling into our Red Rocker; and we complained less about each other when she was in charge because it took so much effort to explain the issues.

No doubt she thought, sitting there on the patio, about moving out west for good, and I imagine her emotions swung with our own. When we were tolerably well-behaved, she probably mused it would be nice to stay forever; and when we were pummeling each other's heads, she likely had second thoughts. She called us *un dolor de la nuca* (a pain in the neck) although she seemed to be only half-serious, most of the time.

Not that she ever considered actually living among us. But Mrs. Miller's house was a haven of peace to which she could retreat at any time, far enough away that her progeny came by ones and twos and invitation only up the winding brick walk to her door.

Anita always assumed that her mother must eventually come to stay, and the birth of her seventh grandchild seemed to snap her last thread of resistance. No doubt she thought that as soon as her back was turned there would be another child on the way; and the fact is that every time she escaped back to New York to her "real" life, she was less and less able to put the distracting, demanding creatures out of her mind.

Back in New York, Lita talked it over with Amalia Bacardí and the others as they sat in Amalia's penthouse drinking her family rum and playing cards. Sometimes they played straight poker for serious money, blowing smoke rings in the air and calling each other's bluff. Other times, for a little diversion, they played *basura* (trash) like "*Alacrán*," where the cards were laid out in the shape of a scorpion and the wildcards kept changing as the tail curled around. "You know," Lita said, "Anita's going to kill herself trying to do everything. *Necia* (foolish), with all those children." "Sarita," Amalia said without taking her eyes off the cards, "she needs you like never before. *Vete a acompañarla.* Go be with her."

And so Lita sold the house in Flushing and moved in with Florence Miller. Her ordinary routine, once she settled in, was to breakfast in peace and then appear at our door in time to chauffeur us along the center of La Jolla Boulevard to school. Returning home, she supervised the housekeeper and the play and feeding of the babies, and made school lunches (peanut butter and grape jelly sandwiches on Wonder Bread, Fritos and Hostess cupcakes) and then crept around Stella Maris Academy, delivering each brown bag to our classroom doors. Before she came back for us at 3:00, she had generally been to the market, and when we climbed in the Chevrolet, we got to count the "green stamps" she collected along with the groceries. One or more of the babies was usually in the back seat happily sharing the smoke from her Lucky Strike. From school we were deposited at Brownies and ballet, Cub Scouts and Little League, and then Lita went home again to watch "Queen for a Day" on our black and white TV before retrieving us. If we didn't happen to have anything to do after school, we sat and watched with her. The gist of the show was that three or four unfortunate women with appalling life stories got up and recounted the details, and we applauded along with the TV audience for the one whose tale was absolutely the most awful. The winner got a washing machine or whatever she needed to make her life bearable. Lita suggested we send her name in as a contestant, but we never did. During the commercials Lita started dinner, rice and *picadillo* (a hash of minced beef and green beans), or tender thin steaks she bought across the Mexican border in Tijuana. When our parents walked in, we ate. The moment dinner was cleared by the maid, Lita left. Her no-nonsense departures might startle a visitor, but they suited everyone else. In these years our grandmother still maintained a certain courtesy with her son-in-law, but the dealings between them were strained at best. It was a relief to our father to see

Lita to her car, and then to immerse himself in the baths and bedtime routines of properly appreciative people.

Except for television, which she came to adore, Lita was rarely idle. And even when she watched TV she usually did something else simultaneously, like darning our torn-up socks on big wooden eggs, or sponging and pasting the gummy sheets of "green stamps" from the grocery into fat little books, and then thumbing through catalog pages of water-resistant watches and unbreakable thermoses for the most desirable prize. Lita was no more able than our mother to read for pleasure and relaxation, although they shared an addiction to "The Reader's Digest" - in Lita's case, the Spanish edition, and in Anita's the condensed books - as a way of getting the most information in the fewest words. My mother, to her great surprise, raised a number of literary children, and was always perplexed that she couldn't convince us to read the abbreviated version of a great novel when the plot was all there in the author's own words and they only cut out the extras.

Lita's export business was transplanted for a time to the west coast, although she had to travel to the wholesale market in Los Angeles, which was two hours north by train. Casting around for a more local enterprise, she looked at real estate and invested the profits from the sale of her Flushing house in a pre-war La Jolla cottage. This she remodeled a bit and resold, and then bought another house, and so on - half-a-dozen transactions in all, including the purchase of a tiny house she called the *gallinero* (chicken coop) which she moved to a better lot and sold for what she thought was a handsome profit. All this buying and selling and interval renting-out gave her a modest but adequate income for many years and, more than that, the pleasure of the game. Rents were low, and once she collected only a blue Wedgwood pot left behind when a tenant fled in the night. But she had almost no expenses except her own tiny rent at Mrs. Miller's; our parents provided everything else, including her car, and so she had the pin money she needed to have some fun.

Lita had sojourned at Mrs. Miller's half a dozen times by 1953, and she already had good friends, Costa Rican emigrés who played cards nearly as well as her New York regulars, schoolteachers and nurses she met at bingo games in parish halls and later on the bus to Las Vegas.

Domestically she found another friendly circle, the other mothers at the country club pool where we children spent the better part of every summer day and most weekends in the spring and fall. There Lita was, enthroned on her deck chair, supervising swimming, toweling heads, yelling at us in Spanish to quit running and yelling, and "signing" for all the deliciously greasy burgers and chocolate malts. She was pretty and lively, and certainly different from anybody else's grandmother.

CHAPTER 22

For the Church and the Pontiff

On the afternoon of her twelfth wedding anniversary, August 8, 1954, Anita stood with Bill before 800 onlookers in Founder's Chapel of the San Diego College for Women and listened to the men's choir of Mary, Star of the Sea Catholic Church sing the ravishing strains of the prayer to the Holy Spirit:

> Come Holy Ghost, Creator blest,
> And in our hearts take up Thy rest.
> Come with Thy grace and heavenly aid
> To fill the hearts which Thou hast made.

Billy and Johnny and I, carrying papal documents and holy water, preceded our parents down the aisle, my brothers in the red and white ankle-length robes of altar boys, and I in a white lace dress with a wreath of roses in my hair. Our two-year-old sister Anita was dressed as I was (which pleased me greatly, as I was passionately in love with her at the time) and the three youngest boys, Tommy, Charlie and Ricky, wore miniature sport coats and slicked-back hair. The seven of us paraded solemnly down behind a mighty procession: Knights of Columbus in full uniform, shouldering the flags of church and state, the bearers of incense and the high gold cross, a flock of larger acolytes, and a crowd of clergy and monsignori in purple-trimmed birettas. Behind us came the deacons of honor. Then our father and, on his arm, our grandmother. And then we children turned to see our mother walking all alone, in a champagne-colored dress with long white gloves, and a white lace mantilla held to the waves of her hair with Spanish combs. Behind her, at the end of the line, was the Bishop of San Diego in his amethyst robes and his miter, blessing his flock with the gleaming crook of the shepherd, and flanked by his Knights of St. Gregory.

The Bishop smiled at us while the music died away, and the congregation listened to the reading of the papal document taken from the cradle of my arms:

> Pope Pius XII deigns to bestow upon Dr. Anita Figueredo Doyle the decoration of the holy cross "Pro Ecclesiae et Pontifice." The Supreme Pontiff considers her most worthy of being so honored with such distinction in recognition of her example, work and life as an outstanding Catholic laywoman.

The Bishop took the golden cross with its fleurs-de-lis, the engraved date 1888 and the face of Pope Leo XIII, and handed it to my father, who pinned it by its yellow and white striped ribbon to my mother's dress. His Excellency turned to our grandmother and offered her his congratulations in Spanish with impressive graciousness:

> O, what an anchor and what a haven, this good mother, who insisted through times of trials and difficulties that her daughter must have the best in education. The mother longed for the day when the daughter would take her place in the medical profession. She saw that day as she sees this, and with us she thanks God for it.

He turned to us, and spoke of the day when the seven "immortal monuments" Dr. and Mrs. Doyle had reared around them "would come from afar, rise up, and call their parents blessed. Our mother, whom the Bishop called a "noble-minded woman and a talented scientist" was not yet thirty-eight years old, but she - and my father with her - had packed what to many seemed a lifetime of Christian service into the seven years they had lived in San Diego.

Tommy was the first Doyle baby baptized at Mary, Star of the Sea, an "architectural gem" of a church erected in 1937 in a perfection of Mission Revival style, with an extraordinary fresco of the Virgin over the front door by the great Mexican muralist, Alfredo Ramos Martinez. The parish church which Anita and Bill joined on their arrival stands near the exact geographical center of La Jolla, and it became in many respects the center of their lives. Bill Doyle had grown up a full participant in regular parish life, but Anita had not; now she embraced the role of Catholic parishioner with her whole heart. Over the years she would fill every lay position in the American Church, with the admiration and blessing of the whole hierarchy of clergy.

It is ironical but true that San Diego, California was in the 1940s a "mission land" of the Catholic Church, an area too primitive religiously to supply its own priests and dependent on such over-endowed states as Ireland. The parish at La Jolla was actually on a rotation for new curates with other such missions as the African bush. The pastor himself, Father Joseph Clarkin, was a large-jowled, humorless autocrat from the old sod (also an excellent administrator) who often said he had never met a woman like Anita Figueredo. He was accustomed to deference, but Anita smiled and spoke her mind. She was willing to lead almost any effort for the church, but on principle she never asked permission when she figured out a new and better way.

The parochial grade school, Stella Maris Academy, opened its doors the year the Doyles come to town, and as soon as Billy donned his navy blue sweater with the yellow star and entered the regimented first-and-second grade classroom of Sister Mary Ancilla, Anita took over the presidency of the Academy Club PTA (not to mention the role of first-grade room mother).[188] Academy Club meetings were packed during her tenure because she had innovative ideas and wasted no time, and because she was always in the thick of things herself: if anybody was sewing curtains for the new parish hall, she was. Even the Mexican families in the parish, who had no experience with parent-participation, were persuaded by Anita to join in. She cajoled them in Spanish after

Mass until they agreed to come and hear, and a few even stood up and had their say.

The teaching order of nuns at Stella Maris were the Sisters of the Holy Cross who wore white starched and pleated haloes like the rising sun. All of them were Anita's patients sooner or later, and her unique credentials as a Catholic woman physician naturally delivered several other convent populations into her care. The strictly cloistered Carmelites, who ordinarily spoke to the outside world from behind a veiled grille, never breached their gates **except** to go to Dr. Anita's. Priests, too, consulted her about symptoms suggestive of cancer, and, of course, Anita never charged any religious person (not the Protestant ministers, the rabbis who came later, not the leaders of the tiniest splinter sects, nor any of their dependents) for her medical services.

Related to this, from 1950 onward she and Bill donated a regular half-day a week at the Guadalupe Clinic, a free health-facility for the poor in southeast San Diego. This good place was efficiently and kindly staffed by the Victory Knoll Sisters under the supervision of their wispy superior, Sister Aurelia, who was tougher than she looked and kept Guadalupe Clinic alive until it was condemned to make room for a freeway in 1963.

Anita's status as a Catholic woman physician, wife, and mother of many also made her a spectacular role model for girls in the Catholic high schools of the 1950s. Nobody knew anybody else quite like her; she was unconventional but trustworthy, and she was asked to speak to legions of girls at Rosary High and Cathedral High and Our Lady of Peace, where before her time the classes on marriage were generally taught by the nuns and priests. (In my own office decades later, the mother of a patient with an earache told me that after thirty years she still remembered the gynecologic details of the talk Anita gave to her class at Cathedral; she said Dr. Figueredo went a little further than the nuns suspected with the sex education.)

1954 was designated by the Catholic Church the "Marian Year," and the faithful were encouraged to reflect on the life of the Virgin Mary and pay her special tribute. Anita developed a lecture on the mother of Jesus which she added to all her others and which was described in the newspaper as being "widely and favorably received."[189] She wrote and spoke what she acted, that "the concept of service is at the very heart of Christianity" and that "Jesus makes it clear that we will be judged according to our responses to him in his many distressing disguises."

CHAPTER 23

Coast Boulevard

In 1955 Anita suffered a miscarriage nearly six months into her eighth pregnancy, and because of that she bought a new house.

Our father insisted that she take one day off from work "to rest"; and it so happened that Betty Stirnkorb was giving a coffee, which Anita could now attend as she had nothing else to do. There she heard a dentist's wife say that her husband was trying to make a clinic of a beautiful landmark, a Spanish colonial villa on Coast Boulevard at the edge of the ocean, but that the owner, an elderly widow named Mrs. David, was being evasive about the sale. Anita knew instantly that this was "417," the walled house south of the Casa de Mañana which she coveted eight years before; and she soon left the coffee and went to pay a call on Mrs. David.

The house stood on four city lots in the center of an almond-shaped island in the coastal road. In front lay the unobstructed sea, and behind, the back door of Scripps Memorial Hospital. The island, called the Pauline Addition, had been developed in 1923, and the central parcel was acquired soon after by a widow[190] who built on it two odd little structures like Chinese pagodas. Then the lady married an artist named Edward Baxendale, a painter of desert scenes and seascapes which were locally admired. It was evidently Mr. Baxendale, in 1931, who supervised the remodeling of the little pagodas into a Spanish Colonial villa and guesthouse with patio, walled gardens, and a perfect painter's studio above the several garages.

The two-story main house faced the ocean, and was a vision of brilliant white walls and red tile roof, with shutters and gates painted Spanish green. A sinuous curve of white balcony hung like a partially opened fan from the upper story, under a deep overhang of all the reds of handmade tiles. The balcony gave the exterior much of its grace; it had nine vertical columns with capitals like wings, and nine supporting beams in triple tiers like fingers toward the sea. On the south wall rose a chimney with a peaked red cap, and generous windows up and down with a view toward the formal garden. To the far left was the red bricked entry with its solid mahogany door as heavy as a man, and its big brass knocker gone green with salt and time.

Anita now pounded the knocker hard against the door, without response. Then, gingerly, she opened the north gate and walked along a broad expanse of grass, past a patio shut away behind a wall, and then out the small back gate and around the three garages to an exquisite guest house dripping with red bougainvillea. Here Anita knocked again, and through the leaded glass pane watched the cranky progress toward her of an elderly woman with clots and wisps of hair in chaotic curlers.

"Yes?" she said, unhappily.

"Mrs. David," Anita said, "My name is Dr. Anita Figueredo...."

"Dr. Figueredo! I have wanted to meet you for years, ever since you saved the life of my daughter-in-law's father. They have sung your praises forever. Please come in!"

Mrs. David pulled Anita into the cool interior, straight through to the bathroom in the back where she was trying to give herself a permanent wave. Here she gratefully sat down and, while Anita deftly twirled the frazzled hair into regular rubber rows, she learned whose life it was she saved (the man with the primary melanoma in his parotid gland), and also the recent history of the house.

The late Judge Walter David had summered in La Jolla from the Texas bench, and in 1945 bought the Baxendales' wonderful home. It was an odd time in the annals of interior decor when such homes were out of favor, and referred to in the trade as "Spanish clunkers." The Judge adored it, but his wife was less sure; and one day when the Judge was back in Texas for the judicial season, Mrs. David brought in a famous Los Angeles decorator who felt that the "only thing to do" was to paint out the architectural details. All of Edward Baxendale's straight-grain mahogany detailing -- cabinets and ten-inch baseboards, ceiling beams and fireplace mantle -- were painted a light yellowish green. Not only the dark wood needed painting out; the ceiling beams were a particular offense as they were radiant in Spanish polychrome, with yellow, blue, green and gold sparkling in medallion-like crossovers. The Persian rugs were stripped from the floors, and wall-to-wall pea soup carpet laid over the whole expanse of random-width mahogany planks and solid brass pegs.

Mrs. David told Anita good-naturedly that when the Judge returned, he said, "My God, what have you done to my house?" and proceeded to rip out a fortune in carpet and reinstall his Oriental rugs. But he left it at that, and the green paint outlived the Judge, who died in 1949. After his death, his widow let out rooms to help with expenses. She herself moved around the property, sometimes inhabiting the main house, sometimes the guest house and now and then the painting studio. The boarders occupied whatever rooms were left; just now there were two maiden ladies in bedroom suites overlooking the garden and the sea. But the upkeep was too much, as her only son pointed out, and Mrs. David supposed she must sell, but to a family who would live in and love the house, **not** to a dentist for a clinic.

Anita said her family would love the house and asked to see it. Mrs. David, in her curlers and endpapers, led her across the patio into a cool interior of perfectly-proportioned rooms, and an entry hall with a rounded niche of the exact size to accommodate an Italian wood Madonna which the Doyles had just acquired. Inevitably, Anita took this as a sign from God and telephoned Bill to come and see their house. Bill protested that they weren't **looking** for a house, but Anita knew her husband was born to have a home like this. Negotiations floundered for a time on the shoals of Mrs. David's ambivalence. Finally Anita and Bill offered to let her stay on in the guest house as long as she wished, and with this and $90,000 they closed escrow in the spring of 1956, and were handed the original grant deed of 1924, which read: "This property shall not be conveyed, leased, rented to or occupied by any person of Mexican, Japanese, or Chinese extraction, or by any person whatsoever, other than one of the White or Caucasian race." Anita's first two hundred dollars of refurbishing money went to have the appalling clause stricken from the deed.

Anita and Bill believed strongly in the concept of private space for children. Here at "417" they not only created special places for themselves, but also for Lita and for every child. Bill gazed ruefully upon the artist's studio with the perfect north light, but then steeled himself and turned it into a comfortable three-room apartment for his mother-in-law. He painted green tiles with the legend "Casa de Lita" and set them in the wall above the landing on the L-shaped stair. Similarly, he looked hard at the second floor of the main house with its four elegant suites of bedrooms and full-tiled baths, and the added luxury of the long balcony for the ocean-front suites and a sun-porch for those facing west and over the garden. My father, with his artist's eye, realized that he was skirting sacrilege in breaking up these rooms. But he had seven children already (with the prospect of more); and so he closed in the sun-porch and erected dividers, and ended up with seven private or semi-private upstairs rooms.

This done, he turned his full attention to the wonderful rooms downstairs. Included in the sale of the house were Judge David's beloved Oriental rugs, some chairs and beds, a hammered-brass pot, shelves of books on lawyers such as Alexander Hamilton and an occasional tract against marriage with Catholics. Bill and Anita, in their "spare" evening hours, moved these things around, and chipped the green paint out of the arabesques in the fabulous wood. Then Anita turned her attention to other matters, and Bill had the leisurely pleasure of laying in thin gold leaf in the letters *Forte et Fidele* on the fireplace mantle, and of choosing beautiful things to fill their home.

For all the years of our childhood, he haunted antique stores and auctions and galleries, and brought back treasures - fine old portraits in carved gilt frames; gleaming andirons and oaken bellows carved with the fiery profile of Savanarola; bronze and marble statues of Aesculapius and Michelangelo; 19th century volumes in pigskin and calfskin on history, and on the lives of the poets and artists (which he invariably read, though some had pages uncut for a hundred years); drawings by Corregio and Caravaggio; and contemporary paintings and sculptures ranging from the sumptuous nudes of Russell Flint and Francisco Zuñiga, to a set of forty-seven exquisite small bronzes depicting Homer's entire *Odyssey*, which a penniless artist sold in exchange for pediatric care.

And then there was the gift from an elderly heiress with a vanished fortune (who mostly dined in later years with the Doyles): an antique Steinway in a rosewood stain, dated 1879, with a gorgeous rococo exterior only slightly less ravishing than its sound. There was music always, Mozart, Scarlatti and Chopin, sometimes from the piano, otherwise from fine machines, and comfortable sofas and chairs with reading lamps which actually cast good light at the proper angle.

Meanwhile, in 1958, Mrs. David relinquished the guest house to Anita, for her office. It had the same graceful proportions in miniature as the main house. Anita's consultation room was carved from the southwest bedroom, which was full of light and looked out over the roses and the lily pond. Waiting patients filled the cool space of the living room, and everywhere they looked they saw the doctor's children, in photographs, in portraits painted by their father, and in person marching through from the patio for an "important" word with their mother.

CHAPTER 24

Mother Teresa

In the winter of 1958, Anita picked up the February issue of *Jubilee*, the avant-garde Catholic "Magazine of the Church and Her People," and saw on its cover the profile of a nun in a white, blue-bordered sari, smiling down at a child she was holding to her breast. The enormous dark eyes of the child stared out at the viewer to whom he was reaching, or pointing.

Anita had happened upon the first report ever published in the United States about the woman called Mother Teresa of Calcutta, and inside she saw words and pictures that burned her mind:

> Centuries of searing days and dank nights, of running-sore pestilence and burning hunger have spawned the modern city of Calcutta, an area of 4,500,000 people in northeastern India. The city's pungent, jangling, macabre life spews out from Kalighat, its ancient fly-infested quarter. And at Kalighat's core... stands a temple of Kali, the...goddess of destruction of the Hindus. Until ten years ago, Kali's presence and power could be doubted by few Indians whose **27-year life**

expectancy was spent huddled and squatting, under-nourished and resigned in Kalighat's alleys.

But, since 1948, a gray-eyed, Yugoslavian nun named Mother Teresa has operated at the temple gates a revolutionary hospital which mollifies somewhat their despair. *Nirmal Hriday* (Pure Heart) accepts only those "incurables" left in the streets to die by Calcutta's already overburdened hospitals. Although medical treatment is freely given, *Nirmal Hriday's* major goal is simply to help the destitute spend their last days as human beings. The bath, food, clean sheets, clothing and compassion the hospital offers are frequently the first touches of dignity in its patients' lives.[191]

The full face of Mother Teresa, plain-featured and nearly-unlined at 48, looked out sadly and directly at Anita from her open door. But in the dozen photographs which followed she was smiling, at the ancient-looking skeletal adults dying of tuberculosis and malnutrition before their thirtieth birthdays; at the mothers waiting in the courtyard sun for milk; and especially at the children, in their clean flowered and gingham smocks at play in *Shishu Bhavan,* her home for Calcutta's crippled and unwanted young.

It was Anita Figueredo's habit all her life, as soon as she began to earn money of her own, to share it with anyone who asked. She was the opposite of profligate; having been poor as a child, she understood very clearly the value of money and wasted nothing. We children had what we needed but not necessarily what we thought we needed. The fine things which filled our house were chosen with care by our father, who really loved them. Our mother scarcely saw them, early on. She was so unattached to things, and so pragmatic, that she casually gave her wedding gown as a costume for children's plays. The day-to-day running of the household was in her charge, and we were generally fed and clothed from discount stores.

Anita recycled instinctively, like breathing. When Scripps Hospital was remodeled and enlarged in 1950, Anita managed to acquire the dismantled pieces, doors and window frames, hardware and old equipment and had it hauled away to Tijuana, Mexico where an entirely "new" Hospital of the Sacred Heart was erected from the discards. And then forever after at Scripps, a network of sympathetic nurses organized by Anita gathered up disposables, scrub brushes and gloves and suturing silk on crescent-shaped needles, and carloads of barely outdated infant formulas and drugs. Part of the job description of Anita's own office staff was to sort and box these things for the *Casa de los Pobres*, a place in Tijuana where Franciscan nuns fed and nursed the poor of *"cartón-landia"*, a riverbed colony of homeless people in cardboard boxes, who were washed out in flash floods year after year.

At home we re-used bottles and bags and saved the stale ends of bread for ducks, but Anita had two odd rooms for special salvage. One was an old brass and mahogany elevator (non-functional in our time), which was filled from floor to ceiling with "previously-owned" wrapping paper and bows, and dedicated to the considerable art of selecting the right materials for covering a gift, so that the existing creases seemed plausible and the slit edges of tape matched up, and flattened shiny curls were persuaded to spring up one more time. When anyone **opened** a gift, in our house or anywhere else, Anita sat forward on her chair with eyes glinting and without the slightest interest in the contents of the box, and watched for a chance to repossess the wrappings before any further damage was done. Some papers had seen as many Christmases and birthdays as the younger children.

The inevitable corollary was the gift closet. Here in the excellent cabinets of a closet so large it functioned as an extra bedroom were most of the presents Anita received in her lifetime, from children and patients and the clubs at which she spoke, as well as anything given to the children to which they paid insufficient attention. These things were recycled endlessly at Christmas, almost always returning to the closet again after the briefest life outside. But they were also handed on to us, re-wrapped by Anita, as presents for the parties of our friends; and my own character was strengthened by watching one girl open stationery imprinted with a shepherdess whose skirt folds spelled

"Sarita," and another unwrap cologne and read aloud from the card, "To Mom with love on Valentine's Day."

Our parents together earned enough to be considered well-to-do, but it goes without saying that the wishes and real needs of a family our size were endless. Yet Anita kept before her the image of another world, with more need. She kept all of the begging letters that, indiscriminately at first and then later very discriminately, found their way to our postman's bag, and which he unloaded around noon each day on our back-door table in teetering piles. I read them with fascination from time to time, heart-rending pleas from dirt-poor parishes on Indian reservations, from boys' towns, schools for the crippled, deaf and blind, soup kitchens, homes for the mentally retarded, quadriplegic artists who painted with brushes clamped between their teeth; and then the picture-stories from abroad of dirty children with bloated bellies, and mothers stretching out their stick-like arms. Anita dealt with these letters as seriously as with all her other bills. First she tore off the stamps, trimmed the ripped edges to ¼" square, and lay them in a shoebox, for later sorting and mailing to the Philatelic Exchange in Spain; the stamps went to collectors, and the money to the poor. Then she began again at the top of the tattered stack, and put checks in each return envelope until they were all gone; and she was not impressed when I noticed repeaters and duplicates, any more than she worried about the possibility of fraud. Her own blessings and comforts seemed so huge to her that she must deal out shares of it all around, even to the occasional thief. On the other hand she went to legendary lengths to make the charities more efficient; she could not bear the waste involved when the same mail brought identical appeals addressed to Anita Figueredo and A.F. Doyle and all the other permutations of her name, and she sent back careful letters with all the mailing labels attached, begging them to purge their lists. And, of course, she actually used the awful greeting cards and the calendars with the name of the mission stamped on top. (She also filled out all the lottery tickets, and once actually won $150; but as the prize was sent along with another begging letter, she sighed, and endorsed the check and sent it back.)

Now Anita sat absorbing the impact of Mother Teresa's story, and considered the fact that although each of them was devoted to healing the sick, she herself lived in great comfort, while this woman with the unforgettable face spent her days in poverty, whether the bare austerity within her convent, or the unspeakable squalor without. Anita closed the magazine, placing it on top of the most stable pile of papers on her desk, and wrote Mother Teresa a check; but she also wrote her a letter about herself. This was unprecedented for Anita. She described her work and her family, and then said that she had always felt drawn to do the type of work Mother Teresa is doing, but instead found herself healing the sick while living herself in luxury. She thanked Mother Teresa for living among the poor and serving them.

Anita was astonished to receive, after many weeks, a thin blue aerogramme from Calcutta addressed to "Mrs. Anita Figueredo, M.D.," and to find that it was a letter from Mother Teresa herself. She wrote, in round British-looking script, that she read Anita's letter to her assembled sisters; that she wished to continue their correspondence; and that she was certain they were destined to meet one day soon. There followed then a slow exchange of letters, by barge evidently from India; and in September of 1960, Mother Teresa sent a note which read (practically in its entirety): "You will be glad to hear I am coming to the States for the Convention to be held at Las Vages [sic]. It is my first time traveling so far after 32 years in India. So say a little prayer for me." That was all. She did not say which Convention, and she did not say when.

On the 27th of October 1960, Anita came home at the end of the day and opened the morning paper. She almost never read the paper. But that late afternoon she picked it up and saw it fall open to the Religion page and a small picture of Mother Teresa (who was still an obscure figure at that time), with a notice that she was stopping over for a single night in San Diego, on her way to a National Convention of Catholic Women in Las Vegas. She would be speaking in a downtown hall in half an hour. Anita picked up her coat and the accommodating Betty Stirnkorb and arrived at Rosary High School to find the auditorium filled with 250 people straining to hear the words of a nervous tiny nun in a sari which was as wrinkled as if she had slept in it, as indeed she had.

Her remarks, in her soft, Indo-European English, were very moving. It has been said of Mother Teresa in recent years that her eloquence is in her work, not in her words. But the tape still exists of her speech on this particular evening, and she was eloquent. She painted a picture for her audience of ninety-four joyful nuns, running everywhere about the city of Calcutta, teaching the children of the slums to read and write and sing, (especially to sing); tenderly nursing the destitute dying, including a man so apparently dead that he is on his way to the burning ghat when he rises up and asks for water; healing the absolute untouchables, the lepers, with medicines and bandages from empty match boxes filled by "society ladies" once a week; feeding and caressing back to health the brutalized children of Shishu Bhavan. When Mother Teresa finished speaking and the clamorous applause died down, the audience was invited to form a line to greet her in person. She had shaken some two hundred hands before Anita, struggling up from the back of the crowded hall, stood before her and said, "Mother Teresa, I am Dr. Figueredo, and this is...."

Whereupon the nun smiled happily and said, "<u>Anita</u>. I knew that we would meet," and embraced her and walked away with her to a corner of the room, leaving the remnants of the receiving line behind. They laughed to find that they were exactly the same size, and they talked for a long time about "everything," their work, Anita's family, and their dreams, cementing a loving friendship that would be refreshed by rendezvous in cities all over the world, Calcutta, Bangalore, Beirut, Amman, Minneapolis, San Francisco, Los Angeles, New York, and would last for more than thirty years. Shortly after the New Year, 1961, Anita received this letter:

> My dear Anita,
>
> I can't tell you how happy your beautiful and loving family photograph has made me. You are just exactly what you have remained in my mind since I saw you in San Diego - "The Smiling Apostle of Charity." What gifts God has given you - your husband - the chosen

one, just made for you... Daily you and your loved ones are in my prayers. From the first time you wrote it has been so. You too must keep on praying for me...

God bless you all

M. Teresa MC

CHAPTER 25

Woman of the Year

"My mother is the best excuse for a human being I have ever known," John Doyle told a newspaper reporter at the turn of the new year 1959. He was commenting on our mother's selection as San Diego's Woman of the Year for 1958. This was an award for the woman whose achievements in her own field exemplify:

> Diligence, high intelligence and rare talent,
> Love for her fellow man,
> Service to her community.

My two oldest brothers and I, all dressed to the nines, sat with our father and Lita at our own round table in the El Cortez Hotel, and applauded for our mother when she rose to accept her silver tray. Now at forty-two, her hair was quite gray, and she was unmistakably mature but still beautiful. It was not apparent to anyone in the overflowing room that Anita, in her fitted strapless black and silver gown, was three months pregnant with her eighth child.

John was eleven at this time, and the rest of his interview (which was published in the *La Jolla Light*[192]) read:

> I think my mother deserves the title "Woman of the Year" because she is the kind of considerate, soft-hearted person any and everyone likes to know. Mommy was taking care of people before I was ever born. Mom is never thinking of herself, but instead she is off to some dark corner scheming a way to help some one less fortunate than she.

And Charlie, who was nine, had this to say:

> I think I know why she deserves the award. Because she never thinks of herself, only the sick and the poor and she shares with most everybody she can. If it hadn't been for my grandmother, though, she wouldn't have it because she helps take care of us when Mother isn't home. Mother loves the whole family and more. She likes everybody in La Jolla that she knows and even in Antarctica and around the world. If you could see her in a picture taken when she was young you might think she was a movie star.

In fact, 1958 was a year of rising at banquets and accepting awards for Anita Figueredo. The Native Daughters of the Golden West inscribed her name in their Roll of Honor.[193] During "National Business Woman's Week", San Diego paid tribute to distinguished women scientists, and Anita was recognized as a physician and surgeon with outstanding contributions in the field of cancer.[194] And the Lion's Club seemed to invent a prize specifically for her: she was the first recipient of the Foreign-Born Citizenship Award, intended to go annually to "a naturalized citizen from a Latin American republic who is considered outstanding as a citizen of the United States."

Anita was still doing all the things for which she had received the "Pro Ecclesiae et Pontifice," and she was also exploring new horizons. In the intervening years, she entered local politics by accepting an appointment as trustee of the La Jolla Town Council. (Anita drew the line at campaigning for political office; but the trustees were, at that time, nominated by committee and voted-in by newspaper ballot.) She was drafted, and agreed to serve for what turned out to be a dozen years of three or more meetings a month, beginning in the summer of 1956. As head of the Youth and Recreation Committee, she directed such things as the Annual La Jolla Tennis Tournament, and the enormous Halloween bonfire which still burns in the memory of all the village children who paraded around it with dazzled eyes.

Anita once said of herself, thoughtfully, that she was a person who never substituted a new loyalty for an old. Her old loves and commitments remained always fresh to her and retained a priority on her time and energy. In this spirit, she became much involved with the Associated Alumnae of the Sacred Heart (AASH) and the board of the San Diego College for Women (SDCW) which opened its doors in 1952.

Not long after her arrival in San Diego, Anita looked up the Religious of the Sacred Heart. The "RSCJs," as they are called (for *Religieux de Sacre Coeur de Jesus*), were Anita's professors at Manhattanville, and she felt that she owed them the fundamental center of her life. She explained later on:

> After four years at Manhattanville College arguing and probing my way through every class in Philosophy and Theology, I had experienced an intellectual conversion which was the first step in a marvelous growth process. Eighteen years after graduation I was invited to return for a panel addressing "What My Manhattanville Education Has Meant to Me." By that time I was a physician and surgeon, living in California with a very busy practice. All this had been made possible by my very fine pre-medical education. It was obvious what I should say and I was prepared to say it. However, I was last on the program, and the other two panelists were a judge and an associate editor of a national magazine. As I sat and listened to the marvels of the pre-law program, and then to the fine courses in English and Journalism, I realized that, in my case at least, pre-med was not the most important thing I learned at Manhattanville.
>
> I set my prepared speech aside and surprised everyone by telling them that the most important thing my

college provided me was the basis for a faith which
has given stability and serenity to my life, which has
ennobled my care of the sick, my practice of medicine
and everything else as well.

The RSCJs had excellent schools all over the United States, and had
just opened their newest college in San Diego. At the helm was the
extraordinary Reverend Mother Rosalie Hill. Rosalie Hill was a
Jeffersonian small dynamo, descended from famous colonial pioneering
stock. On a barren mesa overlooking Mission Valley, she built a
cluster of Spanish Renaissance halls, filled them with the tapestries
and gilt chairs and chandeliers of old San Francisco estates and, more
importantly, with good professors.[195] She also enlisted Anita Figueredo
to help spread the word near and far.

 About this time, requests for speaking engagements began to fill so
much of Anita's calendar that she established a scholarship fund for the
San Diego College for Women and began to ask for a set contribution
wherever she lectured. Then in 1957, Reverend Mother Hill asked
Anita to "go to St. Louis and accept the nomination as President of
AASH." This would inevitably lead to a national alumnae conference
in San Diego; the idea was to publicize the existence of the fledgling
SDCW to the mothers of the country most likely to send their college-
age daughters. Anita, who never said "no" to the Religious of the Sacred
Heart, did go to St. Louis and accept the office (although to me, her
twelve-year-old daughter, the most impressive aspect of this trip was
the fact that, on the return, she ran across the tarmac between planes
to get to my piano recital on time.)

Then, too, Anita took in extra children. Over the course of fifteen years,
from 1957-72, our parents and Lita not only managed their own flock,
but also assumed the care of four teenage Costa Rican cousins, one at a
time, for an average of two years each; and in addition there were a fifth
and sixth in boarding school in Los Angeles who came down to our
house for vacations and long weekends. Usually these young cousins
were just there to learn English and acquire some specialized training
unavailable at home. But, at least once, Tia Sarita and Tia Anita and
Tio Bill were performing a sort of rescue operation, providing a haven

where a youngster from a small and very intimate society could work out his fate in some privacy.

Just before Anita received her tribute as Woman of the Year, she was visited in La Jolla by her cousin, the remarkable Angela Acuña who accompanied five-year-old Anita and her mother on their first journey to the United States. For several decades Anita Figueredo Doyle and Angela Acuña de Chacón were the two best-known Costa Rican women at home and abroad. And in 1958 Angela Acuña was sent to Washington as the first woman ambassador from any country to the Organization of American States. She met her cousins in La Jolla, after a trip to El Paso to receive the title "Woman of the Americas" from the Alliance of Pan American Round Tables (an honor previously bestowed on Eleanor Roosevelt.)[196]

At the time of her appointment as first ambassadress to the O.A.S., Angela Acuña was "just putting the last touches" on a book called *Costa Rican Women through Four Centuries.* This massive work in two volumes documents virtually every aspect of the history of that country's women; and in the chapter called "Costa Ricans Abroad" are two thousand floridly rhapsodic words on Anita Figueredo Villegas and Sarita Villegas Braun, all of it in basic agreement with the matter-of-fact assessments of Johnny and Charlie Doyle.

CHAPTER 26

Angels

On the 24th of July, 1959, Anita sat in the operating room at Scripps Hospital, inserting a radium implant in a patient with cancer of the uterine cervix, when she felt some familiar uterine contractions of her own. By this time, nothing about her labor could surprise her, and so she worked steadily on. The radium was stored in a long metal container full of sterilizing fluid, and when some of this fluid sloshed out on the floor by Anita's stool there was a flurry of anxiety among the nurses who thought she had ruptured her membranes. But, in due course, she finished the procedure and then trundled around the corner to the delivery room and gave birth to her third daughter, Teresa. (Mother Teresa ever after referred to the child as her namesake, and frequently hinted in her letters that God may have sent her a future Missionary of Charity.) Exactly thirty hours after her baby's birth, Anita reappeared in her bathrobe in her patient's room to remove the radium implant as required.

Now this was actually starting over, baby-wise. Ricky, the next oldest child, was six-and-a-half and already at Stella Maris. The year before this pregnancy, Anita and Bill actually almost had their first real vacation together alone since coming to La Jolla. Bill was a serious amateur sailor, and in July of 1957 took part in his second Trans-Pacific yacht race from San Pedro, California to Honolulu. (The first time he did this in 1953, his boat was lost at sea. An old clipping read:

COAST GUARD SEARCHES FOR LA JOLLA YACHT

Bulletin

Honolulu, July 20 - The Coast Guard continued to search today for the 40-foot ketch Marmaduke of La Jolla, Calif., unreported for more than ten days in the 1953 Transpacific Yacht Race.

Anita, waiting at home, was so obviously unworried that Lita was indignant - she thought that a possible widow with her seven little orphans should feign distress, at least. But Bill had explained to Anita that sailboats were hard to sink, and that the *Marmaduke* particularly was a solid little ketch with a wooden hull, not one of these flimsy plastic racers, so that only a really bad storm could turn her over - and there hadn't been a storm. As it turned out, the *Marmaduke* had not lost its men or its way, but only its radio, and sailed across the finish line off Diamond Head after fourteen silent days.)

This time, four years later, Bill wanted Anita to fly out to join him for an adults-only week in Hawaii, and she agreed...although the logistics of placing seven fractious children during summer vacation were daunting, even for Anita. Lita was away in Costa Rica. There was the Mexican housekeeper, but no obvious person to serve as entertainer and referee.

The final plan was that four-year-old Ricky would go with family friends; and that I, who was twelve, would take Charlie and Anita Maria to day-camp every day, and return with them at night. Meanwhile the three oldest boys, Billy, John and Tommy, who were thirteen, ten, and nine, would be sent (much against their natural inclination) by bus to "real" camp in the mountains. Anita stayed to see us all off, cheerfully ignoring signs of mutinous unrest. She and Bill had been nestled in to the Halekulani Hotel in Honolulu exactly two days when the following letter, in laborious pencil on carefully drawn lines, arrived from Camp Marston:

> Dear Mom,
>
> Billy and I are still here but we are not having much fun.
>
> As a matter of fact, none at all.
>
> Tommy left yesterday.
>
> Love, John

It took Anita an anxious few hours by crackling trans-Pacific phone to locate Tommy, who had taken matters into his own hands and left on the first bus out of camp. He ended up sitting on his suitcase in the empty San Diego parking lot for an hour - making sure that the return bus was irrevocably gone - before he confessed to the counsellor; and the counsellor then found Betty Stirnkorb's name listed on Tommy's card "in case of emergency" and called her to come and get him. There he was at Betty's, safe but disconsolate; and Anita and Bill gave up, and flew home from Hawaii.

Nevertheless, our parents seemed as calm and pleased as ever about Teresa, perhaps more so this time as they could focus their attention on just this one infant. She was carried along with them to lunch at their favorite restaurants. Mother's office was now across the patio instead of across town, and our father set up a crib in her consultation room. There Teresa spent her days, adding the sweetness of her laugh to the healing effects of the atmosphere. It so happened that the faithful Betty Stirnkorb was Anita's receptionist that year; and our household help was a mother-daughter pair, so that if Anita was due in surgery or otherwise called away, Betty sat Teresa on her lap as she answered the phone, or the young maid, Alicia, appeared on summons and whisked the baby home.

Anita really savored this baby's infancy, in a way she had not previously done. The only other baby she had by himself was Billy, and the frustrations of that first year out of work had seriously undermined her pleasure at that time. Now she could enjoy this baby without forgoing anything else.

These days Anita woke early in the queen-size bed she shared with Bill, under a glass wall of ocean for their headboard. She slept very lightly, disturbed by tiny corrugations in the sheets or by the press of her own thoughts, and she solved prodigious problems while lying quietly in the dark. The original builders made this room so well that a child with her ear to the door could hear nothing at all; and here Anita and Bill actually had some privacy between the jangling intrusions of the telephone.

Shortly after breakfast, Anita appeared at the hospital behind her house for morning rounds. There she examined her pre- or post-operative patients, and then four days a week returned to her guest-house office where she saw some twenty patients a day. At the hospital she performed an average of twelve to fifteen major operations a month, clustered when possible on Fridays, and in her office four times that number of minor surgical procedures. An aggressive student of her own professional field, she read stacks of medical bulletins and journals, and occasionally wrote for them. A few weeks before Teresa's birth she was the guest editor of the *Journal of the American Medical Women's Association* (June 1959). Her lead article, "Is Melanoma Curable?", recounts long-term survival in consecutive cases of melanoma, a tumor surrounded with an "aura of inevitable doom". Anita wrote, she said, to encourage a more optimistic attitude and "quicker, more 'curative' action on the part of the private practitioner, since a certain paralysis seems to accompany a feeling of inevitable failure." The page-long biography which accompanies this article says, in part:

> Dr. Figueredo is a fine surgeon, equipped with good training, sound knowledge, and devotion to her patients. She finds time to study and keeps abreast of any progress in her field....Although small and feminine, she is a paragon of strength in her determination to succeed in the work she loves, regardless of the obstacles in combining a career with homemaking. She does big things as if they are little and manages all with good workmanship.[197]

Her principal "big" commitment now was the Alumnae of the Sacred Heart (AASH). She assumed the national presidency at the 1959 convention at Manhattanville, two months before Teresa's birth. She had a high school-age daughter (me) at the newest Convent of the Sacred Heart in east San Diego, at El Cajon. And she was swimming along, immersed in French -- still the common language of *Sacre Coeur* -- at Berlitz, in order to represent the 11,000 alumnae of North America at the world conference in Rome, in May of 1960. Our father and Billy and I went along with her to Rome, and from there through Northern Italy and Switzerland to the Loire Valley of France, and Paris. It was the first time our Renaissance man-artist-historian father had been to Europe, and the effect on the rest of us was as if we had accompanied a soul into Paradise.

It was also on this trip that my mother and I shared a feather bed in an attic in a French country inn. We had rarely before had time for intimate chat. (My family name is "Tica," which means "Costa Rican girl" and is used to distinguish me from my grandmother; however my mother's pet name for me is "Serene.") Now she said, from the depths of the big bed, as the rain pattered on the straw roof overhead, "Serene, how old are you?"

"Fifteen," I said.

"And what grade are you in?"

"Eleventh, in September."

She got up on one elbow. "Now why is that?" she asked. "Don't you want to get on with your career?"

Anita Figueredo, at fifteen, had been knocking on the gates of Manhattanville. She was genuinely perplexed as to why anyone with plans might linger this long in high school, even at the Convent of the Sacred Heart, and since I had no strong feelings about it one way or the other, when we returned home she telephoned the mistress-general, Mother Virginia McMonagle, and arranged for me to enter the senior class. It worked out all right, although for years afterwards I had odd gaps in my general knowledge about English literature and history, which are subjects that happened to be covered in the junior year.

For the next twelve months, Anita orchestrated preparations for a national AASH conference in San Diego. Everything else continued on as well, and the list of her worthwhile endeavors was so long, that a writer for the *Catholic Digest* (who was assigned to do a feature on her life in October 1960) wrote to ask for <u>something</u> that would keep the story from "bogging down in complete sweetness."

Always eager to be helpful, Anita confessed to the reporter[198] her sin of perpetual lateness:

> I detest waiting for trains, planes and events to begin; so I arrive just in the nick of time - thus driving my very methodical husband to distraction. Sometimes it isn't only my husband who gets wild, as the time I arrived for a TV program during the introductions, and for a radio interview just as it was going on the air. Mind you, I'm very much ashamed of this characteristic, and am constantly making resolutions to mend my ways; but I'm progressing very slowly!

Betty Stirnkorb later amplified on Anita's tardiness:

> I finally went to work for Anita as her receptionist when her last one quit. Her front-office staff didn't last long because she was always late, her waiting room would be full to overflowing, and then the nuns from Tijuana would walk in the door and be taken care of first. Anita never rushed a patient - they <u>loved</u> her, but they did complain loudly to the staff.

Anita also had advice for the young women of 1960 (which, fairly or no, may still be pertinent in the nineties):

> In my opinion, anyone who wants a career and home must be ready to tackle two full time jobs at once. At least in medicine, this is a wild and hectic arrangement, and requires a particular temperament for success; the alternative is a nervous breakdown. For example, this is no life for a perfectionist. You have to be satisfied to try hard all the time; to do your best, and then to be satisfied

by the results. Otherwise you're constantly frustrated, and that's not good for doctor, wife or mother, and worse still for patients, husband and children! I can't emphasize strongly enough the need for trying ALL THE TIME - simply because the demands of each role necessarily limit the hours available for the others, so each moment must be made to count.

At the time Anita was drafting this reply, she was forty-four and just pregnant, again, but with a difference.

She had begun to feel weak and lethargic, which was uncharacteristic. In her ordinary pregnant state, she was troubled only with sciatica, and she worked up until the literal last moment. But this time Anita was really very sick with an indolent type of hepatitis; when I came home from boarding school on the weekend I was frightened to find her in her bedroom with physicians standing solemnly around. Still, nothing much changed. She not only did her regular work but went on with the enormous task of organizing and then chairing - when she was seven months along - the national conference in San Diego attended by about a thousand alumnae of the Sacred Heart.

I was abruptly graduating from high school just at this time, and it seemed important to my mother that I go to Costa Rica. She herself had not managed a return in a quarter-century. But she wrote at regular intervals to her favorite cousins, mothered various of their children, and had already sent three of her own (with Lita) for stays of many months. Now she insisted on shopping with me for appropriate clothes, since my closet contained almost nothing but convent school uniforms, and she sat heavily in a department store chair with grayness in her face while I modeled my choices. And I did go to Costa Rica, a month or so before my last brother was born.

My mother nearly died while I was gone.

Robert Francis was born on the first of July, 1961. Anita's delivery was not unusual, and the baby was as healthy as all of his brothers and sisters. But nine days post-partum, Anita woke to find she was bleeding, and got up to go to the bathroom, where she collapsed in shock on the floor. Bill heard the noise and found her in a pumping pool of blood, then ran to grab Billy out of bed to help him carry his mother's unconscious and waxen body downstairs to the car. This was done under the terrified eyes of Lita and all the other children. (Lita was so frightened indeed that she left the children huddled with the maids and rushed to church to pray.) The hospital door was only a hundred yards away, and there Bill himself began Anita's transfusion, squeezing the hanging bag of blood to force the flow, until she was wheeled into the operating room for removal of retained placental fragments. The next day she seemed nearly well.

But she no sooner returned home than she was awakened again with chest pain, shortness of breath, and a sense of doom, symptoms of a blood clot to the arteries of the lungs, presumably broken off from the newly-clotted vessels in her pelvis. There was little to be done about a pulmonary embolus in 1961; and Anita's response was to ask Bill to call a priest for the last rites of the Church. The priest came to the bedroom by the sea to administer the sacrament, while Anita cried softly about leaving Bill and Lita with all those little children, and a two-week old baby. But providence was more sensible than that, and she slowly recovered.

The cheerful letters that made their way down to me in Costa Rica never mentioned a thing, and little Bobby was allowed his share of our mother's attentions. Like Teresa before him, he spent his days in the crib in Anita's office, raucously entertaining patients and staff; and at home he was taken up into the tenderness of twelve-year-old Charlie, who ordinarily kept his emotional distance, but had fallen in love with both of his littlest siblings.

Bobby lived eighteen months, and the last thing he did as a member of the family was to ride through the house on Charlie's shoulders. Then, as his parents dressed upstairs for an evening out, his grandmother fussed and settled in her own apartment, five older brothers and sisters sat down to dinner and two maids bustled in the kitchen, he squeezed himself through a pair of heavy doors that no one thought he could open and toddled through the dark into a lily pond so shallow he could have stood in it with help, and drowned.

In the house, a crescendo of anxious searching ended when our mother pulled the blinds overlooking the black garden and Tommy switched on a light which picked out the terrible red of a small jacket in the pool. Until the police, and the ambulance and the newspaper reporters came, Anita and Bill worked in a praying, desperate rhythm over a child whom they knew had slipped beyond their reach.[199]

Lita aged years overnight, pathetically holding the bucket of dripping clothes, the overalls and the little red jacket, and crying at God. Our father wept quietly for his little boy in the living room as he read doggedly through the cascading mountain of letters and cards and telegrams. Anita found peace in action, in arranging for the gentle White Mass, in producing balanced meals from the platters and casseroles stacked on tables and sideboards, and in comforting everyone else around her. She had lived forty-six years without requiring comfort and perhaps now found it awkward; but she also believed in such things as eternal life and the union with God of the blameless soul of her son, and she even considered that the boy had taken an enviable shortcut home.

CHAPTER 27

He Also Serves

It is probable that Bill Doyle did not fully understand what he was getting into when he married Anita Figueredo. It was really her idea, after all, and he was swept along, like a leaf before the wind, by the irresistible force of her conviction. They were in love when they married, they were both doctors, and they were committed Catholics. That was the sum of what they had in common; and it was enough, as Anita foresaw, although she may have been the only person at their wedding who was entirely sure.

As Anita's astonishingly complicated life unfolded, she occasionally joked that what she needed was a good wife. Bill could say the same thing, in the same sense. In fact he came to think that, for him, Anita was the perfect wife; but neither of them had the luxury of a spouse devoted primarily to the care and feeding of the other.

Bill Doyle was accomplished in his own right. To begin with, he was a good pediatrician, and for some years the only one in town, in an era when his own training was the last word in the care of sick children. There were no sub-specialists, there was no university hospital or "tertiary-care center," and at the beginning of his career there were almost no vaccines. Even antibiotics were new. It is hard to imagine a pediatric internship without antibiotics. Yet it was not until 1942, when Bill was two years out of medical school, that he administered the first antibiotic at King's County Hospital, sulfapyridine, to a patient with meningitis, and the patient recovered.

In La Jolla, Bill cared for the tiniest premature infants by himself in the simple nursery at Scripps Hospital. In the same setting he performed the town's first exchange transfusion for a jaundiced baby with "Rh-disease." (This procedure eventually became relatively easy, after the invention of such things as plastic tubing; but originally it involved "cutting-down" on a vein in the leg to drip new blood in, while drawing old blood out from a large sinus in the baby's head, with a needle driven through his "soft spot.")

Bill lived through epidemics of polio, when every phone call in the night about a child with fever and leg pain was a threat of paralysis. He cared for children in prolonged coma with head injuries, with diabetes, with leukemia. In his office he sewed up complex lacerations, set fractured bones, and administered ether anesthesia for his colleague who extracted tonsils. And he made house calls, over a radius which once encompassed the whole of northern San Diego county.

In 1964, Bill was Chief of the Medical Staff at Scripps Hospital, and presided over the emptying of the graceful buildings behind his own house, and the move to a modern brick tower on a sage-dotted mesa just out of town.[200] For a brief span of years, from 1958 to 1964, Anita was able to manage her family and profession by walking briskly around a path about a hundred yards wide, from home to office to hospital and back. Now, and for the rest of her surgical career, she was forced back into her car for a seven-mile commute out of town, along with Bill and all the other physicians in the village. (But whereas Bill drove a well-maintained, late-model car with finesse, and with enough gas, and at the posted speed, driving was always a chancy business for Anita; and she nearly lost her life, in that pre-seatbelt era, during one of those sprints from the mesa. She was actually rushing to a tea for the Religious of the Sacred Heart when she just missed the back of an earthmover, ran her car up the side of a bank, rolled three times, and was found by horrified onlookers hanging in the car upside down from the steering wheel. When the police came along, they turned her car right side up, and Anita went on to the tea an hour late with an unsightly run in her stocking.)

Outside his profession, Bill pursued other interests with a similar intensity. In the 1950s he was a proficient sailor, crewing for his boat-owner friends in serious races which they often won, and occasionally inviting all of his children down to the finish line in such places as Ensenada, Mexico. Then, toward the end of the decade, he gave up sailing for painting.

Growing up in Utica, he had a significant art education. Saturdays and two evenings a week for years he worked as a member of the Art Students League under the eyes of a landscape painter named Chauncey Adams, and the photographer-painter Nicholas Hàz, who was an associate of the famous photo-journalist Margaret Bourke-White. Mr. Hàz tried to persuade the teenager to forego college and devote himself to art, to "starve" for it, if necessary. Bill considered this thoughtfully and decided against starving in favor of Georgetown University and a more reliable profession.

More than twenty years then elapsed before he picked up his palette and brushes seriously again. He never stopped using his camera, and some of his slides, of billowing spinnakers or the pensive faces of children, won prizes. But all during our childhood, we watched our father draw magical beasts on napkins, and illustrations for our school projects. Nativity scenes on the windows of our house (which he painted backwards inside from scaled cartoons) drew crowds of Christmas visitors and prizes from the city. Eventually, in about 1958, he set up a modest studio at home and began to paint real canvasses again. He was a "realist" painter at the height of abstract expressionism, and one of a small group responsible for staging "The 20th Century Realists" show, which introduced to San Diego such giants of representational modern art as Andrew Wyeth and Robert Vickrey.

Bill was deeply religious and faithful to the spirit and the letter of the Roman Catholic Church, its tradition and pageantry. After the Second Vatican Council in 1961, the lives of an army of Catholics exploded with the freedom to change: convents and parish rectories emptied out, and young adults wondered what their sixteen years of Catholic education had been all about. Anita Figueredo was not bothered in the least; she knew what was immutable and what was not, and never cared much for non-essentials. But Bill Doyle was a man who could recite the Latin missal word for word from memory, who loved the High Mass with its tall candles and three priests, celebrant, deacon and sub-deacon arrayed in their golden chasubles, and the men's choir floating its glorious Renaissance hymns over the heads of the kneeling congregation. Yet he knew it was unreasonable to insist on grafting a Latin Renaissance Mass on all the varied cultures of the world; and when all this was replaced in the United States by colloquial English, home-made banners, folk-guitars and, eventually, by lay men and women standing in the sanctuary as lectors and Eucharistic ministers in place of the vanished priests, Bill embraced the new liturgy (although he was always sorry about poor musicianship and running shoes under chasubles); and he was among the first Extraordinary Ministers ordained for Mary, Star of the Sea.

Our father dearly loved the role of paterfamilias. He cherished his own infants in a way our mother did not, loving the feel of their velvet skin and silky hair and the smell of their little powdered bodies, and often walking about the house with a baby nestled under his chin. He conversed with small children in an easy, respectful way and enjoyed their company. He liked the look of his children arrayed in a line, in the pew at church, in photographs, and especially at table.

Precisely at 6:00 every evening our father sat at the eastern head (our mother at the west) of our dining room table and surveyed his children, his children's friends, the current Costa Rican cousin, his mother-in-law, and various semi-permanent guests such as the vague and elderly Miss Mary Romadka who gave us the piano. Our food was more ample than memorable, the operative idea being that anyone was welcome at our table, even at the last moment, and also that most of the people eating were children, and they liked things plain. Our father, whose own mother labored in the kitchen baking and seasoning by the hour, might have looked back wistfully on those days, but he kept his musings to himself. There was all the squabbling, toddler screeching, passing of plates and getting up for something forgotten in the kitchen that one might imagine with a crowd like this, and generally our mother was too busy for sustained conversation. But our father loved to talk to us, and was knowledgeable about everything under the sun; about art and music and medicine, but also sports and old movies, geography and history, books and current events. And, of course, religion and politics, although as his children came of age in the sixties and seventies these grenade-like topics were mostly left alone.

Bill participated with Anita in various civic good works, with the special heroism of the accompanying spouse. By nature a gracious and courtly man, he also spent his workdays talking to the mothers of children; and as he genuinely liked women and understood something of their lives, he was an appreciated guest at banquets and at fund-raising cocktail parties.

More than anything, he did not complain too much about what Anita did, despite the fact that practically every phone call was, in a way, another alienation of his wife's affections. It was not as if there were any requests which Anita was sure to turn down. For instance, she had no particular interest in music, and was quite oblivious to the wonderful sounds emanating from her own living room when Bill was home. Yet in 1964 she took on the presidency of the La Jolla Civic Orchestra. Anita's only criterion for accepting a job seemed to be whether or not she viewed its goals as inherently worthwhile. In this case, she thought, purely theoretically, that music was good for both performers and listeners; and so she not only managed the business of the existing orchestra, but decided that singers should be formally organized as well. And to this end she scrambled around to all the church choirs in the village and invited the members to her home after dinner, to be molded into the La Jolla Civic Chorus.

The novelty of 1964 was that Bill took Anita away on a trip for the sheer pleasure of it. They went to Spain, with no other purpose than immersing themselves in the genius of El Greco, Goya, Velasquez and the Alhambra. The newspaper account is worth reprinting for the astonishing syntax:

> An ardent hispanophile since childhood, their trip to
> Spain in 1964 culminated in a lifelong ambition of Dr.
> Doyle.

Bill was in heaven with the delights of the Spanish masters and the uninterrupted company of his wife, and Anita even perceived that it was lovely to be taken care of now and then, to relax and allow Bill to hold her hand and show her the glories of art, architecture, history, cuisine and luxury hotels. Although she continued to turn her wine glass upside down on the snowy tablecloths, determined to live out her life without alcohol ever touching her lips, Bill sat across from her, sampling wonderful vintages very happily. It would be many years before Anita could go abroad again without some higher purpose than pleasing her husband, but the seed had been planted.

On Mother's Day of 1965, The *San Diego Union* printed an essay by Anita Figueredo in the spirit of National Family Week. It read, in part:

> True love is "patient, is kind" and seeks only one thing:
> the well-being of the loved one and all that flows
> from that. It encourages the full development of the
> recipient's potential; it will be stimulating rather than
> stifling and possessive...[201]

To the interested onlooker, particularly daughters maturing in the pre-liberation decade and considering careers, it looked as though Anita Figueredo and Bill Doyle were oddly and perfectly matched. Individually, each might have been extreme -- one storming the barricades and the other rooted in a glorious past, one a childless socialist in Costa Rica, say, and the other a leader of the Back-to-Latin movement in the Catholic Church -- but together they achieved a remarkable and life-enhancing balance.

CHAPTER 28

Old Ties

I

Mother Teresa

In the fall of 1966, Anita set out with Bill for the Ninth International Cancer Congress in Tokyo, Japan, by way of Russia, India, Thailand, and Hong Kong. Anita was intrigued by the chance to see how cancer was handled in the eastern world, and also to view firsthand the work of Mother Teresa (which was, in a manner of speaking, the way cancer was handled in Calcutta).

In Moscow, as members of an organized delegation of American physicians, they were invited to visit the National Institute of Oncology. This newish facility looked, Anita thought, about like Memorial Hospital in 1940, with large open wards of thirty beds. The staff physicians appeared to be well-trained and conversant with all cancer therapy protocols in established use in the West. They had access to up-to-date journals and current medications, and seemed to be using them to good effect. Then, as now, Soviet physicians were mostly female, although it did not escape Anita's attention that the directors of the Institute were male. Nursing care was competent, with patients who were long-term boarders, sent in to Moscow from the provinces, generally helping out as aides for the months it took to finish their own therapies; there was no arrangement for outpatient care. What seemed a step into another time zone was the operating theater, where blood for transfusions sat in open flasks stoppered with cotton, and anesthetists wrestled with first-generation machines, one step removed from open-drop ether.

After Moscow, they flew south in a sweeping arc to Delhi, and from there to the Bay of Bengal and the steaming city of Calcutta. In the early stage of her friendship with Mother Teresa, Anita received two or three letters a year on the familiar white stationery stamped with the map of India. The letters mentioned things Anita sent: books, medicines, clothing, vestments, money; the birth and then the death of Bobby Doyle and his emergence as the patron saint of Mother Teresa's new order of Brothers; the religious name, Sister Anita, given to the newest Bengali nun; inquiries after the children in general, and always a special word about "little Teresa." Now, though, the last letter was more than two years old, partly reflecting the state of the Indian postal system (in one letter which got through, Mother Teresa wrote, "From Father Anderson I come to know that you did not receive any letters from me. It is too bad because the little I write, if that too is going to be lost, this is really hard.") But it also suggests that even saints have only twenty-four hours in the day.

In any case, Anita had written ahead to say she was coming, and knew the address as well as her own: 54/A Lower Circular Road, Calcutta. She and Bill walked out of the best hotel in the city, threaded their way through the sleeping and squatting forms of a whole colony of street people, and hailed a cab. On impulse, Bill brought with him a box containing a chalice, the golden cup used in the Mass for the sacrament of the Eucharist. Bill's father died a few months before this trip; at ninety, W.E. Doyle was the oldest living member of the Knights of Columbus of Utica, and the Knights presented his family with a chalice, to be given "to any priest who needs it." In planning the Tokyo trip, Bill thought to take the cup to a priest-friend who was head of the Japanese mission. Now all of a sudden he was sitting in a jolting cab in Calcutta with the box between his knees.

As Anita presumed, the taxi driver knew exactly where to go. They pushed their way through milling animals and people on the Lower Circular Road and came to a rattling stop at 54/A. The Motherhouse was a solid, squat, stuccoed affair with an open central yard; at the doorway, they were met by a smiling nun who beckoned them into the tiny bare "parlor" with its few hard chairs, its table, its naked light bulb, and Mother Teresa.

She embraced Anita and Bill, sat them down and asked about their trip, which Anita briefly described; and then they were interrupted by an anxious nun coming in from the hot yard to say that they had just given their last dose of streptomycin, and what was to be done about the snaking line of patients with tuberculosis? "Tell them to return tomorrow," Mother Teresa said calmly. "It will come." The nun nodded and withdrew from the parlor; at which point Bill said, by way of explanation of the box he still held on his lap, "Do you have need for a chalice?"

"Oh, you brought it," Mother Teresa said. "Good. Father Andrew has just been released by the Jesuits to become the first priest of the Missionaries of Charity. Tomorrow he is coming to say Mass here for the first time, and I asked God to send him a chalice."

Bill handed over his box and they accompanied Mother Teresa on a tour of the convent, then rode along in her ambulance to *Shishu Bhavan,* her home for abandoned and brutalized young. There they found 125 bathed and nourished children in gaily-patterned clothes, including ten tiny premature infants and a laughing girl who ran about on her hands, with her useless legs bent crab-like in the air. It appeared that everyone old enough to laugh or sing was doing so, despite the ravages of disease or wounds inflicted by parents hoping for more success in begging.

Anita and Bill returned to their hotel exalted, only to find the rest of the doctors in their company sickened by Calcutta, by the suffocating heat, the appalling visible misery, the noise, and the stench. Two of the group were so struck by Anita and Bill's enthusiasm, setting out next day on a visit to the Home for the Destitute Dying, that they subdued their considerable apprehension and went along. At the convent they found Mother Teresa opening a large box from America of donated drugs, mostly streptomycin. Then they crowded into an ambulance again for the trip to *Nirmal Hriday*. In the Home for the Dying, rows of neat platforms were lined with metal cots, where near-skeletons in clean sheets and robes were attended by smiling young women talking softly, stroking feverish heads, injecting medicines, offering bowls of soup. Mother Teresa explained the screening procedure for patients: the sidewalks of Calcutta, she said, are covered at night by a dark mass of sleeping homeless, packed close enough together to form another living sidewalk. In the morning, whoever doesn't get up is desperately ill or dead; the police make their rounds, haul away the dead, and take the rest to *Nirmal Hriday.*

II

Roberto Figueredo

In 1969, thirty-five years after she last saw her father, Anita encountered Roberto Figueredo again in a hotel room in Guatemala City.

Once, during her residency at Memorial Hospital in 1942, Anita had been approached by another house officer with a Spanish accent. He had seen her name on the new residents' list and wondered whether she could be any relation to his "idol," Roberto Figueredo. The young doctor, Bernardo del Valle, was Guatemalan and an avid soccer fan at a time when Roberto Figueredo was the most famous name in Guatemalan soccer, as player, coach, theoretician, and sportswriter chronicling the history and current state of the national sport. When Anita admitted that Roberto Figueredo was her father, and that she had a number of his gold medals in her jewelry box at home, young Dr. del Valle was fascinated. Anita did not let on that she herself was not feeling particularly impressed with Roberto Figueredo. By this time, it had been nearly a decade since she last saw her father in Costa Rica, during that strange interlude when he appeared out of nowhere to escort her around the town and country day after day. After she returned to New York, he vanished again from her life, and she had heard not a word from him since.

The silence continued nearly another ten years, until one day in 1950 when the saga with her father took a most bizarre twist. Anita read an item in an American newsmagazine with the dateline Cartago, Costa Rica.[202] The article described the collective national outrage over the desecration of the shrine of the Black Virgin of Cartago and the indictment of the suspected thief, one Roberto Figueredo.

The Black Virgin is the special patron of Costa Rican Catholics. Her small ebony form is encased in a jeweled and golden reliquary several times her size, and stands in a niche in the Basilica at Cartago, a four-hundred-year-old city which was once the political and cultural center of the country. *La Negrita,* as the Virgin is called, is sometimes persuaded to perform miracles, generally of the healing sort, and her shrine is surrounded by dazzling tiers of gold and silver *milagros,* body parts (legs, arms, breasts and so on) from the grateful cured. (A decade after the robbery and the restoration of the sacred image, I myself joined the annual pilgrimage on the feast of the Black Virgin, walking with a great crowd through the whole of a rainy night over the continental divide from San José to Cartago.)

It seems that Roberto Figueredo, who was then fifty-five, had moved his household from Alajuela to San José, where one day in early 1950 their former neighbor, the wild and mysterious José León Sánchez, appeared at their door after an absence of several years. In later testimony, Roberto Figueredo described the younger José León as a consummate troublemaker and the scourge of the neighborhood. Sánchez himself wrote that he was backward in school, unable to read or write and considered unteachable. But when he returned to Costa Rica at age 20 and reappeared at the house of the Figueredos, Sánchez was utterly transformed – well-spoken, wearing spectacles and describing himself as a journalist looking for work. He was taken into the family's affections, found a job as a radio reporter through a friend of Roberto's, and fell in love again with his childhood friend Julieta – who sewed for him a special pair of socks.

Months passed. Then, on the night of May 13, 1950, someone entered the Basilica de Los Ángeles, pried out the Sacred Image, tossed her on top of the pulpit canopy where she was lost for more than a week - causing national mourning - and made away with the fabulous golden casing and all the surrounding treasure after killing a basilica guard. Found near the body of the guard was one incriminating blood-stained sock.

Within hours of the crime, José León Sánchez, wet and muddy in Cartago, was questioned by police but released.

Two weeks later, Roberto Figueredo astonished the entire nation by being arrested in the workroom of a dentist friend, where he was melting down some of the highly recognizable gold. Shortly afterward, José León Sánchez was taken into custody for good.

The case was sensational because of the importance of the Black Virgin, but also because Roberto Figueredo was still a national figure and intimate of President Otilio Ulate – in whose office Roberto testified that Sánchez came to him confessing the crime, warned him that Julieta's handiwork was left at the scene, and brought him recognizable gold and jewels and demanded money. Further, Roberto said, that in order to protect his daughter's good name, he agreed to get money for Sánchez by melting down the gold.

José León, for his part, declared exactly the opposite: that he was entirely innocent until he arrived at the house of his beloved, and her father astonished him by showing him glittering pieces of the Virgin's treasure and asking him to dispose of it in the back streets of San José, which he proceeded to do, for love.

Despite friends in high places and improbable goings-on, including the appearance on the scene of the North American FBI, Roberto was indicted as mastermind (*director intelectual)* of the crime and jailed for two years while deliberations dragged on interminably. Finally in 1955, there was a highly public trial during which Roberto defended himself and Sánchez attempted to do the same, since no lawyer in Costa Rica could be found to represent the man now called "The Monster of the Basilica.[203] In the end, Sánchez was convicted and sentenced to forty-five years in prison. Roberto Figueredo was found innocent of any foreknowledge of the crime but guilty of cover-up *(encubrimiento)*, and sentenced to the two years already served. Roberto, his good name battered, left the country forever for Guatemala soon after the trial.[204]

What happened afterward to José León Sánchez is the stuff of legend.

Sánchez, son of a prostitute and brutalized survivor of orphanage and reform school, was confined on the notorious prison island of San Lucas in the Gulf of Nicoya, where boatmen organized tours to see *el Monstruo de la Basílica*. In prison, over time, the "monstrous" Sánchez wrote letters home for illiterate prisoners, and eventually began composing a novel with stubs of pencil on paper scraps torn from bags of cement. In time, Sánchez built a crude mimeograph machine and published the first edition of *La isla de los hombres solos* (*Island of Solitary Men*) which survived deliberate conflagration by the warden, was smuggled out to the mainland, and eventually catapulted the author to international fame.

In 1969, after nearly two decades behind bars, Sánchez was released from San Lucas to the life of a critically acclaimed and best-selling writer of novels and short stories, and earned – among other honors – the Costa Rican National Prize in Literature. And then, in 1999, nearly half a century after the violation of the Black Virgin, the now white-haired and imposing José León Sánchez appealed to the Criminal High Court for reversal of his conviction on the grounds of torture and gross violations of Costa Rican criminal law. His conviction was declared null.[205]

To return to the history of Anita Figueredo and her father, all of these details revealed at the trial were unknown to Anita at the time she first heard of the affair. She only perceived that the father she scarcely knew was thought to be the mastermind of a crime of religious desecration which was a slap in the collective face of the Costa Rican people. Anita was offended in every possible way, by the venality, the assault on religion, the lack of patriotic sentiment and by the sheer ingratitude. For a woman as intensely loyal as Anita Figueredo, it was an unforgivable offense; and while she was in this distinctly unusual frame of mind, she received two letters from Costa Rica.

The first was from her aunt Tita Villegas, Lita's sister, writing in a commiserating way about the terrible trouble Roberto was in and suggesting Anita help. The other was from her father himself, begging money for legal fees, asserting he needed his daughter's support to clear the family name. Anita, who never refused anyone in need, thought about it, and then wrote her father a letter disowning him, "You abandoned me. We are no kin" and so on. And she sent a copy of the letter to her family in Costa Rica.

After the maelstrom of crime and publicity, silence prevailed until one day in the late 1950s when a Guatemalan tuna fisherman made port in San Diego and phoned Anita with the words, "This is your brother, Roberto." Roberto Figueredo, Jr., was perhaps thirty years old at that time (when Anita was forty-two); he had brought his wife and they were both eager to make his famous sister's acquaintance. Anita was distinctly leery about this overture, principally because she knew how offended her mother would be by any such relationship with the Figueredos. Nevertheless, "Robertillo" was cheerfully persistent, and eventually Anita and Bill found themselves entertaining the newfound brother and sister-in-law in their living room at "417" with Anita keeping an anxious eye on Lita's staircase all the while. But her mother did not descend, and as soon as Anita could reasonably plead other commitments, the guests were ushered out the door and all further invitations to "get together" firmly declined.

A few more years passed. And then in January of 1969 Anita traveled with Bill (and Tommy and Anita Maria) to Guatemala City at the invitation of her old friend, Dr. Bernardo del Valle, who was director of the National Cancer Institute there. Dr. del Valle was holding a formal dedication ceremony at the Institute and requested Anita's presence as honored guest. The Guatemalan press played up the event and Anita Figueredo's picture appeared on newsstands.

When the Doyles arrived in Guatemala City, they chose a new hotel, the grandiose El Camino Real. Bill stood in line to register while Anita and the children went on ahead to their room; and then as Bill turned toward the elevator, a vaguely familiar man stepped out from behind a marble pillar in front of him and spoke his name, "*Don* Bill." It was Roberto Figueredo, Jr. He said, "I heard you were coming; it was in the paper. My father really wants to see Anita."

He pressed a card with his telephone number on it into Bill's hand, and Bill continued upstairs to talk it over with Anita, who had found an impressively grand flower arrangement which she assumed was from the Cancer Institute. Bill opened the card, and handed it to Anita, saying, "It's from your father." The card read: "I'm putting my hat in the ring, and hope it will be accepted."

As in all her dealings with her father, Anita was afflicted with the most uncharacteristic, disquieting emotions. Now she was completely nonplussed. Ultimately her practical side prompted her to agree to a meeting, as she certainly could not be going about Guatemala City wondering who might jump out at her from behind every pillar or bush. Bill called the number he was given and invited Roberto Sr. to the hotel that night.

Roberto Figueredo was seventy-four. He was small, perhaps 5'4" to 5'6" with neat gray hair and one scarred cornea from an errant tennis ball. He was a soft-spoken gentleman, refined and poised, still an active journalist. His younger daughters stood beside their father, as he and the accomplished sister they had heard about all their lives embraced. They talked pleasantly enough for a time, and then Roberto prevailed upon the whole party to dine together at one of the sisters' houses, a beautiful modern home.

The party the next night was a steak dinner with Roberto Jr. as expansive chef, very handsome at forty or so, in custom-made boots and a rakish hat. He invited Tommy, who was twenty and had the look of a fellow-adventurer, to go jaguar-hunting with him in the Guatemalan jungle, and Tommy accepted instantly. The party was attended by the whole Figueredo family (minus Anita's stepmother), as well as many of the well-to-do in town, including some other Americans and journalists. It turned out that the younger Roberto led a rather lavish lifestyle, ostensibly on the proceeds from a well-known *churrasco* (grilled meat) restaurant he owned in town, called *La Tablita*. His wife was just home from the hospital with his newest daughter, and he insisted on showing her off to Anita and Bill, who were more sympathetic with the poor tired girl than impressed with Roberto Jr.'s *machismo*. All in all, however, Anita enjoyed the evening and agreed, on taking leave, that Tommy would return to hunt with his charming uncle.

The Doyles left the country soon after for Costa Rica.

The final twist was that when they arrived at Anita's cousin's house in San José, Gladys handed Anita a letter she had just received from a family friend, an urgent warning **not** to let Tommy go hunting alone with Roberto Figueredo, Jr. in Guatemala...that he had "underworld connections"...that Tommy was in danger of being "kidnapped for ransom." The tone of the letter was so alarming that the Guatemalan connection was abruptly cut off, and Tommy placated with trips by car and private plane to the Costa Rican wilderness and a spectacular fishing trip to the Caribbean coast where he boated the first tarpon of the season. With that, the Doyles returned to California. Not long afterwards, Anita and Bill received word of persistent rumors that Roberto Jr. himself was kidnapped and possibly killed in the Guatemalan jungle.[206]

And indeed, nothing more was ever heard of him, or any of the Figueredo family, again until I persuaded my mother in March 1975 that I must write her father in order to understand our family history. The letter was directed to Dr. Bernardo del Valle in Guatemala City; and when the answer came, I was informed of the death of Roberto Figueredo, Sr., ten months earlier, on the 8th of May, 1974.

CHAPTER 29

All Those Children [207]

On August 8, 1967 Anita and Bill celebrated their twenty-fifth wedding anniversary. All of the children, including the four in college and beyond, gathered for the occasion under the wide roof at "417". Besides our eight-year-old baby sister, we ranged in age then from twenty-three to fourteen, all still single though with several intense romances in progress. And all of us filling the front pew during the ceremony of the renewal of our parents' wedding vows, and then later clustered in the church hall, watching movies of the original happening at St. Patrick's Cathedral, wondered about whether we could be so lucky, or so smart, or whatever it took.

Our brother John was the first to try, three months after our parents' anniversary. Then in his senior year at Loyola University, Los Angeles, John had been a sensitive, loving, endlessly good-natured little boy, who once wanted to be a priest. He was about to embark on a career as a math teacher and principal in an inner-city parochial school. In the fall of 1967, while John was finishing a degree in Philosophy and Theology, he married his high school sweetheart at Mary, Star of the Sea.

Anita Figueredo's first daughter-in-law, Kim, was representative of the several she would eventually acquire: an intelligent, competent girl, she was both respectful of, and a little intimidated by Anita; and she may never have been absolutely certain during her married life that her husband admired his wife as much as his mother.

In fact Anita was devoted to John's young wife, as she would be to all of our spouses who came later. Her daughters-in-law and sons-in-law together were drawn from a virtual cross-section of American life, except there were no Irish or Costa Ricans, and also no Catholics among the first half-dozen. The new Doyles, and husbands of Doyles, were Christian Scientist, Mormon, Presbyterian and Lutheran; they were Jewish, Chinese and Polish; and some had been married before. Anita had no notion that any of us could have done better. As a mother-in-law, she was both completely accepting and quick to take charge of any problem which arose. Those of us who had grown up with her did not consider this a paradox, but the newcomers may have been confused from time to time.

In the summer of 1968, when Anita was fifty-one, her first grandchild, John Doyle, Jr., was born at Scripps Hospital, and Anita had the same reaction to the baby as she did to her own infants. She loved him dearly, intellectually, and looked forward to the time when he was big enough to tell her what was on his mind.

Brother John having broken the ice, most of the rest of us ventured into marriage during the 1970s. I myself fell precipitously in love during my last few weeks of medical school at the University of California in San Francisco. Brent Eastman was just departing, when we met, for a year as a surgical registrar in England. On our third date he made me promise to marry him, after which he flew off to East Anglia, leaving me to my internship at the San Francisco General Hospital and returning only long enough at Christmas time for our wedding and a week-long Mexican honeymoon - before flying away again to finish out the English year alone. We were married in my parents' house under a canopy of white flowers one brilliant January day in 1970. Gray whales migrated south, in a sounding and blowing line, outside the living room window. The mother of the bride unexpectedly took her graying, thinning bun to a beauty parlor and emerged with silver white hair upswept in a thick French roll, a dramatic new look for the first time in decades.

Our oldest brother Billy's life was detoured through the Vietnam War, specifically through the Army at Pleiku where his college English major won him a job writing stirring news releases for hometown papers about the troops in the field. Billy refused on principle to apply for a commission, and when he was drafted he got basic training as an artillery surveyor, the key member of a three-man team sent out to make contact with the enemy. At the time he arrived in Vietnam, artillery surveyors were rumored to have an 80% casualty rate.

But Billy Doyle's résumé said "photography and literature," and he was abruptly plugged into the "Hometown News Program," an evangelical mission which called for taking photos of soldiers with their arms around their buddies, "doing their job," and then making up heroic stories for the folks back home, incorporating whatever facts he had. This strange business heightened his already surreal sense of isolation. He was completely on his own, waiting to be told where to go, and it was up to him to get there however he could; so he just packed his gear down to the airport in Pleiku and hitchhiked around Vietnam, staying until he got his story and then moving on.

After his Army discharge in 1970, Billy abandoned a master's degree in English, having come to terms with the fact that what he really wanted to do was to work with his hands. He began by building a seafood cafe with our brother Tommy and a fishing boat for himself, then sailed for months on a tuna seiner before settling down as an architectural welder.

Tommy, our third brother, spent his boyhood with animals, ignoring a smothering allergy to fur and feathers as long as possible, and then turning his attention to the creatures of the sea. We believed he communed with fish; he was an intuitive, expert ocean fisherman, competent with boats at such an early age that by twelve he was working commercially in the waters outside San Diego Bay. He even sang about fish; in the summer of 1969, when he was riding around in an open car in Hawaii with Ricky and Billy - who was on a week's "R & R" from

Vietnam - the brothers composed the following classic, to the tune of "Amóre":

> "When an eel bites your leg
> And you feels like you're dead
> It's a moray.
>
> When the teeth pierce your thigh
> And you swim for the sky
> It's a moray.
>
> For a change from raw fish
> It's a Japanese dish,
> It's a moray!"

By 1970, Tommy graduated in business from San Diego State College, and opened "Ocean Fresh" seafood market-cafe at the south end of La Jolla, a venture spectacularly successful from the outset. Two years later there was a second Ocean Fresh south of San Diego; and by the end of 1975 the original La Jolla cafe was enlarged to twice its former size and transformed into an elegant restaurant with hand carved details of Tommy's own design, palms studded with glistening fragments of abalone, and hundreds of copper fish scales which he cut and hammered in at the roofline, alongside his other builders.

Tommy was remarkably handsome, of medium height, muscular and graceful, with thick, dark hair, a black moustache, and almost perfect features. He had intelligent eyes under dark brows, and a lingering allergy caused him to open his mouth slightly in repose, which gave him a smoldering look. He was a man's man, but women seemed to materialize out of the air and follow him around. Nevertheless, the woman whose company he seemed to enjoy most, at least in a conversational way, was our mother. The two of them had a flair for business, and they were both fearless; they were perfect partners, animated entrepreneurs bending close together over plans laid out on the wide dining room table.

There is a story from around the time of the original Ocean Fresh, which illustrates several Anita Figueredoisms: she and Bill were driving through Belgium, Germany and Austria, having begun in Bruges so that they could aid a Belgian priest-friend who was head of the Japanese Catholic mission, but was ill and resting at home (*combining higher business with pleasure*). Strolling through Salzburg, she spotted lithographs of fish in the window of an antique shop and thought they would be perfect for Tom's cafe (*bringing home souvenirs of every trip for every "child", no matter how old.*) On entering the shop, she was directed to a table covered with "about two hundred" prints, evidently just acquired in an unsorted lot by the proprietor; rifling through these, Anita picked out four or five fish, and then recognized an etching of "Christ at Emmaeus" which Bill had shown her in one of his favorite books on Rembrandt (*missing nothing of what Bill ever taught her.*) Assuming this to be a fine copy, she bought the Christ along with the several fish for the equivalent of thirty-five dollars, and brought it home to San Diego - where it was formally appraised, found to be the original Rembrandt and valued (then) at $12,000.

Charlie was a scientist as long as any of us could remember, raising unsuspecting mice in his room, and launching them in spectacular three-stage rockets, public launchings before a crowd of friends and family shading our eyes and trying to follow the final stage as it sped into the sun, then cheering as the hapless mouse in his parachute came drifting back toward earth.

Charlie wanted to be the first man on the moon, but he was a solitary and idiosyncratic learner, and he found college antithetical. He enlisted in the Air Force in 1969, under the pressure of the Vietnam War. A computer made him a medic, and when he volunteered for the division of "physiological support," he found himself at Edwards Air Force Base in Lancaster, testing space suits in altitude simulators and hyperbaric chambers. Charlie was a distinctly unmilitary type, but he was precise and competent; at one point his picture was posted in headquarters as "Airman of the Year."

Meanwhile, our beloved middle sister Anita Maria (the first of four redheads, as if a suppressed Irish gene suddenly sprang into action) presided with quiet grace as student body president of the Convent of the Sacred Heart in 1969, before winging away to New York for a year at Manhattanville. Then she returned to what had once been the San Diego College for Women, reincarnate as the co-educational

University of San Diego, USD. (Our mother naturally moved from the Board of Trustees of the College for Women to the Board of USD, where she continued to serve with enthusiasm ad infinitum.)

Anita Maria was the child who most inherited Anita Figueredo's spirituality and her concern with the inequities of life on earth. She was contemplative by nature, given to regular meditation, the study of dreams, and a serious preoccupation with peace and the relentless destruction of the planet. Her original degree from USD was in psychology, and she would eventually work as a spiritual psychologist, guiding others to a deepened experience of inner wholeness. She would also found and direct a community resource center for peace. But that was in Montana, later on. Just now, in the middle seventies, she "succumbed to the lure of medicine," as our mother put it, and pursued a graduate degree in child health at the University of Colorado in Denver.

Our youngest brother, Rick, was finding himself in the early 1970s. Rick was wildly energetic, impulsive and frequently in trouble. All this exploding energy often ricocheted off the nearest brothers and sisters, and off the Sisters of the Holy Cross. Despite high intelligence, Rick could not sit still in a classroom and seemed not to hear what he was told. As a last resort, he went to Boyden's, a little old downtown San Diego school where there was a burgeoning understanding of hyperactivity and distractibility. And there, with one-on-one tutoring, Rick did good work, and finished high school a semester early, the week he turned seventeen.

Rick was a man of great enthusiasms, and one of his deepest affinities was with medicine; he would have loved to be a doctor. Yet he could not face eight more years in school. The year he was seventeen, he heard about a six-month course for operating room technicians, and was off to San Francisco. The course so engaged him that he had time to tutor other students while graduating at the top of his class. Back home in San Diego, Rick found work as an "O.R. Tech" at Doctors' Hospital where he stayed for the next three years.

While all this was going on, little Teresa was growing up as something of an only child, mostly in the company of Lita, and the maids, Alicia and Ofelia. She was precocious, having been exposed to uncommon things. When she had just learned to walk, Tommy called our mother and me to a garden window with the shade drawn, and then opened it to show us the baby toddling happily on the grass, with large snakes wrapped around her neck and around each arm and leg. Teresa learned the conventional things easily, and it is a Doyle characteristic to have peculiar intellectual passions; as Tom was unexpectedly devoted to palm trees, for instance, Teresa was to volcanoes. She was also an artist, and sometimes sat by our father's side as he painted, and made her own enchanting drawings. And then Lita took her, summer after summer, to Costa Rica, where she was admired much as our mother was forty years before. Anita's youngest girl more than once appeared on Costa Rican television, singing and dancing and playing the guitar. Although most of the Doyle children ultimately spoke Spanish well, Teresa was the only one truly bilingual all her life.

She would eventually earn a doctorate in physiological psychology. But when I was married in the first week of 1970, Teresa was a ten-year-old flower girl with gleaming red hair to the waist of her purple dress. And when the decade was out - her last older sibling married, and the first ones divorced - she was just coming of age.

Whether or not eight children in one family have ever been raised without pain and trouble to adulthood, I cannot say. Certainly every time and place has its own difficult history, and the 1960s and 70s were no exception for our family. Among them, the children of Anita Figueredo and Bill Doyle suffered and survived - or did not survive - the common traumas of their age: failed marriages, encounters with alcohol and drugs, detours on the search for meaningful work, and loss of religious faith.

Our mother's childhood cannot have prepared her for all this, and our grandmother was loudly scandalized at times that we were not kept more in line. Perhaps the odd thing was that our mother was not scandalized. Here she was, with the strictest sort of moral and religious view for herself, and she was somehow able to look benignly on as we tried to grow up. She never lectured, as far as I know, and she made it clear that her love was unconditional. She prayed, all the time.

When Charlie turned forty in the summer of 1989, our parents were out of town (with Anita Maria's family in Montana) and some of the siblings gathered to celebrate the birthday. The talk turned to our relationships with our mother.

Charlie: She took the time to listen. She had an open-door policy, and was always available. She would stop what she was doing. I was a private person, and didn't like growing up in a "famous" family, didn't like others having preconceived ideas of who I was. But I was proud of Mom, never resentful. And I was delighted to have new babies. I adored them. Mom had a good business mind and good connections [and] co-signed practically anything for her children. She didn't require a financial sheet. She just gave money to anything the children believed in.

John: Mom never thought I was stupid. She always listened, never lectured, let me make mistakes. **I** lectured **them** [Mom and Dad], but Mom never reacted. Mom thought so well of her children and assumed they didn't really mean anything rude. I idolized Mom, and had plenty of her time. I walked right into her office whenever I wanted. I was bothered by their going out at night, and by the phone ringing all through dinner, though it was mostly for Dad. Occasionally an outsider said something negative about Mom, but I knew they couldn't know her.

Billy: I was estranged from the family, except Mom. I could have a conversation with her any time. She was interested in me, and listened without judgment. I never felt cut off from Mom. She was my link to what was going on in the family. I was never resentful [of other demands on her time]. She was accessible to me at all times, capable of waking from a dead sleep and being interested. When I was talking to her, she never looked at her watch.

Dian (Ricky's widow): Rick was so proud of Mom. He thought she was a saint. She loved him in spite of himself, and he was always forgiven. She was always there when the going got rough. She stopped and listened. I myself was intimidated while Rick was alive. It was too hard to accept that Mom was sincere, genuine, that she really gave unconditional love and was free of prejudice; I had come from such a different background. She influenced my life tremendously. She is my role model in forgiveness, understanding, and spirituality.

CHAPTER 30

Sabbatical

In the spring of 1972, Anita perceived that her oldest daughter and son-in-law were about to finish their training in San Francisco as pediatrician and surgeon. She understood that we were not intending to move to La Jolla, that we could only be happy "in the mountains," and that, in any case, we were committed to fellowships right where we were. She understood this perfectly, and only wanted to suggest that we postpone the fellowships one year, come down to La Jolla and take over her practice and Bill's for six months to allow them a little sabbatical. We could earn enough money to travel in Europe before committing ourselves to the rest of our lives in one place.

This seemed like such a reasonable idea that we walked into it with our eyes open, and by the time Anita and Bill returned from their respite, we were so entrenched in private practice that we canceled our fellowships and settled in for the duration, as Anita, of course, had foreseen all along.

The sabbatical took Anita and Bill to the Holy Land. In the fall of 1970, right after Charlie's marriage and before the opening of the original Ocean Fresh cafe, our parents were invested as Knight and Lady of the

Holy Sepulchre, a papal order and the oldest order of knighthood in the world in continuous existence. This high honor of the Catholic Church commits its members to the work of keeping alive a Christian presence in the Holy Land, while helping all the living inhabitants achieve a measure of peace and a decent life.

Newly-invested members generally make a pilgrimage to the Holy Land as soon as possible, and this was the first order of business when Anita and Bill began planning their leave from the practice of medicine. Then it so happened that they attended a Holy Sepulchre meeting in Texas and a keynote speech by the American director of the Pontifical Mission for Palestine. The speech dealt with the Palestinian situation in all its misery. Anita was so moved that she waited afterward to talk to the speaker. The speaker, Father John Nolan, was a decisive man and a quick judge of character; he was due back in New York, but after talking to Anita and Bill for a few minutes, he bought a ticket to California and flew along with them just to talk. Before the plane landed in San Diego and he re-boarded for New York, Father Nolan convinced them to travel in an official capacity to Palestine, in order to assess the medical situation in the refugee camps.

And so they went, under the auspices of the Pontifical Mission for Palestine, to Beirut, to Jordan and to Israel, the week the Israeli athletes were murdered at the Munich Olympics by Palestinian terrorists.

Because of the massacre, security measures were abruptly tightened and interminably long, and Anita and Bill arrived eight hours late in Beirut, about 10:00 P.M. They apologized to their waiting Greek escort, saying that they hoped he would now be able to go home and get a good night's sleep. "No," he said, with a tired smile, "I must return at 3:00 A.M. to pick up a nun from India." Anita and Bill looked at one another, and then proceeded to their hotel in Beirut only long enough to freshen up and eat a small supper. Then they returned to the airport to meet Mother Teresa of Calcutta, and bring her back to their hotel room for what little remained of the night. Mother Teresa did not sleep; she did accept two apples from a basket of fruit in the room, one for her breakfast and one for her lunch.

The travelers compared their itineraries and discovered that they were the same: Beirut to Jordan and Israel, and then New York. Ultimately, the three spent a total of ten days together, mostly in Jordan where Mother Teresa was organizing a house in Amman for the people of the desert.

In Lebanon, Anita and Bill began the work of medical inspection, touring mobile clinics, schools, and orphanages. As it turned out, their exit from Beirut was abrupt and under cover of night. Tension crackled in the city during their stay, and on the fifth day their escort announced, "I cannot permit you to travel by air tomorrow. You must leave here during the night and reach the Syrian border by dawn. I will send my driver at 3:00 A.M."

They thus found themselves in the back of a car, hurtling along due east from the Mediterranean coast in the black Lebanese night. By daybreak they reached the border crossing, and as they approached they were aware of much excitement among the guards. The driver asked and answered questions and, as they drove away into Syria, informed Anita and Bill that the airport at Beirut was closed, having been bombed and strafed within the hour by Israeli forces.

The group stopped for baklava and strong coffee in Damascus on "the street called Straight" (Acts 9:11) and then continued on south, past sun baked mud houses, into Jordan and the desert city of Amman. The distances among the uneasy capitals of the Middle East are small; anyone who has driven around New England in search of autumn leaves will recognize the size of the narrow rectangle of Beirut, Damascus, Amman and Jerusalem, in the route through Vermont and New Hampshire.

The Hashemite Kingdom of Jordan is mostly arid, but the pinkish-white capital sits at some elevation, and Anita and Bill were comfortable in the September sun as they walked through Palestinian refugee camps with their guide. Bill was soon taken off by Irish Franciscan nuns who were resuscitating infants nearly dead from dehydration; the nuns were attempting to set intravenous lines in tiny collapsed veins, and Bill was a master of this particular art.

Meanwhile, Anita was taken to see a little pathology lab where nuns were reading Pap smears and referring women with cervical cancer for hysterectomy, the only treatment available at that time, no matter how early the lesion. In the West, conization - removal of a cone-shaped bit of cervical tissue through the vagina, under anesthesia - is standard treatment for very early cancers. But Islamic law prohibits vaginal exam or treatment by men, and so women in the camps with abnormal Pap smears were subjected to abdominal hysterectomy (whenever they could get it), or nothing. Anita, therefore, gathered the nuns together and taught **them** the proper vaginal exams and therapies. Years later she learned that she had revolutionized medical treatment of women in the camps.

Anita and Bill were two weeks in Amman, and when Anita was not in the camps she was with Mother Teresa who set about the business of making a home in the city for "the mentally and physically impaired." These unfortunates had been carted off into the desert by the municipal authorities to a clump of little concrete huts, and left to care for themselves between weekly visits from the outside. Water distribution, Anita observed, was by a mentally-retarded boy who carried the precious liquid around in a leaking can, with a trail in the dust as he went. The Missionaries of Charity were "invited" to live with these folk in the wilderness, but Mother Teresa informed the government that the inmates belonged in the city where the people of Amman could learn the joy of caring for them properly.

From Amman, Anita and Bill proceeded west again into Israel, where their guide was a portly Franciscan priest named Father Godfrey, who is **the** guide in Israel for all visiting VIPs, including U.S. presidents; Anita and Bill had him all to themselves for ten days as they followed the pilgrim's route from Jerusalem to Galilee, Bethlehem and Nazareth.

From Israel, they flew to Rome and a private audience with Pope Paul VI to whom they reported on their mission. (A marvelous picture of the three of them, Anita in a black veil, was printed in the *La Jolla Light*. This was clipped out and sent to them by a friend with the handwritten comment, "Anita - Bill - Beautiful Picture! Who's the guy with you?") From Rome they flew into New York and a final visit with Mother Teresa in Harlem, and then home. A few months later, a letter from Calcutta began, "I still think of you in Amman - how Jesus brought us together..."

Back in La Jolla, Anita Figueredo and Brent Eastman began surgical practice together, taking turns seeing patients in the office in back of "417," and assisting each other in surgery at Scripps Hospital. (Likewise, my father and his partner Dr. John Welsh and I formed a comfortable alliance until my father's retirement in 1977.)

It was a very happy interlude for Anita. She had never had a surgical associate in her own office, and missed the camaraderie of her residency days. Working every day with Brent was "like an infusion of new life." She thought him a surgeon with "gorgeous skills." Their daily interaction was "terrific, exciting, wonderful"; and as Brent admired her as much, they had a lovely time.

The partnership lasted two years. Then, over the Christmas holidays of 1974, the four Eastmans and Doyles were out to dinner and discussing cases, as we often did. Brent was describing a patient having "crescendo transient ischemic attacks" or "T.I.A.s," meaning rapidly increasing symptoms resembling minor strokes. A week later, when we were all out to dinner again, Anita found herself looking around for a draft: she had the uncomfortable sensation of cold air blowing across the left side of her face. Then she realized she was numb along the left side of her tongue, her lips and her cheek. The sensation lasted thirty or forty minutes.

The next day the symptoms reappeared, disappeared and reappeared, until they were present nearly all the time. Soon her left arm and leg became numb, although so far there was no paralysis. Characteristically, Anita perused her full calendar and decided she could see a doctor Saturday morning, several days away, before an operative case at 11:00 A.M. Her calendar was especially crowded at this time because she was in the process of founding a bank.

The year before, she was persuaded by a local group of professional and business-women that something must be done about unfair banking practice as related to women. In the early seventies, it was still difficult for a woman to obtain credit on her own. Anita Figueredo herself had no such trouble by then, but she was always intrigued by injustice. As soon as she agreed to join the organizing board of The Women's Bank, she found herself in highly technical and sometimes rancorous meetings which began after work, consumed most Saturdays, stretched on into the night, and sometimes involved flying off to Sacramento. After a staggering amount of work, the bank charter had just been granted, and Anita elected chairman of the board, when she first felt the ominous "draft" across her face. By the time the Saturday appointment with her doctor rolled around, she was dizzy, and when her blood pressure was found to be alarmingly high, she was admitted to the hospital.

Up until this point Anita was more mystified than ill. She was fifty-eight, and had enjoyed spectacularly good health all her life, except for an annoying pain in the neck for the last three or four years. (The neck pain, which began at the base of her skull and radiated up over her head into her eye, was the end result of a several-week marathon of sorting and re-packaging **two tons** of sample medications for urgent shipment to Mother Teresa - hours and hours of bending over from her desk to rummage among boxes on the floor. The cure for the pain was to not bend her head; alternatively, she could wear a thick cervical collar, and for years she did, eventually acquiring a wardrobe of colorful scarves as camouflage, including white satin for formal wear.)

This time, however, was different. No sooner was she hospitalized than she became profoundly weak, unable to walk without assistance and scarcely able to lift her head. After a state-of-the art work-up, the final diagnosis was "transient ischemic attacks from spasms of the left vertebral artery." There was no real explanation for this and, what is worse, no real treatment. Her physicians could only recommend that she rest, take certain drugs every day to prevent clotting in her constricted blood vessels and forestall a stroke, and to retire for at least a year from surgery and hospital practice.

The distress of this loss was blunted to some extent by Anita's overwhelming weakness and fatigue. She could scarcely move, let alone operate. On discharge from the hospital, she was totally incapacitated and had to be carried upstairs to bed by Charlie and Bill. After a time her operating shoes, an ancient pair of small white oxfords, were brought home by Tom from her hospital locker, and bronzed.

CHAPTER 31

Illness

The decade of the 1970s was divided very neatly in half by Anita's illness. For the first five years she was well, her children were healthy (if not without personal struggles), and she herself was continuing her amazing balancing act: rolling the ball of her medical practice under her nimble feet, while twirling The Women's Bank, the Co-Workers of Mother Teresa, the University of San Diego, the Order of the Holy Sepulchre, and *Casa de los Pobres*, and still all the while juggling a clutch of romantic and financial family projects, not the least of which was a complex real estate transaction involving most of her own and Bill's retirement income.

Then all of a sudden, Anita's surgical life was swept out from underneath her, along with her stupendous energy. For a time she was unable to do anything more than lie in her bed at home under the glass wall of sea, with her mind active and clear behind closed eyes, trying to work out the words to persuade Bill to have her files brought upstairs. She imagined that she might install herself somehow on the balcony with a typewriter and a telephone. Before long, she modified her goals to just sitting up.

Weeks passed, and finally she could make her way downstairs to lie on the living room couch. After a little more time, she went out with Bill for her first ride in a car. She returned to find on her doorstep the get-well gift of a watercolor (shimmering grey doves) by her painter-friend, Eileen Monaghan Whitaker, and she fainted from excitement. Emotional lability was by far the oddest aspect of her illness; in this regard, she was totally unlike the "old" Anita. Heretofore, she was as unsentimental as a cat, and she never had her feelings hurt. Now she was easily wounded, or swooning from strong emotion. In fact, she first realized she was improving after an extraordinary argument with Bill, when he walked out of the room and she was so frustrated by her inability to follow that she threw a telephone at him - and did <u>not</u> pass out.

At any time, it would have been hard for Anita to "rest." Resting made her restless; she was not good at it. Even now she felt a pressing need to be on her feet. Primarily, she wanted to return to her patients. She loved being a doctor, even a non-operating one, and she looked upon her return to work as the only real symbol of restored health. Also, her income had ground to a halt, at the very moment her decades-worth of careful investments were slipping into the sinkhole of a self-destructing office building in Orange County. Brent Eastman had departed to a general and vascular surgical group based at Scripps; and Anita's excellent disability insurance was just enough to cover the salaries of her three office staff, whom she did not have the heart to let go, and who were sitting in the empty office, awaiting her return.

On top of this, just before Anita first took to her own bed, her mother was put to bed in Costa Rica with a re-fractured hip. (She broke it the first time in 1971, flattened in the dark driveway by Ricky's impossibly heavy motorcycle. She recovered, only to skid on a hall rug and into a closet within days of arriving in Costa Rica to visit Gladys.) Now Lita was dragging herself up, after a confinement of five months, and returning home weak and unsteady, to Anita.

Then, too, that spring, the city of Saigon was falling to the army of North Vietnam, and, as Anita's annual Christmas letter put it, this tragic event "provided her the opportunity" to install a Vietnamese family at "417." Our mother knew someone in Saigon, a Catholic nun named To Thi Anh; and now, from the living room couch and resting between sentences, Anita wrote "Anh" offering to sponsor her if she would flee to the United States. The blue envelope battered with tire tracks and mud reached Anh in March 1975.

Anh replied quickly that she could not leave her people, but asked that her younger sister and nieces be given her place instead. What was instantly needed, among other things, was a letter from the President of the University of San Diego awarding a full scholarship to the sister, To Thi Dien.

By this time, there were neither a Vietnamese postal service nor regular flights to Vietnam, and Anita still could not move more than briefly to her elbow to dial her phone. What transpired is documented in a letter from Anita to President Hughes of USD, in which she recounts the "chain of rescue" which somehow gets the precious document to the chaotic and terrorized city of Saigon, and out from under the cap of a stranger on a bicycle into the hands of To Thi Dien.[208] Dien and her children left the country within hours, taking with them two suitcases, one containing a change of clothing, and the other a pound-and-a-half of gold and Dien's diplomas from the Sorbonne and from Duke University. Only the suitcase with the clothing arrived in the United States.

In the last week of April, I found myself driving my mother, lying back in the cranked-down passenger seat, through an immense refugee camp in Oceanside, California, looking for this sister of a friend and her two little girls, aged seven and ten. As it happened, it took more time to find the family at the camp in Oceanside than to get them out of Vietnam. Anita and I gave up after searching for what seemed miles of Marine Corps brush and sage, and leaving notes on tent flaps. Only some days later was the exhausted trio actually found and packed into our car and then into the Doyle home.

Anita's stamina gradually improved and, before her Vietnamese guests moved out on their own about five months later, she forced herself to return to her office half-days or, to be precise, alternate half-days from 9:00 to 12:00, followed by a recovery period of the rest of that day and all the next. Between patients she sometimes lay on her office carpet.

Her office practice always defied traditional categorization because she was a surgeon-specialist who also provided primary care to patients without surgical problems, by way of her regular cancer detection exams. And since, in addition, she had a small army of recovered cancer patients whom she followed for life, Anita was able to give up hospital practice and still stay as busy as she could manage.

It **was** hard, though, for patients who needed surgery to adjust to being referred elsewhere, and Anita briefly wondered about attempting to operate again whenever she recovered. But finally she decided that she "wouldn't get any better at surgery after being out for a year, and then perhaps wouldn't have the sense to quit." She decided that she had fallen into a fortuitous semi-retirement. Members of her extra-curricular boards came and met around her living room couch in the afternoons, and discussed their business as Anita lay staring at the ceiling.

The pictures of this time show nothing unusual. Here she is, with her upswept white hair, smiling and accepting an award from the Soroptimists[209], and here cutting the ribbon for The Women's Bank. She even made another trip with Bill to the Holy Land and Rome; and then, as the months rolled around into 1976, to her 40th reunion at Manhattanville College, to Minnesota on retreat with Mother Teresa, and seemingly all over the southwest and Mexico on Holy Sepulchre business with Bill, who was Head of the new Western Lieutenancy of the Order.

None of this activity, she later said, was as difficult for her as their regular Friday nights at the symphony, where she had to sit up straight and crane her rebellious neck to glimpse the musicians, and she generally fled to the ladies' room couch to lie down after intermission.

By the end of the second year, Anita felt that her life might really be returning to normal. She could work longer half-days in succession, and her devastating fatigue was appeased with shorter naps. She had not had a stroke, and her left-sided numbness bothered her less often. And then Tommy began having headaches.

It was during the year he finished the big restaurant. There was the stress of the business, of course, the almost crushing success. There was something of burning the candle at both ends, of late nights at the burnished mahogany bar and of beautiful women. His old allergies. Migraine. But ultimately, none of these explanations was enough, and one day Tommy entered the waiting room of a specialist in headache, sat down in a chair, and had his first convulsion. The brain scan that afternoon showed a tumor the size of an egg buried deep in the left side of his head.

CHAPTER 32

Tommy and Lita

The tumor in Tommy's brain was discovered just after Christmas 1976, and partially removed in the first days of 1977. He was twenty-eight years old. Before his surgery, Tom was rather less concerned about dying than being paralyzed or left helpless. We were all cheered somewhat by the fact that he was left-handed; the tumor lay in the left hemisphere, which was the dominant side for the average right-hander but seemed less threatening to Tom. Gathered around his hospital bed, we tried to fix him in our own brains as he was then. He was his mother's son in the face of adversity, smiling and reassuring, helping us all through a trying time.

On the morning of surgery, the family sat and stood, waiting, in the hospital chapel - except for Anita who slipped into her operating clothes for the first time in two years, and stood at the neurosurgeon's elbow. What this good man thought about having the patient's mother looking on is not recorded, but he had known Anita for a long time, and did not attempt to dissuade her. When the tumor was isolated, a biopsy specimen was sent for analysis, and the little group in the operating room waited in silence five minutes or so, until the pathologist's somewhat hesitant voice was heard over the loudspeaker: "I have the report...Shall I give it now?" The surgeon looked at Anita, who nodded, and they heard that the tumor was a "Grade 3 astrocytoma" meaning highly malignant and, so far, incurable.

Cancers of the brain are different from cancers elsewhere in two respects: on the one hand, there is no fear of distant metastasis, they do not spread far; on the other hand, they are almost never cured by surgery. The principle of "wide excision" is useless where every cell removed takes with it a bit of normal movement or personality. In Tommy's case, what was done was to "de-bulk" the tumor, and to hope for the best from radiation and chemotherapy.

After a long while, Anita came in to the chapel to report that Tommy was awake in the recovery room and had raised his right hand to show that he was not paralyzed. She told us about the cancer with a sad gravity, as if she was sorry to be the bearer of bad news, but not as though she herself was crushed.

That first night after the diagnosis, however, Anita went to bed intensely worried and praying for guidance; and this came to her suddenly, she later said, as "a flooding of my being with all the scriptural passages I had ever heard relating to death - 'though I walk through the valley of the shadow of death, I will fear no evil, for thou art with me'; 'O death, where is thy sting? O grave, where is thy victory?'; 'I am he that lives, and was dead; and behold, I am alive for evermore', and so on. I realized that I was having a tremendous spiritual experience in which God was speaking to me, and the effect was that my anxiety for Tom, and for ourselves, floated away."

A day or so later, a friend told Anita that it was "cruel that Tom should have the very disease you have devoted your life to curing." But Anita did not agree. "On the contrary," she said, "I feel that I have been in training all my life for this very thing - to help Tom and sustain us all."

Tom was "given" five years to live, and he exceeded his allotted span by four months. In the end he survived his cancer, but not the cure. His disease was treated very aggressively, as he himself wished, and he had a "good" ten months, a second operation (in which a cyst was found in the old tumor site, but no cancer), another good several months, and then a long and poignant decline. Early on there were subtle changes evident to the family, the most startling of which was that Tom agreed to a proposal of marriage.

Our dark and handsome brother had spent his young manhood evading matrimony. At his side during the first hospitalization was a lovely-looking, sweet girl who never seemed to grasp the significance of what was happening to the man she loved. After surgery, Tom's brain underwent several weeks of radiation, and then months of chemotherapy. With time he became more docile, less able to think things through. Charlie, who left the Air Force, assumed the running of Ocean Fresh with his brother only nominally in charge. Tom still appeared at the restaurant most days, with his bald head covered by a series of old caps, and his growing confusion peeking through. Then he announced that he was going to be married.

There were conferences with his intended, who smiled radiantly in response to all doubters. There was a bridal shower, a rehearsal dinner, and a garden wedding in which all the participants, including the central couple, moved like actors in a strange play. The best man was the elderly widower who lived next door to the Doyles; Commander Gregory loved Tom like a favorite grandson, and was unhappy about the proceedings. Yet Tom on his wedding day was nearly his old self. He was persuaded to trade his cap for a white fedora with a wide brim which he wore at a rakish angle, above a neatly trimmed full beard and thick moustache. His wine-red velvet jacket was beautifully cut, and a handsome counterpoint to his bride's long white gown.

A month or so later, Anita wrote in her annual Christmas letter under a picture of the wedding party that the event was "a particularly joyous occasion...because it marked a public affirmation of faith in the future which in January would have been unthinkable." By that time, however, the bride was having second thoughts, and within a year or so she left.

Tom was bewildered by his wife's defection and lonesome in a way that he had not been before. He kept a separate house with a sea-urchin gatherer named Mike as a roommate, but spent most of his waking hours with our parents and Lita. Our father retired from medicine after thirty years of practice in order to paint full-time; he and Tom did projects around the house, laying Mexican tiles in the garden, and nurturing the rare varietal palms that Tom had planted in his International Palm Society days. The two of them cruised to Scammon Lagoon off Baja California, to the winter home of the gray whales, and much of what Tom, the fisherman, once knew about whales seemed to come back to him.

Anita realized only slowly how much Tom had changed. He began to spend long hours just sitting in our parents' living room, looking out to sea, and Anita was distressed by the seeming aimlessness of his days. She kept thinking that the "old" Tom, whose energy nearly matched her own, would hate having nothing to do. She sent him for occupational evaluation and was astonished by the social worker's report, which began: "This apparently healthy, disheveled young man..." Anita's son, who once turned heads with his stylish grace, now drew curious looks with his lopsided wig and shuffling bare feet in old Mexican sandals.

Nevertheless, Anita kept trying to rehabilitate Tom, although she realized, at some level, that he was happy as time passed just doing nothing. She talked him into work-outs at a gym, and an evening art class at the university on the edge of town, to which he rode the city bus. At last, one midnight the doorbell rang, and there was Tommy. He missed the bus, and waited and waited in the dark until he became frightened and started walking. A woman passerby watched this elderly-looking young man wandering through the trees of the dark campus, and picked him up in her car, and brought him home to his mother. With that, Anita abandoned rehabilitation.

Tommy and Lita slid away from life together, and they became very companionable in their last years, as they never were when they were both strong and strong-willed. Their relationship ruptured completely for a time while Tommy was a teenager, over Lita's discovery of a young woman in his bed, and it was only his illness which restored him to his grandmother's expressed affection.

Lita herself changed drastically during a trip to Costa Rica in the summer of 1977. Ordinarily these visits lasted months, as if Lita finally meant to live out her old age there, surrounded by properly attentive relatives, with or without Anita. But this time, she wrote within a few days of her arrival, asking to come home because she was "exhausted." This remarkable request was alarming in itself; and when Lita returned, thin and frail and struggling anxiously through customs, it was clear that something had happened to her. Usually she reappeared from Costa Rica revitalized and plump from all the creams and cakes of afternoon tea.

Lita was losing certain faculties, probably from minor strokes. She who managed the household accounts was now unable to keep track of her own money. She complained of not being able to read, and had her glasses changed more than once before we realized that the problem was not her vision but her comprehension of the written word.

As it happened, Lita was only a little ahead of Tommy in these losses, and he slowly caught up. He began mounting the steps to his grandmother's house and sitting happily with her in front of the television, sharing her deep-fried pork-rinds and Pepsi-colas. When Tommy needed to nap, Lita lay down with him on her pink bed under the delicate porcelain angels, and Anita often found the two of them asleep together in the late afternoon.

It was Lita who raged against Tommy's death when it came and, clomping down her stairs and out the front gate, threatened to throw herself into the sea. The final event was a long seizure commencing in Tommy's own living room under the eyes of a hapless salesman, and ending two weeks later at Scripps Hospital. On the night it began, Tommy walked down the front steps of his house on his mother's arm and lay down in the ambulance at her request, but his eyes were vacant, and by the time he reached the hospital he had slipped into a twilight state from which he never awoke.

The family had many days to sit by his bed and ponder the metaphysics of Tommy's state, and we came to somewhat different conclusions. This was mine

For Tommy
1948-1982

My brother's gone. He left here Thursday
On the night train,
His sweet soul working out its passage
From his hurt brain
To God knows where. His strength and beauty
Wit and grace
All gone before, how could he stay?
Still that lost face
Had loving eyes, and which of us
Has so much
Love that this loss doesn't matter?
The wound is such
An old one now, you'd think mere time
Would wilt the pain.
But here's the old familiar anguish
Fresh as rain,
Here's the wishful thinking like cinder
In the eye,
And I cry for all the years of watching
Tommy die.

Our mother wrote an old friend that "Tommy's was as kind a death as you can imagine."   And she gave the eulogy at the overflowing funeral mass, a feat which the rest of us thought ranked with her more remarkable.   She spoke mostly, she said, to reassure the congregation that the doctors did their best, and that Tommy was greatly pleased to have beaten the odds against his living five years. Anita Maria's journal entry speaks of our mother as eloquent in her description of Tom's heightened "incandescent" awareness, the experience that he had "arrived," free of ambition at last, as there was nowhere left to go. After the service, the family gathered on the beach in front of "417" and watched a friend on a surfboard paddle out into the setting sun and scatter Tommy's ashes into the sea.

Lita lingered three more years, and died at the age of eighty-eight, in April 1985. Several months before, Anita found her mother in a heap on the floor by her bed, in the aftermath of a febrile convulsion. Lita was admitted to Scripps Hospital and properly treated for pneumonia; and when she woke up, was much annoyed at finding herself still alive. She extracted a promise from Anita never to take her to the hospital again.

Lita was too weak after that to climb stairs. In my parents' house, she was installed in a small sunny bedroom next to the kitchen; she had a walker and shuffled around her contracted world, looking for Anita, though often Anita had been there five minutes before. She did have to go to the hospital just once more, when she slipped on the dining room rug and broke her good leg, but Anita brought her home again as soon as she could be moved. And finally, Lita slept away her days in the family room itself, in the very midst of all the human traffic in and out the back door, so that she was not lonesome.

No one was surprised that Anita, joined by several of her children at the pulpit, gave Lita's eulogy.   She thanked the congregation for joining her in paying tribute to her mother and then gave an account of their shared history:

> Against the advice of her family, against the advice of nearly everyone (because it simply did not make sense), she decided to immigrate to the United States, a country she had never visited, with a language she did not know. She had no skills, except those of an upper class young lady of Latin America: she could sew, which means hand-stitching, embroidery and such. But her daughter, then age 5, wanted to become a doctor. All of you who have children know that you simply don't pay attention to what a five-year-old says she wants to do, because it can change at any time. But she did pay attention, and she decided that it could not be accomplished in Costa Rica, and that she would leave and come to the United States, and somehow arrange for that to happen. And so she did.

...in spite of the fact that I was in boarding school (for which she was struggling to pay), there was never any question in my mind that she was completely devoted to me. I never had a problem with my identity or whether I was being rejected by being sent away - there was never any question about it. And so I got the impression quite clearly that there was more to having your children know you love them than just "being there" - there was something else. And this was an extremely important thing for me to know in my subsequent life.

..she worked as a seamstress for many years. She had great pride in the fact that she had been selected to make Mrs. Roosevelt's inaugural dress...

In addition to this work as a seamstress in what we would now call sweat shops, she would do additional work because, of course, she never made enough at that to pay for my schooling. And so she would take out piece work. Many of you may not know what that is, but she would pick up [sections of garments that needed special work], threads drawn or embroidery, things like that; she would take the pieces out, distribute them to a group of people she had working for her, pick them up and return them to the shop.

And then in addition (because you couldn't make ends meet even with that) she ran a boarding house. One of the clearest memories of my high school or college days was getting up in the morning and finding that Mother had not yet gone to bed. She had worked the whole night through and she was ironing sheets. But this was the way she lived, and nothing was too hard for her.

But then, on the side, and this is probably the most important thing, she was the unofficial consul for Costa Rica. She never had the title, but everyone in New York who was Costa Rican or remotely related to Costa Ricans, somehow went to our house. They would get fed, they would get shelter if they needed it, they would get comfort, they would get help with their shopping - whatever the problem, Mother took care of it or would help them to take care of it. She was one of those people who could always solve problems. I was aware of this, because every time I would come home on vacation I would find strange people at the house; they were all part of the family. They were students who didn't have enough to eat and were homesick. They were sick people who had come from Costa Rica for treatment, who would get taken to the hospital.

A long time later, when I was on a voyage to Costa Rica after thirty years away, people, countless people, really dozens and dozens, came to me and said, "I'm so grateful to your mother, because when I needed it, she helped me." Or "I was out of a job" or "I was lonely," whatever, "and your mother helped me." So there are many, many people out there who owe her a great deal. And I feel that when it was my turn to need her, after we had married and moved out here to California, she came out to live with us, to help us raise the children.

I want you to know that it was she whose light guided my footsteps. It was she who taught me that nothing is unattainable, that if you work hard enough and you want something hard enough, you will do it. There were no barriers to be considered. There was never any thought of "You can't be a this or a that because you're a woman." That never came up, I never remember it being mentioned. You could do whatever you wanted to do if you really wanted to do it. You could never be too busy to convey to your children the fact that you loved them, and they'd never feel that you didn't really care just because you weren't always there. You could show them that you love them, and you could be happy. And I am so grateful to her for having been that kind of an example to me.

CHAPTER 33

Carrying On

If the 1980s were rewound like a video and played out again, one would see Anita Figueredo moving from joy to sorrow and back again, over and over, as though the machine had gone haywire.

Just before the decade began, she was sixty-two and had recovered enough physically to assume that she wasn't going to get any better. She was used to her neck pain and fatigue, wore her collar and lay down in the afternoon, and agreed to represent "AMASC at WUCWO". This translates as flying to the muggy interior of southern India as delegate of the International Alumnae of the Sacred Heart to the World Union of Catholic Women's Organizations. Bill sensed that this would not be his type of trip and stayed home.

On February 6th he got this letter:

> Darling -
>
> You can't believe how much I miss you! You were so right not to come. Absolutely nothing to do except for the meetings 8 hours a day, then the Eucharist (in 6 languages & 3 different rites so far) followed by dinner.

> You would die, but I'm getting along fine - it's much more my style than yours. I've even gotten to like cold fried eggs. They make them all at once about 6 AM and leave them out on a table until we pick them up for breakfast and wave away the flies a couple of hours later. The day starts with meditation - I'm squatting - at 7 AM before breakfast, then AM prayers. We bathe out of a bucket - really very comfortable when you get the hang of it. You collect some hot water from a trickling spigot & add it to a large bucket of cold, then dip out what you need....

This journey started with Anita smuggling chalices for Mother Teresa (who was the keynote speaker at the meeting.) The first step in San Diego was going around to local clergy and asking for extras. Anita's simple approach - "You only need one" - prompted a dozen disarmed priests to hand over their surplus gold. Then she appealed to Baskin-Robbins for a giant ice cream carton, and eventually made her way unbothered through Indian customs, hauling her treasure along in a barrel with a knotted string handle labeled "Metal Cups." Mother Teresa was pleased, and she wrote our youngest sister from Bangalore, "My dear Teresa, I am so happy to have your good mother here with me."

In the fall of this year, Anita's friend won the Nobel Peace Prize. The self-effacing little nun traveled to Norway for the ceremony, and that morning wrote Anita about it on the back of a little card stamped with the words "Oslo - December 10, 1979" and the Prayer for Peace of St. Francis. A few months later, Anita wrote back, formally requesting that Mother Teresa bring her nuns to Tijuana, Mexico. Anita had spent most of her adult life caring for the poor across the border, and her great dream was that Mother Teresa would join her there in founding a permanent house. And she finally did come in 1988. By the end of the decade, Anita had the deep satisfaction of getting to know the more than fifty nuns, priests and brothers of the Missionaries of Charity in residence in Tijuana - more "MCs" in one place than anywhere else in the world, after Calcutta.

Other exhilarations this decade included the garden weddings at "417" of Rick and Teresa; the births of five healthy grandchildren, in California, Montana and Oregon, for a total of ten; and the gathering of Anita and Bill and most of their progeny in a cottage on the Mexican coast to celebrate their fortieth anniversary.

A half dozen major honors also came Anita's way, including a four-year term as delegate to the National Advisory Council for American Bishops, for which she traveled every several months to Washington, D.C. There were two of these lay delegates, male and female, from each of thirteen regions in the country; so that Anita Figueredo was the one woman from California, Nevada, Hawaii and Guam most trusted to tell the Bishops what the faithful had in mind. And then there were other awards: "Living Legacy"; Ecumenical Tribute; San Diego Press Club Headliner, and American Cancer Society Honoree [210] - so many that the Doyle siblings abandoned our ordinary family dinners and just gathered in our evening clothes and brought each other up to date in the hotel ballrooms of San Diego.

In the background of all this, up to 1985, was the dragging decline of Tommy and of Lita. A photograph of Anita after Lita's funeral exposes the strain; she looks weary and almost gaunt, after more than five years of constant vigilance. But the next two years gave her breathing room, and she recovered, as always. She was most proud of the Honorary Doctorate of Humane Letters bestowed by her beloved University of San Diego in 1985 (only days after her return from carrying Lita's ashes home to Costa Rica.) Anita was the first member of the USD Board of Trustees to be honored in this fashion, reflecting several decades of service through good times and lean.

It is likely, in retrospect, that when Reverend Mother Hill built her lovely Spanish Renaissance school in Alcalá Park in 1952, the heyday of the women's college was already past. There is no question that the San Diego College for Women offered a fine, Catholic, classical education. The question was how many "modern" young ladies would continue to want it; and the answer seemed to be fewer and fewer as the 1960s dawned. I, myself, had a chance to offer that opinion when I enrolled as a freshman at SDCW in 1961. I actually had fantasies of winging away east to college, someplace like Wellesley or Vassar, at least **close** to some intellectual boys; but then I "won" a full, four-year scholarship to SDCW, and my fate was sealed. It was only when I interviewed my mother for this book that she confessed that *she* won my scholarship; it was her personal reward from Reverend Mother Hill for organizing and chairing the huge national alumnae conference on campus that same year.

The Religious of the Sacred Heart had always administered their own schools, but at SDCW they begin to look outside the cloister for fresh ideas; and by the mid-sixties, Anita Figueredo and one (Protestant) gentleman banker were asked to join the board of nun trustees. The burning issue before the new board was whether or not to merge the College for Women with the College for Men on the other side of the locked high gates, across the street. This question was extremely complicated by the lack of parity between the two schools. No professional teaching order, no Jesuits or Augustinians, were running the men's college; rather it was being held (barely) together by ordinary priests of the diocese, some reasonably well-qualified to teach, and others not. Academic standards and morale and finances were at a low ebb, and it is not clear who was in charge; the treasurer's reports were vague, but there seemed to be a lot of red ink.

For at least two years, from 1967-69, Anita attended one exploratory meeting after another, while the boards of the two schools tried to reconcile their differences so that a "merger" would not mean a "sinking" of the College for Women. The Women's Academic Dean, Sister Sally Furay, devoted herself to finding ways to unify disparate departments and curricula, and to eliminating duplicates without wholesale loss of jobs.[211] Each time the task force met, the Women's delegates set forth a list of requirements for upgrading the Men's College before union could proceed; and each time the Men's trustees agreed, and retired - and then at the next meeting, the same ground was covered again.

Then, in 1969, the new Catholic Bishop of San Diego, Leo T. Maher, arrived on the scene. Bishop Maher was a man of action who was ultimately devoted to the University of San Diego, and an energetic chairman of its trustees for many years. Now, however, he was annoyed to find that so much time had been "wasted" in non-productive talk about a merger. The Bishop convened a meeting of the two college boards. "I had never met the Bishop before," Anita said, "and he did not ask our opinion about anything.

> He stood before us, quite imperiously, and addressed his remarks to a place somewhere above our heads. He said he was appalled to find "this thing" dragging on for two years; he said he wanted the merger done and that he had come to lay down the law, which was that there was to be no more discussion.

> In the vacuum which followed these remarks, I looked around me. The other members of the Women's board were nuns who certainly could not defy their Bishop, and a Protestant gentleman who had no wish to offend. So I stood up and said, "Bishop Maher, I am Anita Figueredo, and I am speaking for the College for Women. If there really isn't anything to discuss, as you have just said, then there is no point to our staying in this room. We have been working on this union for years, trying to get the cooperation of the College for Men all that time, and until we get it, we cannot merge. If there is no room for further discussion, we consider that this meeting is adjourned, and we are leaving the table." And I turned on my heel, hoping the nuns would follow me out.

> There was dead silence. Then the Bishop said, "Wait, wait - wait a minute. There's no need for a Latin outburst like that. Come back and sit down, and we'll talk."

> So I did sit down, and we were allowed to explain what had been holding things up, what our problems were, and what needed to be worked out before we could merge. After that, things sped up. The Bishop insisted that the College for Men comply with our requests. It took another three years of hard work before a healthy University of San Diego was born in 1972, but it was a school of which we all could be justly proud.

On the USD Board of Trustees, Anita was vice-chair to her friend Bishop Maher for the next ten years, and then chair of the Academic Affairs Committee, and "a million other things." (By the time she had served forty continuous years, she was the only person to have taken part in both search committees - a quarter century apart - for university president: the first in 1970-71, for the enormously popular Author E. Hughes, Jr.; and the second in 1995, for Alice B. Hayes. "Under their leadership," Anita said,

> "I have had the opportunity to be a part of something that just keeps getting better. It has been a constant gratification to me to be associated with this University, now viewed by so many as a pearl of great price. Everything I see at USD is positive, working, developing, strengthening; it's a triumphant thing, USD!"

So now, on May 26, 1985, Anita Figueredo joined the procession of nearly nine hundred candidates for bachelor's and advanced degrees, at the Thirty-Second Commencement of the University of San Diego.[212] Tiny, in an academic gown trimmed with the velvet green of medicine, Anita lifted her head joyously to receive the sky blue-and-white satin hood of USD from the hands of Bishop Maher. President Hughes told the audience that Dr. Figueredo's life story had already inspired hundreds of modern young women at USD, and that she was a "role model for women who combine their dedication to home and family with a lifelong professional career." Then Anita stood on her mother's old footstool to deliver an address which was a straightforward call to the service of one's fellow man, both as a force for good, and as the talisman of personal happiness.

Nearly two years passed without serious incident. Then, at the age of thirty-four, our brother Rick drowned in full diving gear in shallow water.[213]

Bill got the call at home, from somewhere near the harbor, the call that said Rick had had an accident. The voice on the end of the line reported that Rick was on his way to University Hospital; when Bill pressed, the voice unhappily conceded that there had been no heartbeat for fifteen minutes.

That clear spring morning when she arose, Anita prayed in an unaccustomed way: Dear Lord, I offer you my prayers, works, joys and sufferings of this day. Then she said to Bill, as they dressed, "That's pretty easy, since we have no sufferings." The words were on her mind as she and Bill were driving to what awaited them in a small closed room, now redolent of the sea and the anguish of the youngest Doyle wife.

Anita's relationship with Rick always revolved to some extent around pain. She thought him the sweetest of her babies, and he remained that way always in her mind, but he was afflicted with physical pain from his teenage years, especially migraine. Blinded with headache, Rick called for his mother, and Anita responded; when he lived at home she tried all the conventional remedies, one after the other, and when those failed, she tried something else. Eventually intravenous Marezine, a drug for motion-sickness, brought relief; and after Rick married, Anita still got the desperate calls and climbed the steep hill to his ramshackle house, with her black bag in hand. Rick had back pain, also, the result of diving into barely-submerged rock, and a more-or-less failed laminectomy. Anita said, "I always had such a tender spot in my heart for Rick, because he suffered, and was so grateful for anything I could do."

And yet the years at Doctors' Hospital, where he worked assisting surgeons as an O.R. technician, were also happy ones for Rick, years to enjoy three of his favorite enthusiasms: his work, his love for all things Hispanic, and his great friendship with Tommy, who was four years his senior. That first winter of 1973, Rick was just twenty and Tom twenty-four, already the proprietor of Ocean Fresh Cafe. Tom took Rick with him fishing, ate and drank with him at Ocean Fresh, and welcomed him into his circle of friends.

In November of that year, the brothers joined our parents and sisters on a most memorable trip to Spain, a trip on which their first airplane turned back over the Atlantic with engine failure (and weeks later crashed in Spain); a trip on which Tom and Rick took off by themselves on a wild ride along the Costa del Sol, with Rick for once in charge and with the prettiest girl, on account of his fluent Spanish.

At "Doctors", Rick was assigned to the Emergency Room, which he liked and where his Spanish was very useful. Rick loved being half-Costa Rican and - with his red Irish hair and freckles - delighted in listing himself as "Hispanic" on his employment applications, in those early days of affirmative action. One day the hospital sent him as the lone medic on a small chartered plane to El Salvador, where his mission was to pick up, restrain and bring home a sailor who was psychotic and violent. Anita Figueredo happened to be attending a cancer meeting in Mexico City, where she got a pre-dawn phone call from "Rick Doyle in El Salvador" asking for advice about sedatives. Once she got over her disorientation, she gave him detailed instructions, and he brought off the mission as directed.

After that, there were two life-changing events: the first was that he began to lose Tommy, his idol and friend. Second, in a class at City College where he was making another try for a formal degree, Rick met his future wife, Dian. Dian herself at that time was beginning a recovery from despair, and she and Rick very slowly built a haven for one another - not always strong enough at first to keep the demons at bay - but eventually a place of comfort for both of them. Rick told Dian that what he wanted most in the world was a marriage like our mother and dad's, and that he thought he could have it with her.

Before their marriage, Rick got the "perfect job", as poison control specialist at UCSD Medical Center. He loved Poison Control, he loved being at a hospital like UCSD with its rescue helicopters, and its state-of-the-art Trauma Center. Everything in emergency medicine excited his interest.

About this same time Rick began ocean diving and, along with it, underwater photography which became another passion, and indeed a small business. Rick had long been a fine photographer and his pictures both in and out of the water line the walls of all our homes. He was especially proud of his prints of the Life Flight helicopters.

Rick and Dian worked and traveled, achieved their R.N. degrees and dived in the azure waters of Bon Aire. They wanted a house but bought a boat instead, and named it "Antidote." The year before Rick's death was the best in their lives. And in the end Rick died doing what he loved, and in the arms of his friends from Life Flight.

Anita stood up, once again, before a murmuring throng of mourners and spoke in a steady voice about her sweet and loving boy. This time, as the somber crowd filed out of Sacred Heart Church, a woman with brimming eyes embraced her and said, "Anita, how can God do this to you?" And Anita was heard to repeat the words of St. Teresa of Avila, who one day complained, "If this is the way He treats His friends, no one wonder He has so few of them."

But later Anita reflected:

> I am truly protected from the emotional reaction to disaster by placing it in God's hands. I do not suffer anguish. I am spared assigning blame, or grieving about what might have been, because I view it as part of God's plan.

A picture of my mother that will always stay with me is this one from 1988: seventy-two years old today, small and strong, grey and beautiful, still remarkably and radiantly beautiful. Seven of us who love her are celebrating her birthday, although my father is called away from his first glass of wine by the recurring illness of a widowed sister.

Our remaining party sits in a restaurant dining room. I have not seen before tonight the building's current reincarnation with its motif suggestive of the six days of creation, all the walls and ceilings studded with the remains of sea life, starfish, sand dollars, abalones and clams, and the spaces between tables filled with white plaster land animals from every continent and curious stuffed-suede cactus. Before this, though, two owners back, it was Ocean Fresh Cafe, our brother Tom's place.

I sit directly across the table from my mother, who is flanked by two of our surviving brothers, Billy and John. At the table ends are the last brother, Charlie, and my husband Brent, and then our son, Roan, who is fifteen years old. We have finished dinner. The focused light from the ceiling track bathes my mother's face and shoulders, and half-lights the faces of Billy and John, who are turned toward her in exactly the same posture of tenderness. I feel as though I am gazing at a fresco in a church. Mother is holding Billy's hand and talking to us about herself.

She is the person who consistently fascinates all of us. The least-guarded of women, she nevertheless rarely talks about herself in a family group; and thinking about it later, I realize that it is our father's absence which allows the conversation to settle as it does. Ordinarily, when our parents are together with us at table, the talk is of the details of their still-busy lives, their adventures and plans, and Mother is content to let Dad's enthusiasm speak for them both.

This evening starts off badly with some careless political jokes which I, usually over-sensitive to our father, inexplicably start; and he is provoked. Then the predictable cascade around the table of chagrin and annoyance, until our mother claims the right of honored guest and forbids further political talk. In the ruffled silence she tells her own joke - actually complete and actually funny, about an aged couple on a second honeymoon who can't recall what they did on the first - and comfort is restored.

CHAPTER 34

Ad Infinitum

In 1992, Anita and Bill celebrate fifty years of marriage. They spend the entire year doing it, before and after the actual magical weekend of August eighth.

For the weekend itself, they escape with their six grown children and spouses to the high desert of Santa Fe, New Mexico. We are fourteen altogether: Mother and Dad; Billy and his wife, Cecelia Smith; Brent and I; John and his wife, Sally; Charlie; Dian; Anita Maria and her husband, Ira Byock; and Teresa and her husband, Tom Liu. Charlie has spent months making a biographical video called *Remarkable Union* from a lifetime of pictures and papers; we sit together for the viewing in the library of La Posada Inn, sipping wine and laughing and wiping away tears. We gather in the cool morning for Anniversary Mass at old St. Francis Cathedral. We eat fine food, browse among paintings by Georgia O'Keefe, stroll through an 18th century Spanish colonial ranch, and sit under brilliant stars while the strains of Mozart's *Don Giovanni* fill the desert night. Altogether, it is a lovely enough weekend to be practically worthy of the occasion. Afterwards Anita and Bill go on alone to Taos for a private celebration of their own.

They have been home only a few weeks when they embark on their longest adventure of the year, a month-long cruise down the eastern coast of North America from the St. Lawrence River to the tip of Venezuela, and home through the Panama Canal by way of Costa Rica. At seventy-six and seventy-seven, they claim to be the youngsters on the cruise and in general are pretty spry, although Anita is nursing a wounded leg.

She has had a tiny sore which - on a little side-trip to Anchorage, Alaska - blows up overnight into a fulminant, raging infection which threatens "necrotizing fasciitis," meaning extensive destruction of the soft tissues of the leg. The original germ, a rare invader called *Nocardia,* may have come from her own garden. With very aggressive surgery by Brent, and industrial-strength antibiotics which poison her a little along with the *Nocardia*, Anita boards the "Crown Jewel" as planned. By the time the ship docks again in San Diego, she is walking without a limp; her skin is a little jaundiced, and she has been mostly too dizzy to eat, but she considers that something of a plus, as at least (she says) she doesn't have to diet.

In February of 1993, Anita and Bill are robbed of all their formal clothes, gold decorations and jewels. They have packed these things for a regional meeting in Pasadena of the Order of the Holy Sepulchre. As they are to gather with Cardinal Mahoney of Los Angeles, the occasion calls for white tie, black robes and, in Anita's case, black lace mantilla with Spanish comb. Also gold pilgrim shells, Crosses of Jerusalem, diamonds and pearls, and mink for the winter night, when the elegant robes are laid aside. As Anita Figueredo is not an acquisitive person, all these things have been given her as gifts, most of them by Bill. The spectacular triple-diamond ring, three perfect whole carats side by side on a platinum band, was presented years ago by a grateful patient. The woman had a cancer of the face, and was the widow of a Florida physician; she had moved, after losing her husband, to the Casa de Mañana. When cancer was suspected, she found Dr. Figueredo, who removed the lesion but refused to accept any payment. The patient argued; surely professional courtesy no longer applied, as her husband was dead and, in any case, could never have referred Dr. Figueredo a patient from Florida. No matter, no payment was due. The widow returned to have her sutures removed. Out of her handbag she drew a small purse, and from that a diamond ring. "I have no heirs," she said, "and you will do me another kindness by accepting this ring."

Since then, the amazing diamonds have rested entwined among the pearls (from Japan and from Spain) in a zippered case of Chinese brocade, except when they briefly adorn the most formally dressed Anita Figueredo. Indeed, they are resting in the little case inside the neatly packed bags, inside the trunk of Bill's car, inside the parking lot of the Norton Simon Museum of Art (where Anita and Bill have run in to see a few pictures, as they are in the neighborhood) - when the whole lot is stolen under the noonday sun and never seen again.

In due course it is found that, although there is a $2500 deductible on the contents of the car in general, the diamonds are insured separately for $10,300. When the check arrives, it transpires that $10,000 is precisely the amount needed by the nuns at Casa de las Pobres for their "City of Mercy," a home for the impoverished mentally ill on a barren rise overlooking Rosarito Beach, Mexico, and the check is passed on. All in all, Anita considers the robbery a gift from God, as do the Mexican nuns.

On Mother's Day, 1993, Anita is invited as speaker and honored guest to the one hundred and twenty-sixth commencement of the Southern Virginia College for Women - formerly Southern Seminary College. Dad and I go along. We set out on a sunny spring day for a flight to Roanoke, Virginia via Atlanta. Anita wears a sky blue dress with silky bow tie. She seems thrilled to be going back to "SEM." A quarter-century has passed since she was last summoned to Buena Vista to help celebrate the school's centennial.[214]

We have the last three seats on the plane. The tail flips from side to side in the turbulence so that our coffee sloshes heavily into our omelets, but Anita is unperturbed. For reading material, she has brought along a manila envelope postmarked "28 Aug 1985", across which she had written in big letters "READ!" This document has surfaced *after nearly eight years* from a great pile on her desk of papers which could not be thrown away until read; she says air travel gives her the perfect chance to catch up. In this case, the contents are political cartoons and commentary sent by a man who had heard Anita speak at the 1985 USD commencement, when she received her honorary doctorate, and who had been sent a copy of her remarks. He wrote:

> a note of thanks for sending your 'response' at the USD commencement. I've copied it and given it to all our children and kept the original for regular review. There is so much in it...a new and beautiful facet every time it's read.
>
> It has been a genuine honor and pleasure to know you... You bring to mind Mark Twain's description: "the calm confidence of a Christian with four aces."

Anita writes her correspondent a very charming letter, as if no time had elapsed worth mentioning, and Dad and I go back to our usual sorts of books. I am re-reading Fawn Brodie's *Intimate History of Thomas Jefferson*, in preparation for a visit to Monticello, and Bill is studying Dante's *Inferno* for a seminar in Fiesole, near Florence, Italy, where he and Anita are headed next. Anita will learn everything she needs to know about these two subjects by asking us.

At 6:00 that evening we are met at Roanoke Airport by a college van and two very kind members of the staff. An hour's drive through green forests and blue hills takes us into Lexington and the Inn at Union Run. This is a "bed and breakfast" filled with antiques; we have big rooms with high, soft beds and thick comforters, ceiling fans, and verandas.

After dinner in the private parlor, we are escorted to the May Ball at SEM. At the entrance to "Old Main" (Main Hall, Anita's school as a teenager), we find a large display on an easel of Highlights from the Life of Anita Figueredo: photographs, letters and clippings, and a current press release to community papers regarding this event.

The day of Commencement dawns sunny and warm. We are up at 7:30 A.M. despite our jet lag, and Anita appears for coffee in a pretty pink and gray dress with pink jacket made by her housekeeper, Ernestina, her primary couturier. On one lapel she wears a Jerusalem brooch with a large opal in gold filigree, with hanging small rubies and emerald. She looks distressed.

"I forgot my speech," she says.

There was a time when Anita never spoke from notes, but in recent years she has felt she gets "inspired" less reliably, and not always when in front of a microphone. So she has begun writing things down, though hardly longhand. Today's speech lies at home on her computer which was a seventieth birthday gift from her graying children.

Modern technology still triumphs. There is a faxed copy of the speech in the President's office, where Anita peruses it over Danish and more good coffee. I help dress her in her academic gown with its green doctoral stripes, overlaid with the hood of USD; instead of a mortarboard, she wears a soft, black velvet cap, which makes her look somehow otherworldly, like a small medieval alchemist.

Commencement takes place on the lawn sweeping down from Old Main, by the intimate Grecian colonnade where Anita received her high school degree in 1932. Today there are fifty-seven graduating seniors in violet cap and gown, in procession with Anita, the President, the Chairman of the Board of Trustees, and the academic faculty and deans. Dad and I sit looking on proudly from the front row.

Anita gives an address which is a thoughtful restatement of her remarks at USD eight years before. She begins by expressing her delight at being back at SEM, in its fresh identity as Southern Virginia College for Women, and speaks of the women's college in general as a proving-ground for female leaders, and of the confidence she herself had gained by "total immersion" in such institutions. She goes on to say that, as a private citizen, she has no earth-shaking news to impart except her own experience, and that

> My credentials as an advisor are that I have lived a very
> happy, full and fulfilled life. After 76 years, I would
> not want to change any of it. Living as I have been
> blessed to do is a wonderful experience.

She says that she attributes her "abiding joy" to several essentials, and encourages the graduates to consider them for themselves:

The first is FAITH, an unshakable belief in a personal God who loves us and who always deserves our trust. Such faith has given stability and serenity to my life...If you have not yet found it, seek it. Devote your energy and ingenuity to the search. And when you do find faith, cherish it, and watch it grow and flower and enrich your life.

Another...is PERSONAL INVOLVEMENT. Nothing is as expansive as love. The more you give, the more you have; the more you have, the easier it is to give, and the more satisfaction you get from giving. This world is full of the hungry, the oppressed, the sick, suffering and persecuted. We have the means, but must develop the social will to put an end to these evils.

Mother Teresa of Calcutta teaches us that we do not have to look across the world to find those most in need of our love and concern. They can often be found sitting across from us at the breakfast table, or at the next desk.

Finding them requires the development of yet another skill: CONCERNED AWARENESS. We must strive to develop awareness of others' needs with the same concern with which we recognize our own. To do this is to become involved, and involvement is risky and time-consuming, and may create more demand...We must learn to say "yes" when asked to help. Better still, we must learn to **offer** help, but that is an advanced stage in the development of this talent.

It is amazing, when we are willing to take this risk, how often it takes relatively little effort to do much good. If all of us use our talents, not just for ourselves, but for the good of others...then we will be loving one another and will perhaps fulfill the prophecy of Teilhard de Chardin when he said:

"Some day, after mastering the winds, the waves, the tides and gravity, we shall harness for God the energies of love. Then, for the second time in the history of the world, Man will have discovered Fire."

The warmth of the applause suggests that there are many in this small school "family" who share Anita's vision of the well-lived life. President Ripley rejoins her at the podium and bestows upon her the first honorary Associate Arts degree from Southern Virginia College for Women.

That evening, we have dinner at Tracye House, the President's Greek Revival style residence. In the intervening few hours Anita and I have walked the campus from upstairs down and end to end; the three of us have barely escaped a thunderstorm under the great arch of Natural Bridge (which was owned by Thomas Jefferson, and which has the initials of George Washington, surveyor, carved in its side), and have attended Mass at St. Patrick's Church in Lexington, where the pastor guesses Anita's identity from her picture in the paper, and says he is honored by her presence.

On the way back to college we drive through the adjacent campuses of Washington and Lee University and Virginia Military Institute, where Anita danced in her tender adolescence. At Tracye House, we find sympathetic souls, good food and wine, so much affection, and an annual tribute lavished on "the most distinguished alumna."

AFTERTHOUGHTS

The writing of this book ends here, in 1993, after the trip with my parents to Southern Seminary, and it ends because I have been researching and writing it for twenty years and Anita Figueredo shows no signs of slowing down. She could outlast me. It is time to assess whether or not I have answered the questions which drove me to write in the first place.

After all the documents are filed, all the interviews transcribed, Anita Figueredo is not fully explained. She possessed: intelligence, intellectual curiosity, academic aptitude, non-threatening physical beauty, grace and dexterity, predominant good health, stamina, the will to ignore illness, emotional stability, resilience, prevailing good mood, optimism, personal magnetism, friendliness and the will to listen, leadership, eloquence.

She also had: a transforming belief in the goodness of others, courage, the strength of her convictions, unwillingness to be offended, high energy, selective focus, organizational / management skills, willingness to take risks, impulse control / ability to delay gratification, thrift and a horror of waste, generosity, compassion, sense of fair play, resourcefulness, eyes to see and the will to do and cheerful disregard of obstacles in pursuit of a good cause. She was gifted with self-confidence, sound judgment, loyalty, the ability to love unconditionally, fertility and joy in family life and a pervasive and dynamic religious faith. Anita also had: one devoted parent, opportunity, sufficient wealth, live-in help, the freedom of the self-employed and an excellent life partner.

She lacked: perfectionism, introspection, a compelling need for peace and quiet, prejudice, any notion of personal limitation because of sex, destructive addictions, materialism. And she was fearless.

Many of Anita's best traits are direct genetic gifts from her parents. In her petite beauty, grace and physical dexterity she most resembled her father, and she also received Roberto Figueredo's charisma, open friendliness and generally sunny outlook. From Sarita Villegas came tenacious will and indifference to adversity, courage, high energy, selective focus, thrift and resourceful management, and generosity to those in need. Roberto and Sarita were both intelligent; but in her academic achievement Anita most resembled her German great-grandfather, Dr. Juan Braun, and she must have received at least some of her great intellectual curiosity from the voraciously self-educated General Rafael Villegas.

Anita's religious life was not familial. Of her direct lineage, only her mother's mother was traditionally pious. The rest of the family, including her father and his parents and Sarita's father General Villegas, were either truly irreligious or freethinkers. Sarita Villegas herself was of two minds during her lifetime - early on she was rebellious and willing to be married outside the church. Later on she returned to the weekly Mass, while holding herself aloof from parish life; and on her deathbed professed an Act of Contrition she had written out by hand on an old piece of paper. But Sarita was neither animated by faith, nor protected from the grief of her losses and disappointments. Unlike her mother, Anita was disposed by temperament to give thanks, possibly the heart of a God-centered life, and she never blamed those she loved - including God - for what sometimes went wrong. Then, too, at just the age when she was seeking her true spiritual home, she encountered the highly intelligent and attractive Religious of the Sacred Heart and cast her lot with them.

Apart from religion, Anita always believed that her mother's self-sacrificing devotion was the key to her success and, of course, Sarita's role was huge. But a different child exposed to exactly the same chain of events might relate the following history when she grew up:

I came from a broken home. My father's infidelity drove my mother away within a few months of my birth and she and I had to squeeze ourselves into my grandmother's small house with a lot of other struggling relatives. There was no future for a divorced woman in Costa Rica. When I was five years old, I was uprooted again and sailed off with my mother to an uncertain life in New York.

My mother had no English at first and no marketable skills other than sewing, so she worked day and night as a seamstress and still had to take in boarders to make ends meet. My father contributed nothing to my support except one $20 gold piece and I never saw or heard from him again during my childhood. Over the years my mother had various boyfriends and I used to pretend that one or another of them was my father.

During the day I was left in the care of neighbors, or even alone in an upstairs apartment. Then, when I was eight years old I was sent away to boarding school, and saw my mother once a week, if I was lucky, until I was twelve. After that we actually lived together part of one school year, but even then she was hardly ever home and I had to earn my lunch by walking a neighbor child to and from school.

I found my own high school - a girl's seminary in Virginia - arranged for my own admission and left home again within a month of turning thirteen and without even the proper clothes. My mother never managed to visit the school until the day of my graduation three years later.

By the time I returned to New York for college, and then medical school, Mother had her own life and we didn't have a lot in common. She was certainly proud of my becoming a doctor - that was her goal for me - but then I spoiled it all by deciding not to return with her to live out our lives in Costa Rica. I got married instead, and she never forgave me or my husband.

This bleak revision of Anita's history is factually true, yet completely false to Anita's own loving and completely positive interpretation.

After several decades of considering the question, I have come to believe that Anita's life flowered from the most felicitous assortment of genes and that her natural gifts both created and allowed her to take full advantage of opportunity. She was indeed blessed in her mother, her native and adopted countries, her teachers, her husband, her children and her wide community - and they in her.

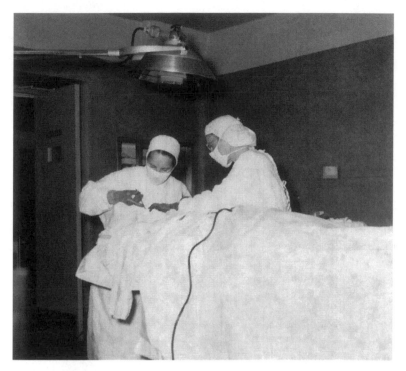

Anita plunges into her role as the first woman surgeon in San
Diego, 1948. Two years later, the *San Diego Union* publishes
this photograph of Anita as Mother of the Year, at home with her
five children, age six and under.

The Doyle home at 417 Coast Blvd, La Jolla. Inset: Anita's medical office at 418 S. Coast. Bird's eye view shows the proximity of the home and office to Scripps Memorial Hospital where Anita performed surgery.

1954: Receiving the papal medal "Pro Ecclesiae
et Pontifice" as her seven children, their father
and grandmother Sarita ("Lita") look on. Insert:
Anita at her office desk, looking serene. The 1961
Doyle Family Christmas photo is the only one showing
all nine children; the youngest, Robert, died the following year.

L - R Standing: Bill, Billy, Sarita, Charlie, John, Tommy
Seated: Anita, Bobby, Rick, Anita Maria, Teresa

Tommy   1948-1982   Ricky   1952-1986

Billy   Sarita   John   Charlie   Anita   Teresa

La Jolla, California   1988

Bill Doyle is an artist before becoming La Jolla's first pediatrician, and he continues to paint throughout his life. Costa Rican attorney and feminist Angela Acuña brought her cousins, Anita and Sarita, to the US in 1921; three decades later, she visits them in La Jolla, when she is honored as *Woman of the Americas.*

Anita begins a written correspondence with Mother Teresa in 1958 and meets her for the first time two years later in San Diego. These photos record a 1966 visit by Anita to Calcutta, cementing a loving friendship that will be refreshed by rendezvous in cities all over the world – and leads to the establishment of Mother Teresa's nuns and priests in the San Diego border city of Tijuana, Mexico.

 Through the charitable foundation established with a handful of close friends, Anita serves the poor of northern Baja California. The tradition continues as her youngest daughter, Teresa Doyle, takes over day to day operations.

317

1947

Love Story

1992

Spending the Night

A poignant phrase, *spending
the night*, conjuring coins
of time in a steadily
emptying purse. My old room,
the smallest and best,
tucked in the northwest
corner upstairs in this
seaside house, welcomes me
in as if thirty-five years
away is no time at all.

I was adolescent here,
a convent school girl, while
my youngest siblings went on
being born; and weekends
home from college I lay
on the bed reading Yeats
and St. Vincent Millay
as the tide of life
in the great house pulsed
and lapped outside my door.

Tenant here a decade
through the dream-time of my teens,
I'd emerge to play the Steinway
while my father painted portraits
and our mother saved the world.

She was glorious at forty
in the full flood of her beauty
and her will to be of service.
And here she is at ninety
still tiny, trim and upright,
still a force of nature
sorting medicines and castoffs,
reading out epistles
as the Friday morning lector
striding through an honor guard of love.

I've come home to keep her
company while Charlie is away,
so we dine by summer starlight
at the Cottage Café,
and then mount the stairs together
as we did when I last slept here
on the eve of my wedding -
when the circle of her arms
was so joyful in its blessing -
but no more so than tonight.

SDE - 2006

Epilogue

Anita Figueredo Doyle

August 24, 1916 – February 19, 2010

Anita Figueredo died exactly as she had lived, transcendently.

Shakespeare wrote in *MacBeth* of a flawed man who died bravely: *Nothing in his life became him like the leaving it.* But our mother Anita died exactly as she had lived, and **everything** in her life led directly to the way she took her leave.

We had a remarkable mother - Billy and I, John, Tom and Charlie, Anita and Rick, Teresa and Bobbie – and nothing in my own life, after marrying Brent Eastman and mothering our children, has given me as much pleasure as writing about Anita Figueredo. Condensing that life, that light, into 300 pages left Anita in her mid-70s, with 17 years unaccounted for, so this is a brief summary of what came before and what happened afterward.

Although Anita Figueredo no longer performed surgery after 1975, she did not abandon her beautiful office overlooking the rose garden but went on seeing hundreds of faithful patients, all survivors of cancer, until she finally retired from the practice of medicine in 1996 when she was 80 years old and celebrated with a sentimental journey to her beloved Costa Rica.

The following year Anita lost her friend Mother Teresa of Calcutta, thirty-six years after their first encounter in San Diego in the auditorium of Rosary High School. In a life full of accomplishment and joy, one of Anita's most joyful was to welcome the Missionaries of Charity to Tijuana and San Diego in 1988 and the MC nuns and priests into her home and into her heart. And in 2003, when approximately 350,000 of Mother Teresa's admirers gathered in Rome for her Beatification, Anita took her daughters, three of our children and a son-in-law and daughter-in-law as witness; and in the great, pulsating crowd spilling out from St. Peter's Square to the Tiber River, we watched on the big screen as the 87 year old Anita Figueredo sat in the front row with the new Superior of the Missionaries of Charity, Sister Nirmila, to receive Communion directly from the hands of Pope John Paul II and to honor her old friend.

Our father Bill Doyle, the husband whom Anita and God picked out on the first day of medical school, died in May 2000 after a struggle with pancreatic cancer that was mercifully brief. Anita and Bill had been absolute opposites and perfectly matched and they became their best selves in one another's company. Our mother and father had their first seven children in eight years and their ninth when Anita was 44 years old; they had two huge medical practices between them; they were pillars of the church, school, town and the wider community ad infinitum, and they never fell out of love.   Anita, along with her children, nursed Bill at home until he died in the bedroom they shared since they first entered the house on Coast Boulevard in 1956.

After our Dad died, and we children began organizing our days and weeks around our mother – not out of duty so much as the fact that we were all crazy about her - we used to joke that God must have other things to do besides keeping an eye on Anita Figueredo. We would take her out to lunch in an impossibly crowded La Jolla, and a parking space would appear, a table for four on the patio materialize out of nowhere; the clouds would gather when we needed shade and part when we wanted sun.

So it did not surprise us, when it came time for Anita to die, that she suffered a cerebral hemorrhage on Thursday February 4th – at her own dining table, with Anita Maria by her side – not on Wednesday the 3rd when Brent was far away; not on Friday the 5th when she would have been trapped with me and John on an Amtrak train bound for the Consulate of Costa Rica in Los Angeles, where Anita at 93 was applying for dual citizenship. She was at home with her daughter who caught her as she fell, and with Charlie and Satya nearby to summon help; she was taken directly to the hospital she loved and served her whole career, Scripps Memorial, where she was cherished and honored in return; and at the emergency room door she was met by Brent, returned from Haiti twelve hours before.

She had two days of brilliant and compassionate state-of-the-art intensive care at Scripps, which was just enough time for all her children to gather in the library named for her there, and to remember what she had told us about the inevitable prospect of her death - which was that she did not want extraordinary measures to extend her life, and did not want to die in an ICU. And on the third day we took Anita home.

In her beautiful, balconied upstairs room, the big bed she shared with our dad was moved to the southeast corner, and her hospital bed set up facing the ocean – which was wild those two weeks in February, with wind and rain and crashing surf some days, and others brilliant sun.

Anita was surrounded by her entire extended family. We signed up for four hour shifts, but the reality was that there were hardly ever fewer than half a dozen of us (and up to 19 or 20) at her side or reading in nearby chairs. We watched with her out her windows where shorebirds, pelicans and gulls wheeled around and tide pools stretched out practically to the horizon in the very low winter tides. Friends and relations, priests and religious from all over San Diego and Baja California came and went. Orchids, roses, tulips, stargazer lilies and "a host of golden daffodils" were everywhere.

Most of the time the first week, Anita slept peacefully, but woke to look at us carefully and speak to us softly in both English and Spanish. We read to her from *A Trail of Light* in both languages. On the fifth day, she held each of us individually in her arms for several minutes, touching our faces as if memorizing them for the journey, and caressing our hair. On the eleventh day, when Anita had refused food and drink for many days and seemed to have slipped beyond our reach, three of Mother Teresa's contemplative nuns came to visit and serenade her on the Echo Harp, and when we all laughed and clapped, Anita opened her eyes, smiled at them joyfully and clapped her hands high in the air. Anita took us with her as far as we could go and it was so like her to leave us with that last memory of joy and grace.

ENDNOTES

The Rich Coast

Chapter 1 - The Rich Coast

[1.] Calvo, Joaquin Bernardo. The Republic of Costa Rica. Trans. and edited by "L.de T." Chicago and New York: Rand, McNally & Co, 1890.

[2.] Jones, J. Bascom and Scoullar, William, Eds. of Latin American Publicity Bureau, Inc. The Blue Book of Costa Rica, 1916. San José, Costa Rica: Imprenta Alsina, 1916, p.46.

[3.] Guerra, Francisco. "Medical Education in Iberoamerica" in The History of Medical Education, C.D.O'Malley, Ed., Los Angeles: Univ. of Calif. Press, 1970. "The medical schools of Central America appeared rather late. Nicaragua, Honduras, El Salvador and Costa Rica depended on the University of Guatemala (1676) during the colonial period. Panama was part of Colombia until the opening of the Canal; its medical students went to Bogotá until 1951. Nicaragua established a medical school in 1814; El Salvador in 1847; Honduras in 1882; and **Costa Rica at San José in 1957, after an early trial in 1887.**"

[4.] Nelson, Harold D., Ed. Costa Rica: A Country Study. Area Handbook Series. 2nd Ed. Washington, D.C.: US Government Printing Office, 1970, p.11.

[5.] Blutstein, Howard I., et al. Area Handbook for Costa Rica. Washington, D.C.: US Government Printing Office, 1970, p.11.

6. Melendez, Carlos and Villalobos, José Hilario. <u>Gregorio José Ramirez.</u> San José: Ministry of Culture, Youth and Sport, Dept. of Publications., 1973, p.21.

7. Ameringer, Charles D. <u>Democracy in Costa Rica.</u> From <u>Politics in Latin America. A Hoover Institution Series.</u> Connecticut: Praeger Publ., 1982, p.33.

8. Fuentes Baudrit, Dr. Hernán, President of the Academy of Genealogical Sciences of Costa Rica. Letter to author, 18 Jun 1987, enclosing extracts of *reseñas* (historical reviews):

1. "Carrillo Family, I and II", by Eliado Prado. *Revistas de los Archivos Nacionales, 1940, Tomo IV, Nos. 7-8, 9-10.*

2. "Alonso Bonilla, founder of the Bonilla Family", by León Fernández. *Revista No. 2 de la Academia Costarricense de Ciencias Genealógicas,* 1955.

3. Genealogical tables of the Bonilla and Carrillo Families, *Genealogías de Cartago, Tomos I y II,* by Mons. Victor Manuel Sanabria y Martínez, 1957.

Chapter 2 - Betrothal

9. "Compromiso Matrimonial Figueredo-Villegas". Engagement announcement in unidentified newspaper, San José, 1915.

10. Medals in possession of Roberto Figueredo's daughter, Anita Figueredo.

11 Padilla, Rosario de. <u>Antología de Poetas Costarricenses.</u> Private printing, 1946. Roberto Figueredo is represented by six poems with the translated titles: "Sphynx"; "Post- humous"; "Immortal Harmony"; "Love's Clock"; "To You, Bird Off-Course"; and "Why Did You Come?" RF is described by the anthologist as a "magnificent conversationalist who has contributed numerous and varied articles to newspapers and journals...He lived many years in Guatemala and has travelled in Cuba, Mexico and the United States."

12. Carta de Naturalización del señor don Rafael Villegas. Acuerdo No. LXXV. Palacio Nacional, San José. Julio 31 de 1882. Presidente de la República Próspero Fernández. Decree conferring naturalized citizenship on Rafael Villegas for important services to his country.

13. Baptismal Record, "Raimundo Rafael" Villegas. Parish of Nuestra Señora del Carmen, Abejorral, Antioquia, Colombia. Book 16 of BAPTISMS, **1852**; Folio 18, No. 78. Christened 13 Jan 1852 at "a few days of age," the son of Estanislao Villegas, a farmer, and Raimunda Arango, of that parish. Paternal grandparents: Nepomuceno Villegas and Josefa Bernal. Maternal grandparents: Miguel Arango and Higinia Montoya.

14. Arango Mejia, Gabriel. Genealogias de Antioquia y Caldas. Abejorral: 1st Ed., 1910. Medellín: 2nd Ed., 1942. Vol. 2., pp. 532-545: "Villegas." The "correct" Villegas lineage begins with don Felipe Villegas y Cordoba who was born in 1714 in Revilla del Campo, Burgos, Spain, and who emigrated to Antioquia, Colombia between 1740-42. The "Arango" lineage is given in Vol. 1, pp. 35-56; the emigrant was don Antonio de Arango Valdez, who was born in Villagonzay, Asturias, and who left Spain in 1655.

This entire vast work is replete with direct and collateral ancestors of Rafael Villegas Arango.

15. Decreto No. XXXXV. Presidente de la República Bernardo Soto. Avril 28 de 1885. Decree promoting Rafael Villegas to the rank of General of Division, for his role in the campaign against General Barrios.

Chapter 3 - The General and Chola Braun

16. Fischel, Gladys Mora de. Interview with Anita Figueredo 1984, San Diego.

17. Villalobos, Asdrubal. Editorial. "La Muerte del General" in the newspaper *La Prensa*, San José, 20 Sep 1922.

18. Gutiérrez Braun, Hernán. "Reseña de la Familia Braun" in *Anales de la Academia de Genealogia e Historia de Costa Rica 1974-1976.*

19. Cementerio General, San José. Tomo 3 Folio 283. Elena Bonilla de Brawn (sic) 17 Jan 1883. Juan D. Braun 12 May 1885.

20. Vargas Coto, Joaquín. From the obituary "La Muerte del General Villegas" 21 Sep 1922. Reprinted in *La Nación*, 10 Feb 1970 in the column "El Dia Histórico."

21. Marriage Petition, Rafael Villegas and Rafaela Braun. Curia Metropolitana, San José. Book label 257 - 1856 - I. No. 300. 9 Julio de 1886. Recaredo Bonilla appears as witness as closest male relative.

22. Villegas letter, 13 Jul 1886. Rafael Villegas to his fiancee, Chola Braun, from the town of Carrillo, Costa Rica.

23. Villegas, Rafael. Páginas de Antaño San José: Imprenta y Libreria Trejos Hnos., 1927.

24. Calvo 1890, p.273.

25. Villegas letter, 1 Dec 1886. Rafael Villegas to his wife Chola Braun.

26. Fernandez Peralta, Ricardo. "Familia Villegas-Braun. Hijos del Gral. don Rafael Villegas Arango y de doña Rafaela Braun Bonilla." Un-named publisher, San José.

Chapter 4 - The Birth of Sarita Villegas

27. Fernandez Peralta. "Familia Villegas-Braun."

28. Villegas, Páginas 1927.

29. Salvador 1892. Bulletin No. 58 of the Bureau of the American Republics. Washington, D.C.: 1892. Revised to March 1, 1894.

[30.] Acuña de Chacón, Angela. La Mujer Costarricense a través de Cuatro Siglos. Vol. 1. San José: Imprenta Nacional, 1969, p. 279.

[31.] Calvo 1890, p. 156.

[32.] Villegas letter, 1 Dec 1886.

[33.] Salvador 1892.

[34.] Villegas, Páginas de Antaño 1927. These are Rafael Villegas' memoirs of the years 1894-97, published in bound form 5 years after the General's death. The first half consists of the "Autobiography" preceded by a eulogy. Following this are 14 essays on various topics, and finally a second eulogy.

One day in 1908, the General was stung by a letter to the editor of the newspaper *La Republica* which accused him of being an agent in the 1890s of the notorious Ezeta government of El Salvador. This was a particularly vile slander because - as General Villegas began to write - he himself was a hunted enemy of the Ezetas, and had gone on to lead the revolutionary army which eventually threw them out in June 1894. His detailed account of events was published by the paper in serial form, and then later collected in a permanent volume.

Chapter 5 - A Household of Women

[35.] Pacheco, Otoniel, Ed. Directorio de la Ciudad de San José - 1895. San Jose: Tipografía Nacional, 1895, p.III.

[36.] Ferráz, Juan F. "San José de Costa Rica" in Almanaque Ilustrado. Guatemala, Dec 1893. Reprinted in Otoniel Pacheco's Directorio de la Ciudad de Costa Rica - 1895.

[37.] Villegas letter. Rafael Villegas to his daughter Elena, from Guayaquil, Ecuador, Nov 1898.

[38.] Villegas letters. Rafael Villegas to his 12-year-old daughter Elena from Quito, Ecuador, 28 Jul / 2 Aug 1902.

39. Secretario de Gobernación, Archivo Nacional, San José. Nos. 11986/88/89 - Serie I -Guerra Y Marina - Fo. 150,225.178. Mayo 1900/Sep 1901/Mayo 1902. Inspector General of the Army releasing a pension to General Villegas of 300 colones/mo., then 250 additional.

40. Doyle, Henry Grattan. <u>A Tentative Bibliography of the Belles-Lettres of the Republics of Central America.</u> Cambridge, MA: Harvard University Press, 1935.

41. Segarra, José and Juliá, Joaquín. <u>Excursion por América. Costa Rica.</u> San José: Imprenta de Avelino Alsina, 1907, p.218.

42. The original serialization in *La Republica* (1908) was republished in 1927 after General Villegas' death, together with several of his essays in a volume called <u>Páginas de Antáno</u> <u>(Pages from Yesteryear.)</u>

43. Fischel, Gladys Mora Villegas de. Personal interview with author, Jan 1988.

44. Calvert, A.S. and Calvert, P.P. <u>A Year of Costa Rican Natural History.</u> New York: The MacMillan Co., 1917, p. 29.

45. Velloso, W. "Presenting our First Ambassadress." *Américas, The Journal of the Organization of American States.* 10:32-33, November 1958.

46. Blutstein 1970, p.151

47. Calvert, Amelia Smith and Calvert, Philip Powell. <u>A Year of Costa Rican Natural History</u>. New York: The MacMillan Co., 1917, p. 30. The number of girls at the Colegio de Señoritas in 1908 was 306.

Chapter 6 - The Cuban Connection

48. Calvo, Yadira. Ángela Acuña: Forjadora de estrellas. San Jose: Editorial Costa Rica, 1989.

49.   Santa Cruz y Mallén, F.X. <u>Historias de Familias Cubanas. Vol. VIII</u>, p. 90-94: "Figueredo."

50.   Wright, Irene. <u>Cuba.</u> New York: The MacMillan Co., 1910.

51.   Jones, J. Bascom and Scoullar, William, Eds. of Latin American Publicity Bureau, Inc. <u>The Blue Book of Costa Rica, 1916.</u> San José: Imprenta Alsina, 1916, p.444.

52.   Humboldt, Alexander. <u>The Island of Cuba.</u> Translated by J.S. Thrasher. New York: Derby & Jackson, 1856.

53.   Strode, Hudson. <u>The Pageant of Cuba.</u> New York: Random House, 1934.

54.   <u>La Enciclopedia de Cuba. Vol.8.</u> "Municipios: Las Villas. Camaguey. Oriente." San Juan y Madrid: Enciclopedia y Clásicos Cubanos, 1974.

55.   Black, Jan Knippers. <u>Area handbook for Cuba. 2nd Ed.</u> Washington, D.C.: US Government Printing Office, 1976.

56.   Jones and Scoullar 1916, p. 444.

57.   Rosa's baby daughter **Guarina** Lora will give her great-niece Anita Figueredo her odd middle name.

58.   Acte de Mariage, Confédération Suisse, République et Canton de Genève. Extrait du Registre des mariages de L'arrondissement de l'état Civil de Gneve Ville. Vol 1931, page 494, No. 4. 3 Novembr 1931: Figueredo, Viriato Saturnino Dario, ne le 19 Décembre 1893 a Santiago de Cuba, fils de Jose et de Ana née Lora.

59.   Fernandez Peralta, Ricardo. "Familia Villegas Braun. Hijos del Gral. don Rafael Villegas Arango y de doña Rafaela Braun Bonilla." San José. Lists all children and spouses with dates of birth, marriages and deaths.

60.   Pérez Cabrera, José Manuel. *Un Héroe del 24 de Febrero: El General Saturnino Lora y Torres.* Monograph read before the Academy of Cuban History, 25 Nov 1958, the centennial of the birth of the illustrious Cuban patriot. Havana: Imprenta "El Siglo XX" Muñiz y Cia., 1958.

Biography of **Saturnino Lora y Torres**: born 29 Nov 1858 on farm near village of Baire, Jiguani, Oriente, Cuba; father Mariano Lora y Fonseca, mother Josefa Torres y Mora; married Rosa Yero Castellanos; died 29 Sep 1921. Document lists five brothers   and six children; and states that, in 1894, daughter Ana Lora was married to José   Figueredo and already the mother of two sons, living at 72 lower San Carlos Street in Santiago.

61.   *Diario de la Marina* (Cuban newspaper.) "In the Centennial Year of General Saturnino Lora Torres. He Gave the Cry for Independence in Baire on the 24th of February 1895." Havana: 22 June 1958. Has full-length portrait of Saturnino Lora Torres, his wife Rosa Yero Castellanos, and daughters Isabel and Guarina Lora Yero.

62.   *Indice Alfabético del Ejército Libertador de Cuba* [Alphabetical list of the liberating army of Cuba] Lists José Yero Castellanos (his brother-in-law) as a captain in General Saturnino Lora's Division. José's parents (and Rosa Yero's) are listed as "SalustianoYero and Inés Castellanos."

63.   Corona, Ramon. "Saturnino Lora" in <u>Todo por Cuba</u>. Madrid, Spain: Colección Livre, 1972, pp. 42-43. "The famous leader was of medium height, lean, with a close beard, pale complexion, spare gestures and a kindly expression. One of his aides told me that he had seen in few other men such great nobility and magnanimity."

64.   Casasus, Juan J.E. <u>La Emigration Cubana y la Independencia de la Patria.</u> La Habana: Editorial Lex, 1953. Map showing the principal "triangle of exile" during the War of Independence as = to New York - to Santo Domingo - or to Costa Rica.

65. Archivos Nacionales. Procedencia Sala 1era, Apelaciones. No. 366. Divorcio. Figueredo vs. Lora 1896-1897.

66. Chacón Pacheco, Nelson. Alajuela de Ayer. San José, Costa Rica, 1985, p. 108. Also, Jones and Scoullar 1916, p. 402.

67. Biesanz, Mavis; Biesanz, Richard; and Biesanz, Karen. Los Costarricenses. San José: Editorial Universidad Estatal a Distancia, 1979.

68. García Soto, Esaú. *Anécdotas Manudas.* Alajuela, Costa Rica: Museo Histórico-Cultural Juan Santamaría, 1994.

69. *Libros de acuerdos del Ministerio de Relaciones Exteriores de Costa Rica, 1917-1940.* Biblioteca del Instituto Diplomático Manuel María de Peralta, Ministerio de Relaciones Exteriores y Culto de Costa Rica.

70. Jones and Scoullar 1916, p.444.

71. Henríquez Ureña, Max and Lora, Guarina. Telegram addressed to Lic Roberto Figueredo Lora. 'S-Gravenhage (The Hague) 26 Apr 1940. "Viriato falleció esta mañana habiéndolo asistido mejores médicos aquí agotándose todos recursos ciencia punto entierro tarda tres 3 días abrazamos te. Max Guarina." Death Certificate. Viriato Figueredo Lora. 1 – T181 – F311-A621, del Registro Civil, San Jose. "44 years old (*sic*; actually 46), unmarried (*sic*; actually married since 1931 to Christianne-Henriette Stattler), resident of Switzerland, died 4 May 1940 (*sic*; actually 26 April), The Hague, Holland, buried in San Jose 22 Mar 1944" in a cemetery plot reserved for members of the College of Physicians and Surgeons.

72. Bureau International de L'Education, *Annuaire International de L'Education et de L'Enseignement.* Geneva: 1935. Mentions Viriato Figueredo as Consul of Costa Rica in Geneva.

73. Fernández Morales, Jesús Manuel. *Las Presidencias del Castillo Azul.* San José, Costa Rica: Imprenta LIL, 2010, p. 320.

74. Alarmvogel. (Francisco Picado Soto.) *Apuntes para la Historia de la Ciudad de Alajuela 1782-1966.* San José, Costa Rica: Imprenta Nacional, 1966.

75. Ferráz (Pacheco) 1895, p. XI.

Chapter 7 - Fire and Ice

76. Marriage record, Roberto Figueredo Lora and Sara Villegas Braun in <u>MATRIMONIOS</u> Vol. 22, I., p. 356, No. 16620, Civil Registry, San José Costa Rica. [Also Microfilm #1104588, LDS Library, San Diego, CA]

"In the city of San José at seven in the morning of the 30th of January 1916, the Governor of this state was present in the house of doña Rafaela Brown Bonilla de Villegas, located on 8th Street North between 3rd and 5th Avenues...to celebrate the marriage of **Roberto Figueredo Lora,** adult, 21 years of age, single, Costa Rican, Bachelor of Law and resident of Alajuela, legitimate son of José Figueredo, merchant, Costa Rican, and Ana Lora Yero, housewife, Costa Rican, both residents of Alajuela; with Miss **Sara Villegas Brown**, 19 years old, single, employed at home, born in El Salvador, Costa Rican and of this vicinity, legitimate daughter of Rafael Villegas Arango, journalist, Costa Rican, and of Rafaela Brown Bonilla, housewife, Costa Rican.

77. "La Boda Figueredo-Villegas" and "La Boda de Hoy". Undated newspaper clippings.

78. History Center, Volcan Poás. Visual display, 1988.

79. Calvert and Calvert 1917, p.324.

80. Birth Record, Anita Guarina Figueredo Villegas. Registro de NACIMIENTOS de la Provincia de Alajuela, T107 - P40 - AS79.

81. "Figueredo ya es Papá" Undated newspaper clipping.

82. In the Civil Registry office in San José, the heavy book with the entry for Anita Figueredo's birth is quite near the old register of

her parents' marriage and divorce. In the space-saving system of the Registry, the minute details of the marriage are written out in a clerk's clear hand, densely covering two legal-sized pages; and then running into the script of the marriage contract along the whole left margin are another clerk's tightly cramped curls and swirls which a magnifying glass reveals to be the divorce:

"In a final judgment delivered by the Third Civil Judge of this province, at 10:30 A.M. on the 18th of March of the current year.... the marriage of Roberto Figueredo and Sara Villegas Braun, the persons referred to in the adjacent entry, is declared dissolved."

San José, 20 March 1944.

Chapter 8 - Interlude

83. Acuña de Chacón 1969, p.278.

84. Velloso 1958.

85. "Bautizo" Baptism of Anita Figueredo in Alajuela, recorded by unidentified newspaper, 26 Jul 1917.

Chapter 9 - The Death of José Figueredo

86. *La Prensa Libre* (San José newspaper), 15 Oct 1917. "The Horrible Tragedy which Unfolded Yesterday in the City of Alajuela. Don José Figueredo Shot to Death. His Funeral an Imposing Manifestation of Sorrow." Long article and commentary (6000 words) with 3" central photograph. All the details of the movements of the principal characters before and after the event are taken from this report.

87. Archivos Nacionales. Procedencia Alajuela. Juzgado del Crimen. No. 3894. R948. 157 Año 1920 Febrero 21. Sección Jur Clase JI Serie II Materia C. Asunto Homicidio. Reo: Hernán Cortes Castro. Ofendido: José Figueredo Figueredo. Acusador: don Roberto Figueredo Lora. Iniciada el día 14 de Octubre de 1917. Fallada el día 9 de abril de 1919.

88. Chacón Chaverri, Tranquilino. *"José Figueredo - Un Sensible Fallecimiento"* ("A   Painful Loss"), 1922, reprinted in <u>De Ayer y de Hoy</u>. San José: Imprinta Alsina, 1930. "He undertook to write a book on the history of Cuba, which he finished about eight days before his death."

Chapter 10 - A Digression on Family Medicine

89. Doeblin, Prof. Dr. Jurgen. Letter to author, 6 Jul 1993, enclosing extracts from records of *Bistum Augsburg*, the Catholic church of the Augsburg region of Bavaria; the original files are from the *Pfarrei Diessen* (Catholic church of Diessen.)

St. Alban is part of Diessen, which was named Baierdiessen in the last century. It is located near the *Ammersee* (Lake Ammer), thirty miles southeast of Munich. Johann   Braun was born in St. Alban / Baierdiessen.

"**Johann Baptist Braun**, born 3 Jan 1825 @ St. Alban; son of Joseph Braun, joiner, b. 24 Feb 1792 @ Hostetten, who married 20 Feb 1821 Mechthild Astaller, day worker, b. 23 Nov 1786 @ St. Alban. Paternal grandparents: Bartholomaus Braun who married 31 Mar 1788 Magdalena Babenstuber, b. 9 May 1762 @ Hostetten. Paternal great-grandparents: Mathias Braun von Stoffen and Agnes _____.; Martinus Babenstuber and Barbara __.   Maternal grandparents: Sebastian Astaller, day worker, of St. Alban, and Christina Reder."

From *Landsberger Kreisheimatbuch* [The Homecounty Book of Landsberg-am-lech and Ajacent Towns] edited by Bernhard Muller-Hahl, 1992, p.675-76: St. Alban is an ancient fishing village, with a church built in 1410, and with five houses in the 18th   century. The **Braun** family lived at number 2 from 1810 onwards.

90.. Carr, Albert Z. <u>The World and William Walker.</u> New York: Harper and Row, Publishers, 1963 .

91. Gutierrez Braun, Hernán. "Reseña de la Familia Braun" in *Anales de la Academia de Genealogia e Historia de Costa Rica 1974-1976.*

92. Doeblin, Prof. Dr. Jurgen. Letter to author, 22 Jan 1992, enclosing extracts from records of the University of Munich 1843-46. Grobgeschaidt 223-8501, Heroldsberg, Bavaria, Germany.

"Johann Baptist Braun studied at the University of Munich during 1843-1846, the only student of that name:

1843/44 study of philosophy (home town: St. Alban)

   address in Munich: Veterinarstrasse 1/1

1844/45 study of philosophy (home town: Baierdiessen)

   address in Munich: Sonnestrasse 19/0

   1845/46 study of medicine   (home town: Baierdiessen)

   address in Munich: Lerchenstrasse 16/0

There was no student or professor of that name after 1846."

93. Puschmann, Dr. Theodor. <u>A History of Medical Education.</u> Facsimile of 1891 Edition. "Modern Times: The German States." New York: Hafner Publishing Co., 1966, pp. 576-81.

94. Simmer, Hans H. "Principles and Problems of Medical Undergraduate Education in Germany during the Nineteenth and Early Twentieth Century" in O'Malley, C.D., Ed., <u>The History of Medical Education</u>, an International Symposium held Feb 5-9, 1968, UCLA School of Medicine. Los Angeles: University of California Press, 1970, pp. 173-176.

95. Norwood, Wm. Frederick. "Medical Education in the United States Before 1900. The Reluctant Years, 1801-1860" in O'Malley, 1970, pp. 476-486.

96. O'Connell, Charles D., Special Assistant to the President, The University of Chicago Office of Alumni Affairs, Robie House / 5757

Woodlawn Avenue, Chicago, IL 60637. Letter to author, 26 Aug 1987.

97. Marriage petition of Juan Braun and Elena Bonilla. La Curia Metropolitana, San José: Book label *Indice de: Espedientes matrimoniales y Documentos varios de 1855 a 1875.* Folio 20 / Asiento 041, **1856**, p. 6, 65/266, num. 3786.

98. Sáenz Carbonell, Jorge Francisco. *Don Joaquín de Oreamuno y Muñoz de la Trinidad.* San José: EUNED, 1994, p. 232.

99. Jones and Scoullar 1916, pp. 28-32.

100. Keen, William Williams, Ed. Surgery: Its Principles and Practice. Vol. 1. Philadelphia and London: W.B. Saunders Co., 1906, p. 61. "It was a shrewd American dentist, W.T.G. Morton, who established publicly the use of ether as a safe and sure anesthetic, in 1846...at the Massachusetts General Hospital."

101. Chloroform was first utilized in Costa Rica in 1848 by dental surgeon Jose Maria Montealegre. See "El Doctor Montealegre ha ensayado entre nosotros la virtud del cloroformo" in *El costarricense* (periodical), San José: September 1848.

102. Sheldon, George, Professor and Chairman, Dept. of Surgery, University of North Carolina at Chapel Hill. Personal communication with author, 14 Jul 1993.

103. Baptismal Record, Rafaela Braun. La Curia Metropolitana, San José. Book Label B - 23- 1 Julio 1857 - 25 Avril 1859. Pg. 154 / asiento 287. "Elena Josefa Rafaela," 6 Junio 1858. Legitimate daughter of Juan Braun, a native of Bavaria, and Elena Bonilla, of Costa Rica.

104. Guerra, Francisco. "Medical Education in Iberoamerica" in O'Malley 1970.

105. Velloso 1958.

106. Chacon Pacheco, 1985, pp 96-97

107. Fernández Morales, 2010. "Sobre el gobierno de Tinoco y la represión política."

108. Fisher, Leonard Everett. Ellis Island: Gateway to the New World. New York: Holiday House, 1985.

Chapter 11 - Taking Leave

109. Lora, Anita. Letter to Sarita Villegas, 22 Dec 1919, Alajuela, Costa Rica.

110. Vargas Coto 1922.

111. Allen, Frederick Lewis. Only Yesterday: An Informal History of the 1920's. New York: Harper and Row, Publ., [1931] 1964.

112. Sullivan, Mark. Our Times. The United States 1900-1925. Vol. VI. TheTwenties. New York: Charles Scribner's Sons, 1935.

113. "Relación detallada de los juegos olímpicos centroamericanos verificados en Guatemala con motive del centenario – La actuación del equipo 'Costa Rica' – Impresiones de un deportista." *Detailed account of the Central American Olympic Games staged in Guatemala on the occasion of the Centennial – Impressions of a sportsman."* Diario de Costa Rica*, sábado 15 de octubre de 1921, p 2.

114. Advertising circular for the Great White Fleet of the United Fruit Company, including cabin plans and pictures of staterooms for the *SS Ulua*. From files of the SSHSA (Steamship Historical Society of America, Inc.), University of Baltimore Library, 1420 Maryland Ave., Baltimore, MD 21201.

This Side of Paradise

Chapter 12 - Risking the Person

115. "Passenger and Crew Lists of Vessels Arriving in New York, 1897-1942" Microcopy Vol. 6950 - **November 13 1921**. Ship's Manifest for *S.S.Ulua*. Washington, D.C.: National Archives.

116. Wurman, Richard Saul. NYC Access. New York: Access Press Ltd., 1989, p.16.

117. Szucs, Loretto Dennis. Ellis Island: Gateway to America. Salt Lake City: Ancestry, Inc., 1986, p.13.

118. Bonilla, H.H. Reminiscencias: Mi Familia y Yo. San José, Costa Rica: Editorial Texto   Limitada, 1983, p. 242-73.

119. "The Times of Your Life", Vol. XXI, No. 98. Atlantic City: 1988. "In 1921, annual income in the United States was $2,134 or $178/month."

120. Sullivan, Mark. Our Times. The United States, 1900-1925. Vol. VI: The Twenties. New York: Charles Scribner's Sons, 1935.

121. Acuña de Chacón, Angela. La Mujer Costarricense a Través de Cuatro Siglos. Vol II. San José: Imprenta Nacional, 1970, p. 137.

122. Anthony, Susan Brownell. The Revolution (woman suffrage newspaper). March 18, 1869.

123. International Ladies Garment Workers Union. Our City - Our Union. 40th Anniversary. New York: 1940.

124. Kolchin, Morris. "The Ladies' Garment industry" in American Federationist, 36:1472-77. Washington: Dec 1929. An historical description of the garment industry.

125. Henry, Alice. "The Way Out" in Life and Labor 2:120-121, April 1912. In aftermath of Triangle Waist Co. fire, investigation of safety and shop conditions.

126. Van Dyk, Jere. "Growing Up in East Harlem" in National Geographic Vol. 177, No. 5, May 1990, pp. 53-75.

127. Villalobos, Asdrubal. "La Muerte del General" editorial in newspaper La Prensa. San José: September 20, 1922.

Chapter 13 - Scholar

128. Visit by author to Chestnut Hill College, Philadelphia, site of original Mt. St. Joseph Academy, Jun 14, 1988.

129. Sister Mary Alacoque, R.D.C. Letter to author with historical data and photographs of Good Counsel, Oct 4, 1989.

130. Sister Mary Teresa Brady, R.D.C. Letter to author enclosing records of Anita Villegas Figueredo at Good Counsel, Jun 13, 1983.

131. Clurman, Harold, as quoted by Bruce Bliven, Jr., in New York: A Bicentennial History. New York: W.W. Norton & Co., Inc., 1981, p.170.

132. Santiago Chamberlain Zeledón, 1887-1967. www.RootsMagic. com Archivo Genealógico Eduardo Chamberlain Gallegos.

133. Fernandez Peralta, Ricardo. "Familia Villegas-Braun." Roberto Figueredo Lora married (2) Teodora Padilla Bolanos in Guatemala, 15 Dec 1926. Roberto's second family of children had the surnames Figueredo Padilla.

134. "Passenger and Crew Lists of Vessels Arriving at New York, 1897-1942." Vol. 9788 - **February 25, 1929**. Ship's Manifest for Honduran SS Virginia. Washington, D.C.: National Archives.

135. Telegram 28 Feb 1929 from Roberto Figueredo (in Guatemala) to Viriato Figueredo Costa Rican consul in Geneva: "mama murió ayer inconsolables abrazamos te - Roberto"

136. Mack, George "Bud". Letter to AVF, November 1942, recounting days at St. Gregory's. The "December" issue of <u>Look</u> was issued in November.

Chapter 14- Southern Seminary

137. <u>Southern Seminary - Buena Vista, Virginia.</u> Announcements for 1929-30. Register for 1928-29.

138. Carroll, Roger. "Chronicle of Southern Seminary is the Story of a Family." in <u>Lexington News-Gazette</u>. Lexington, VA, 16 Nov 1966, p. 6A-7.

139. "The Virginia Reel." Southern Seminary Junior College. Vol.IX, No.1, 1867-1967, Centennial Year.

140. Robey, H.Russell. <u>As I Remember It.</u> Private printing, after 1968.

141. Sheaffer, Annie Parks Moore. Letters to author dated: 6 Sep 1989; 8 Sep 1989; 11 Sep 1989; 24 Oct 1989. 328 E. King St, Shippensburg, PA 17257.

142. Bliven 1981, p.175-76. "By the time [Governor Al] Smith ran for the presidency in 1928, New York was perhaps the best-run state in the nation....The campaign was needlessly savage. Smith was the first Catholic ever nominated, a fact that bigots...exploited to the full."

142. Wiencek, Henry. <u>The Smithsonian Guide to Historic America: Virginia and the Capital Region.</u> New York: Stewart, Tabori & Chang, 1989.

144. <u>The Maid of the Mountains.</u> Published by the Senior Class, Southern Seminary. Buena Vista: 1930, 1931, 1932.

145. "Hermoso Laurel" in newspaper <u>La Nueva Prensa</u>. San José: 12 Jun 1930.

146. Marulanda, Francis. Letter to Sarita Villegas, dated 10 Nov 1930. The text mentions Sarita visiting a friend in the hospital; Francis says he is "once again admiring your little heart of gold - how much pleasure it takes in helping the less fortunate, and how it has wasted on me its treasures of sweetness and affection."

Chapter 15 - Manhattanville

147. Bliven 1981, pp. 177-78.

148. Encyclopedia Americana, 1974. "International Ladies' Garment Workers Union."

149. "Manhattanville 1841-1979: Distinction Built on a Tradition of Excellence." Historical review, extracted from alumnae publication, 1979.

150. Harrison, V.V. Changing Habits: A Memoir of the Society of the Sacred Heart. New York: Doubleday, 1988.

151. Clark, Mary T., RSCJ. Letter to AVF dated 2 Aug 1989, and enclosing picture of Mother Grace Damman, RSCJ.

152. The Tower 1936. Yearbook of Manhattanville College.

153. AVF in Manhattanville Yesterday and Today edited by Mother Loretta Corcoran, RSCJ. Purchase, NY: 1953.

154. "El Dia de la Madre", La Tribuna, San José; 15 Aug 1932. A 6" oval portrait of "Doña Rafaela B. viuda de Villegas, with whose photograph La Tibuna offers a tribute of respect and admiration to the Costa Rican mother."

155. "Figuras de nuestro fútbol: **Roberto Figueredo**". Undated Guatemalan newspaper clipping. A chronicle of RF's career in Guatemala.

156. Mario Leiva Quirós, 1913-1990. Graduated University of Costa Rica School of Law 1936. Magistrate of the Supreme Court 1955,

and President of the Legislative Assembly 1961-62. www.asamblea. go.cr/galeria/president/congre18.htm.

157. "Anita Figueredo V. Maid of Honor to the queen of the ball, on the ninth anniversary of the San José Athletic Club" in souvenir program "Souvenir de la Independencia 1821-1934."

158. "Passengers & Crew Lists of Vessels Arriving in New York, 1897-1942" Vol. 11,958 **October 1 1934**. Ship's Manifest for **SS Virginia** sailing from Canal Zone September 25 1934. Washington, D.C.: National Archives.

159. Lang, Catherine Illyne. Letter to author, 1 January 1995. 519 Washington Road,   Woodbury CT 06798.

160. *Diario de Costa Rica* 25 Jun 1936.

Chapter 16 - Medicine and Love

161. Bliven 1981, p.178.

162. Medical Education in Brooklyn: The First Hundred Years. SUNY, Downstate Medical Center. Brooklyn: 1960.

163. Jablons, A., Ed. History of the Long Island College Hospital, Long Island College of medicine, and the State University of New York College of Medicine at New York City, 1856-1955. New York: 1955.

164. Doyle, James. "Last Will and Testament - 19 May 1878" Rome, NY. Lists property in Rome, and three children: James, Mary Ellen and "Edward William" (later known as "William E.") James Doyle died 28 May 1878, aged about 62. His wife Ellen Cosgriff Doyle, aged 41, predeceased him by two weeks, 15 May 1878. Her obituary in the Rome Sentinel states that her physician had prescribed laudanum for some ailment, and that she drank it

off in one draught, thus dying - intentionally or otherwise - of an overdose of opium.

165. The Doyle-Knower stores in Utica, Binghamton and Syracuse.

166. Elizabeth Mabel Carroll, born 20 Sep 1880, in Port Dickinson, NY, the 4th of 5 daughters of Henry Harrison Carroll, a cooper, and Nancy Maria Severson. Marriage Record, William Edward Doyle and Elizabeth Mabel Carroll: married 21 Dec 1902, Binghamton, Broome, NY.

167. Program, Tenth Annual Commencement of the Long Island College of Medicine,

Academy of Music, Brooklyn, 6 Jun 1940. Prize of the Class of 1898 awarded to Anita Villegas Figueredo.

168. Acuña de Chacón, Angela in *La Tribuna*, 16 Jun 1940. Also, *Diario de Costa Rica*, 15 Jun 1940.
Chapter 17 - The Path to Memorial, Marriage and War

169. Baker, Rachel. The First Woman Doctor: The Story of Elizabeth Blackwell, M.D. New York: Julian Messner, 1944.

170. del Regato, J.A. "James Ewing" in Int J Radiation Oncology Biol Phys 2:185-198, 1977. The history of Memorial Hospital is given on p.189.

171. *La Tribuna*, San José, 10 Aug 1942, in *Mundo Social*.

172. Bill Doyle kept a journal for the eventful year 1942, and the journal, along with the letters between the newlyweds, gives a detailed account of the early days in the South Pacific.

173. *Utica Daily Press*, May 7 1943: "Officer on Sick Leave Lauds Care Given U.S. Armed   Forces.

174. Hailey, Foster. "Dive-Bombing Attack" in <u>Pacific Battle Line.</u> New York: Macmillan Company, 1944, pp.306-318. Mr. Hailey was a war correspondent for the *New York Times* assigned to the *Nicholas* at the time of the sinking of the *DeHaven*.

Chapter 18 - Washington and Motherhood

175. Zegrí, Armando. "Cirujana, Joven y Bonita" ["Young, Pretty Surgeon"] in <u>Norte</u>, March 1945.

Chapter 19 - Cancer Detection and the Call of the West

176. Reyher, Becky. "Latin Americans to the North" in <u>Mademoiselle</u>, March 1946, pp. 179 and 289-90.

A Heaven of Blackred Roses

177. cummings, e.e. from <u>W [ViVa]</u> (1931) as published in the collected <u>Poems 1923-1954.</u> New York: Harcourt, Brace & World, Inc., p.253.

Chapter 20 - The New Frontier

178. Morgan, Neil and Blair, Tom. <u>Yesterday's San Diego.</u> Miami: E. A. Seeman, Publ., 1976.

Brandes, Ray. <u>San Diego: An Illustrated History.</u> Los Angeles: A Rosebud Book, 1981.

Christman, Florence. <u>The Romance of Balboa Park. 4th Ed.</u> San Diego Historical Society, 1985.

<u>Eileen Monaghan Whitaker Paints San Diego.</u> Text by Don Dedera. La Jolla: Copley Books, 1986.

179. Randolph, Howard S.F. <u>La Jolla Year By Year.</u> La Jolla: 1955. La Jolla's population in 1940 was about 5000; it was about 10,000 by the end of the decade.

      Dawson, Barbara. "Dr. Anita Figueredo" from "Outstanding La Jolla Women", in <u>Inside LaJolla 1887-1987.</u> La Jolla Historical Society, 1987.

180. Anita Figueredo Doyle. Certificate of Naturalization. Petition No. 13988. Superior Court, San Diego County, Dec 17, 1948.

181. Sara Villegas. Certificate of Naturalization. Petition No. 14416. Superior Court, San Diego County. September 7, 1949.

182. Letter from Fred W. Stewart, M.D., Memorial Cancer Center, to Scripps Hospital pathologist George Hartley, Jr., M.D., October 12, 1953.

183. Cope, Elizabeth N. "Pattern". 13 July 1950.

184. <u>The San Diego Union.</u> "News Show to Star Cancer Society Aid." 19 April 1951.

185. Joseph V. Barca, D.D.S.

186. California Federation of Business and Professional Women's Clubs. Fall Conference of Southern District, Calexico, CA: 25 Oct 1952.

Chapter 21 - The Second Coming

187. During the early 1900s, Johnny - a native of Texas and always called "*Mr. Martinez*"– was the kindly conductor on the Alajuela-San José train, which Sarita rode often during the difficult years from 1916-1921. He later retired to New York. Chacón Pacheco: pp 81-82.

Chapter 22 - For the Church and the Pontiff

188. *The Star*, magazine of Mary Star of the Sea Parish, Oct and Nov 1950. *La Jolla Light*, Society and Club News, 2 Nov 1950.

189. <u>La Jolla Journal</u>. Thursday, June 17, 1954, p. 3.

Chapter 23 - Coast Boulevard

190. History of "417 Coast Boulevard"
      Otherwise known as **Lots I,J,K and L of the Pauline Addition**

----

1. 31 Dec **1923** - Map of Pauline Addition filed
2. 7 Jan **1924** - Ada George grant to Southern Title Guaranty Co. of Lots J,K,L,M,N,O,P
3. 13 Mar **1924** - Southern Title Guaranty Co. grant to Jennette T. Gay, widow - Lots J & K
4. 10 Oct **1927** - Lot J, Notice of Completion [Book 84 - Page 301]
5. 21 Feb **1931** - Notice of Completion [Book 100 - Page 84] Both lots filed same date.
6. 9 Oct **1942** - Executrix of estate of Jennette T. Baxendale, deceased, grant to Edward Snowden Baxendale = Lots J,K,L
7. 12 Apr **1943** - Probate of estate of Jennette T. Baxendale grant to Edward Snowden
Baxendale as his separate property: Lots J,K,L and Lot I
8. 3 Feb **1945** - Edward S. Baxendale grant to Walter F. and Mabel B. David Lots I,J,K,L
9. 10 Jun **1949** - Aministration of estate of Walter F. David, deceased, grant to Mabel David Lots I,J,K,L and the residence known as 417 Coast Blvd. (adult son Jennings Roy David, only other heir)
10. 8 Feb **1956** - Mabel B. David, widow, grant to William J. Doyle and Anita F. Doyle Lots I,J,K,L

Chapter 24 - Mother Teresa

191. *Jubilee*. February 1958, pp. 28-35.

Chapter 25 - Woman of the Year

192. Reggie. *La Jolla Light.* Thursday, January 29, 1959, p.1A.

193. July 1958. The Native Daughters of the Golden West inscribed AVF's name in their Roll of Honor for "women not eligible for membership", *i.e.*, not born in California, "who have performed some signal service for the State of California." Despite having been established in 1910, the Roll of Honor contained the names of only 20 women altogether, half of whom were dead, and with the most various claims to fame. One "Patty Reed Lewis" was listed as a member of the Donner Party trapped in the Sierras in the terrible winter of 1846.

194. *The San Diego Union* Oct 5, 1958. "Banquet sponsored by Business and Professional Clubs in San Diego County to honor outstanding women scientists in this area."

195. Engstrand, Iris and White, Clare. The First Forty Years: A History of the University of San Diego 1949-1989. San Diego: USD, 1989, pp. 1-15.

196. Gilpin, Gertrude. "Life Dedicated to Women" in *San Diego Evening Tribune*, 16 Nov 1958. Biography of Angela Acuña de Chacón. She pioneered in winning the vote for Costa Rican women in 1949. Mentions her late husband Dr. Raul Chacón, attorney, author and professor; her only daughter Isabel and son-in-law Dr. Rodolfo Trejos, studying dentistry at Ann Arbor, MI. States Angela Acuña taught *Introduction to Spanish Literature* and *Commerical Spanish* for four years at the University of [Southern] California.

Chapter 26 - Angels

197. Le Marquis, Antoinette M.D. "Anita Figueredo, M.D. - Guest Editor" in *J.Amer.Med.Wom.Assoc.* Vol.14, No.6, June 1959, pp.493-498.

198. AVF Letter to Kay Sullivan, *The Catholic Digest*, New York: October 1, 1960.

199. Wood, John. "La Jolla Child Drowns in Patio Pond" in *The San Diego Union*, Jan 10, 1963.

Chapter 27 - He Also Serves

200. *La Jolla's Hospital Dilemma - How Did it Come About?* Pamphlet produced by La Jolla Community Hospital Foundation, 1963.

In 1989, the Greater San Diego Chamber of Commerce held a North City Forum at which they answered the question, "Why did the physical boundaries of La Jolla extend past the village, giving some in the Golden Triangle a la Jolla address? The answer was: Due to Scripps Hospital's need to expand, and the desire of the La Jolla City Fathers to ensure Scripps Hospital remain a la Jolla-based hospital, land outside the village (and within a four mile radius of la Jolla) was annexed to accommodate their wishes.

201. *The San Diego Union* May 9, 1965. "True Love Key to Family Unity" by AVF.

Chapter 28 - Old Ties

202. "Miracle Occurs in Costa Rica – The Black Virgin Returns Again", Life Magazine, June 5, 1950, pp. 37-40.

203. The courts went so far as to create a special law permitting senior law students to take on the case, at a considerable remuneration. One of these students, Jorge Alfredo Robles Arias, assumed the defense of the other individuals accused of participating in the crime or handling the stolen goods, but Sanchez refused Robles's offer to defend him as well. *Interview of Jorge Alfredo Robles Arias by Jorge Saenz Carbonell*, San Jose, Costa Rica: January 19, 2010. Attorney Robles Arias went on to have a long and successful career in the law, and also served as Ambassador from Costa Rica to Portugal, Russia and Brazil.

204. Noticias del crimen de la Basílica: periódico *LA NACION*: 12 y 13 de mayo, 27 de mayo – 15 de junior 1950. San José, CR. Declaración de Roberto Figueredo Lora: cita textual *Expediente No. 35-50. Crimen de la Basílica de Nuestra Señora de los Angeles. Tribunal de Cartago, 1950.* Gómez, Juan Carlos: *Escandaloso sacrilegio la inocencia.* San José, C.R.: Editorial Educativa San Judas Tadeo, 2001. Sánchez, José León. *Cuando nos alcanza el ayer.* Miguel Hidalgo, México, D.F.: Editorial Grijalbo, 1999.

205. *Sentencia de la Sala Tercera de la Corte Suprema de Justicia de Costa Rica de 15 horas de 14 de octubre de 1999, exp. 97-000418-0006.* www.aciprensa.com/notic1999/octubre/notic776.htm *La isla de los hombres solos. Diariovasco.com www.diariovasco.com/20080817/gente/isal-hombre-solos-20080817. August 17, 2008*

206. In reality, Roberto Jr. apparently died of natural causes. A friend of his wrote: "I didn't see Roberto for many years while I was working in Switzerland and only learned of his death on my return to Guatemala – it was not a kidnapping, but a natural event." Calvo Aparicio, Mario. Email message to Jorge Saenz, December 8, 2009.

Chapter 29 - All those Children

207. In 1968, Anita begins writing an annual Christmas letter which details the lives of each member of the family. The letters are complete from **1968-1980**. There is a gap from 1981-85, during the decline of Tommy and Lita. The letters resume and are continuous from **1986-1994.**

Chapter 31 - Illness

208. AVF letter to Dr. Author Hughes. April 18, 1875.

209. Woman of Service, May 28, 1975.

Chapter 33- Carrying On

210. 1986 - Living Legacy - Women's International Center of San Diego

1987 - Ecumenical Tribute - San Diego County Ecumenical Conference

1988 - Headliner-Humanitarian - The San Diego Press Club

1989 - Honoree, Outstanding Physician/Philanthropist - The American Cancer Society, La Jolla League

211. Engstrand and White 1989, pp.39-43

212. Official program, The Thirty-Second Commencement at the University of San Diego, May 26, 1985.

213. *Los Angeles Times* Apr 16 1987, "Diver Drowns While Working on Boat."

The San Diego Union Apr 16 1987, "Autopsy set in unexplained death of diver."

The San Diego Union Apr 17 1987, Obituaries: "Rick Doyle."

Chapter 34 - Ad Infinitum

214. Buena Vista News, May 18, 1967. "Seminary's 100th Graduation Program Begins Wednesday [May 24th]. California Alumna is Featured Speaker"

INDEX*

A

Academy of Our Lady of Good Counsel, The, 90–98, 92–93

Acosta, Ricardo, 59

Acuña Braun, Adelita, 47

Acuña Braun, Jorge, 81

Acuña Braun de Chacón, Angela, *14,* 40, 47, *76,* 126, *315*

    article on Sarita and Anita, 137

    education, 35–36

    emigration to New York, 70–71, 79

    honors and awards, 227

    influence on Sarita, 36, 66

    law school and, 49, 66

    women's rights and, 35–36, 66

Adair, Frank, 150, 156, 181

Adams, Chauncey, 241

Alajuela, Costa Rica

    in 1916, 44

    Anita's birth in, 16

    Figueredo family relocation to, 39–40

    Roberto and, 41–42

    Roberto's political activity in, 66

Alajuelan Soccer League, 41

Alicia, 260–261

American Cancer Society, 191, 291

Ammerman, Harvey, 159

Andrew, Father, 247

---

*Italicized page numbers indicate figures; an *n* after a page number indicates endnote. Regarding the discrepancies between Spanish surnames in the index and those in the text: Spanish surnames in the index follow standard Spanish practice; however, the text of this English edition generally follows the practice in English-speaking countries, which is to use abbreviated versions of Spanish surnames.

S